m

WITH...

D1337258

007953313

Violence and the Social Services
in Northern Ireland

Studies in Social Policy and Welfare
Edited by R. A. Pinker

Violence and the Social Services in Northern Ireland

Edited by

John Darby
Arthur Williamson

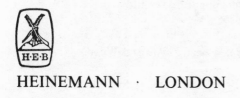

HEINEMANN · LONDON

Heinemann Educational Books Ltd
LONDON EDINBURGH MELBOURNE AUCKLAND TORONTO
HONG.KONG SINGAPORE KUALA LUMPUR NEW DELHI
NAIROBI JOHANNESBURG LUSAKA IBADAN
KINGSTON

ISBN 0 435 82261 6

© John Darby and Arthur Williamson, 1978

First published 1978

Published by Heinemann Educational Books Ltd
48 Charles Street, London W1X 8AH
Filmset in Great Britain by
Northumberland Press Ltd, Gateshead, Tyne and Wear
and printed by
Richard Clay (The Chaucer Press) Ltd Bungay, Suffolk

Contents

Preface

The connection between violence and political and institutional developments can hardly have escaped the notice of anyone who has even a casual awareness of the troubles in Northern Ireland. The introduction of the British army in 1969 and internment in 1971, as well as the prorogation of Northern Ireland's parliament in 1972, were all widely publicized examples of political initiatives in reaction to a deteriorating security situation. The relationship has not always been so direct. A major difficulty in assessing the effects of violence on Northern Ireland's institutions is that its prevalence between 1969 and 1977 coincided with an abnormally large number of administrative initiatives which had been determined before 1969. The intention to reorganize the administration of health and personal social services, education, housing and local government all preceded 1969, as did the decision to introduce the office of Ombudsman. However, all these changes came into operation after the violence had started, and all of them were affected by it. The decision to reorganize local government, for example, was taken in 1967, but the reorganization itself took place at the height of the troubles in 1973. As a consequence, its terms in part reflect the early civil rights demands for franchise reform, the abolition of the company rate and a more equitable means of housing allocation.

The centralization of housing administration is perhaps the case which demonstrates most clearly the interaction between violence and social change. Since 1922 provision and allocation of public housing had been the responsibility of local government, together with the Northern Ireland Housing Trust in the period 1945–71. Post-war improvements in housing provision did little to quieten growing dissatisfaction about discriminatory allocation of houses and the exercise of political influence by local councillors. The highlighting of these issues during the Civil Rights campaign led to the introduction of a uniform system of housing allocation in November 1968. However, the violent upheavals of August 1969 persuaded the British Home Secretary, James Callaghan, that more radical reforms were needed to satisfy minority pressure. As a result, the Northern Ireland Housing Executive was established. This replaced more than 60 local councils and assumed responsibility for both the provision and the allocation of houses throughout the province.

The influence of violence in administration is not confined to these well-publicized political initiatives. In a community where civil disturbances have pervaded the very fabric of society, no institutional or administrative change can totally ignore it. At a local level it has influenced medical emergency procedures, school catchment areas, the operation of public transport, housing allocation policies and indeed every facet of public administration. This book is designed to examine the ways in which Northern Ireland's social services have been affected by eight years of civil disorder, and their responses to the pressures it has created. As the significant growth of community groups' activity in Northern Ireland since 1969 implies their wider interpretation of social service, the book also considers the implications of violence for community organizations, and the consequences of this for statutory social service agencies.

John Darby
Arthur Williamson
New University of Ulster, 1977

Chronology

1916	Easter rising in Dublin.
1919–21	Anglo-Irish war—the war of Independence: first meeting of Dail Eireann (Southern Irish Parliament) in 1919.
1920	Government of Ireland Act: partition established.
1921	Anglo-Irish treaty.
	First Northern Ireland parliament opened.
1921–2	Violence in Northern Ireland: 232 people killed in 1922 alone.
1922–3	Northern Ireland established its institutions: Civil service; Local Government; Royal Ulster Constabulary; Civil authorities (Special Powers) Act (1922); Education Act (1923)—the Londonderry Act.
1925	Colwyn Committee recommended that the financial contribution to Ulster should be based on the difference between her revenue and her actual and necessary expenditure taking into account average standards in the two countries and also 'any lower general level of . . . standards of comfort or social amenity which may exist in Northern Ireland as compared with Great Britain.
1930–9	Northern Ireland's unemployment rate did not fall below 25%.
1931	Planning and Housing Act (N.I.) based largely on the model of the English Town Planning Act, 1925.
1932	Mental Treatment Act (N.I.) introduced a more enlightened code enabling voluntary and temporary patients to enter mental hospitals.
1932–5	Intermittent violence in Northern Ireland.
1934	Unemployment Act (N.I.), 1934, created an Unemployment Assistance Board to pay money to many of the unemployed who had no right to insurance benefit.

1937   New constitution for Irish Republic: 'Special position' of Catholic church recognized, as was the claim that 'the national territory consists of the whole island of Ireland'.

1939–45   Second World War: economic boom in Northern Ireland. IRA campaign in Britain.

1943   First housing survey ever made in Northern Ireland conducted by the Ministry of Home Affairs (Cmd 224). Recommended 100,000 new houses to meet immediate needs; double that number would be required to eliminate slums and overcrowding.

1944   Planning (Interim Development) Act (N.I.), followed the English Town and Country Planning Interim Act of the previous year. Little positive planning took place in Northern Ireland for the next twenty years.

1944   Ministry of Health and Local Government set up; embraced all health functions of Ministry of Home Affairs and other departments.

1945   Housing Act (N.I.) created the Northern Ireland Housing Trust to build and manage houses at Exchequer expense.

1946   National Insurance Act (N.I.), introduced Beveridge-style social insurance provision.

1947   Education Act (N.I.), 1947. Established the duty of local education authorities to make available efficient educational provisions at primary, secondary and further education stages. Introduced selection at age 11+.

1948   Health Services Act (N.I.), provided for the introduction of the National Health Service in Northern Ireland.

1949   The Ireland Act guaranteed Northern Ireland's position within the United Kingdom.

          Social Services (Agreement) Act (N.I.) passed. Covered national assistance, family allowances, non-contributory pensions and the health service. If the costs of these services were proportionately higher in Ulster then the United Kingdom Exchequer would bear 80% of the excess.

1954   Tanner Committee set up to examine informally the working of the health services in Northern Ireland. (Reported 1955.)

1956–62   IRA campaign in Northern Ireland.

1963	Terence O'Neill replaced Lord Brookborough as Prime Minister.
1964	Northern Ireland government recognized the Irish Congress of Trade Unions.

Campaign for Social Justice in Northern Ireland began.

Disturbances in Belfast during elections.

Matthew Report: *Belfast Regional Survey and Plan*, 1962. Recommendations and conclusions had been published the previous year. Recommended a stop-line around Belfast and creation of a new city in County Armagh.

White Paper: *The Administration of Town and Country Planning in Northern Ireland* (Cmnd 465), stressed the need for a planning system answerable to Parliament; 37 planning authorities should be replaced by 10 local development committees covering the whole province.

White Paper: *Educational Development in Northern Ireland* (Cmnd 470) proposed to narrow the differences between secondary (intermediate) schools and grammar schools, working gradually towards non-selective secondary education.

1965   Premiers of Northern and Southern governments (O'Neill and Lemass) met at Stormont.

Lockwood committee recommended that a new university be established in Coleraine.

Wilson plan for economic expansion heavily concentrated growth areas in the east.

Ministry of Development established.

1966   Ulster Volunteer Force (Loyalist) declared war on 'the IRA and its splinter groups'.

Malvern St murders: UVF members convicted and jailed.

1967   Northern Ireland Civil Rights Association (NICRA) formed.

Republican Clubs declared illegal.

White Paper on reform of local government.

1968

June   Austin Curry took possession of house in Caledon, County Tyrone, which he claimed had been unfairly allocated.

August	First Civil Rights (NICRA) march from Coalisland, County Tyrone, to Dungannon.
October	Civil Rights march to Derry defied government ban. RUC charged marchers and rioting continued during the night.
	Five Civil Rights organizations in Derry form the Derry Citizens Action Committee.
November	Terence O'Neill announced reform programme, including a points system of house allocation, an Ombudsman, a franchise reform, a review of Special Powers Act and the dissolution of Londonderry Borough Council.

1969

January	People's Democracy (PD) march attacked by loyalists at Burntollet.
April	Terence O'Neill resigned: replaced on May 1 by James Chichester-Clark.
July	White paper on *Reshaping of local government*: 73 councils to be replaced by 17. Education, health and social services to be the responsibility of nominated area boards.
August	Apprentice Boys' march in Derry attacked; Bogside stormed by RUC; rioting which later led to establishment of 'Free Derry'.
	Rioting spread to Dungannon, Dungiven, Lurgan, Newry and Armagh.
	In Belfast four men and a boy killed.
	Units of British Army intervened between Falls and Shankill roads in Belfast, establishing what later became the 'Peace line'.
	Joint communiqué from British and Northern Irish Prime Ministers.
September	Cameron report on August riots.
October	Hunt report on police reform: RUC to be disarmed: 'B' Specials to be abolished: security to become a military responsibility.
November	Commissioner for Complaints (Ombudsman) office established: John Benn first Commissioner.
December	Maurice Hayes became first chairman of Community Relations Commission.

1970

January

Two hundred and fifty-seven delegates walked out of Sinn Fein congress in Dublin—they were to form the nucleus of the Provisional IRA.

February

Public Order (Amendment) Act: stricter control of marches and demonstrations.

April

Alliance party formed: policies moderate and 'firm on the constitutional issue'.

July–August

Intermittent rioting in Belfast and Derry.

August

Social Democratic and Labour party (SDLP) formed.

1971

March

Brian Faulkner became Prime Minister, replacing Chichester-Clark.

July

SDLP announced boycott of Stormont following two deaths in Derry, and set up alternative assembly.

August

Internment introduced; 300 people arrested; widespread violence and intimidation; 11 deaths and 240 houses burned down; rent and rates strike. Emergency followed.

Thirty prominent Roman Catholics withdrew from public office, to be joined three days later by 130 non-Unionist councillors.

October

Payment for Debt Act passed to combat rent and rates strike.

Democratic Unionist Party (DUP) formed by Rev. Ian Paisley.

November

Compton report on interrogation of internees; found evidence of ill-treatment, but not of brutality.

1972

January

Northern Ireland Housing Executive established.

'Bloody Sunday' in Derry; thirteen men killed by army; followed by four days' rioting in Derry, Belfast and Dublin.

February

Maurice Hayes resigned as chairman of Community Relations Commission.

Ulster Vanguard launched by William Craig as umbrella movement for traditional unionists.

March

Parker committee's report on interrogation procedures. Found, Lord Gardiner dissenting, that methods were justified in exceptional circumstances.

Amnesty International report on treatment of internees. Found that the 'ill-treatment used amounted to brutality'.

British proposals to Northern Ireland government included Border plebiscite, phasing-out of internment and the transfer of 'law and order' to Westminster.

Stormont parliament prorogued; Direct Rule introduced with William Whitelaw as Secretary of State; Vanguard called two-day strike.

July   'Bloody Friday': 22 IRA bomb explosions in Belfast; 9 dead and 130 injured.

Operation 'Motorman': Army moved into positions in Andersonstown, Belfast and Bogside, Londonderry.

Claudy, County Londonderry car bomb; 8 killed.

October   Provisional IRA laid down three demands: the Irish people should decide Ulster's future; a date for withdrawal of British troops; an amnesty for political prisoners.

December   Diplock report suggested temporary changes in administration of justice, including trial without jury.

1973

February   Burges report advocates the abolition of educational selection at age 11+.

March   Border referendum: 41% abstained; 57.4% favoured maintaining the British union; 0.63% voted for a united Ireland.

White paper proposed an 80-member Northern Ireland Assembly, proportional representation and a Council of Ireland.

April   Northern Ireland (Emergency Provisions) Act passed, based on Diplock report.

May   Local government elections; the first on universal adult suffrage.

June   Elections to Northern Ireland Assembly.

July   Northern Ireland Constitution Act, abolishing Stormont parliament, became law.

First meeting of the Northern Ireland Assembly: Loyalists staged a sit-in.

October	Reorganized structure of local government, education and health and social service boards took effect.

1974

January	Northern Ireland Executive took office. Official Unionists, Vanguard Unionist Progressive Party (VUPP) and DUP withdrew from the Northern Ireland Assembly as protest against Executive.
April	Basil McIvor, Minister of Education, announced intention to introduce 'shared schools'. Ivan Cooper, Minister of Community Relations, announced plans to abolish the Community Relations Commission.
May	General strike called by Ulster Workers' Council (UWC) as protest against Executive. 'Emergency' situation until 28 May. Unionists, forced by UWC strike, resigned from Executive, which collapsed: direct rule restored.
June	Brian Faulkner and his followers formed new party, later named the Unionist party of Northern Ireland.
July	British government White paper proposed elections to a Constitutional Assembly.
November	Prevention of Terrorism Act allowed deportation of people from Britain.

1975

January	Gardiner report recommended continuation of detention.
May	Elections for Northern Ireland Constitutional Convention. Loyalists won 44 of a total of 78 seats. British Government granted £50 million to save Belfast shipyard.
August	Prevention of Terrorism Act extended to Northern Ireland.
November	Northern Ireland Constitutional Convention Report published.
December	Detention without trial ended officially with the release of the last detainees from Long Kesh.

1976

March	Northern Ireland Constitutional Convention ended with the loyalist group's report demanding majority rule.

| July | Mr Christopher Ewart-Biggs, British Ambassador in Dublin killed in a landmine explosion near Dublin. |

August — Report by European Commission on Human Rights substantiated 1971 torture allegations against British Army in Northern Ireland.

The first peace rally marked start of the Women's Peace Movement.

September — Emergency Powers Bill passed in Dublin; provided for unprecedentedly stiff sentences against terrorists.

October — Publication of Quigley Report on economic development of Northern Ireland.

Publication of Northern Ireland Household survey, detailing the extent of housing deprivation.

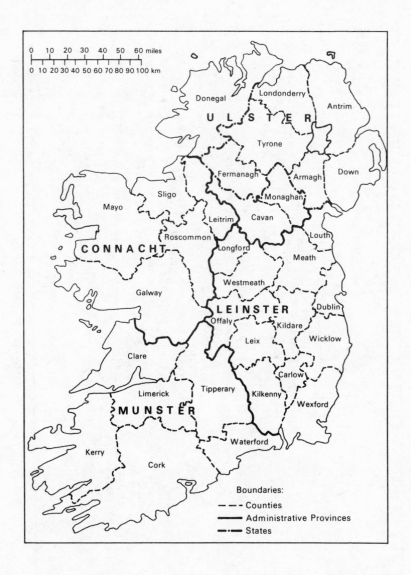

Map I   Ireland

Map II Northern Ireland

1 Violence, Institutions and Communities in Northern Ireland

John Darby and Arthur Williamson*

To think that the special problems which plague Northern Ireland suddenly emerged in the late 1960s is to be seriously misled. Many of the seeds of the present violence had been lying close to the surface of society before that time. The social services have been attempting to deal with these special problems for many decades, in addition to the other problems facing social agencies anywhere in the British Isles.

Most of these problems sprang from economic or political causes. Possessing few natural resources and situated on the periphery of Europe, Northern Ireland had relied for a century on agriculture, textiles and shipbuilding. It was her misfortune that all three suffered from simultaneous depressions during the post-war years. While parity of social services with the rest of the United Kingdom guarantees minimum standards of service and benefit levels, an unemployment rate of between two and three times worse than that in Great Britain has severely strained the social services as well as providing a gloomy backcloth to the public services.

This picture of disadvantage is duplicated in many other areas of social life in Northern Ireland. Personal income levels in 1972 were only 75% of the average for the United Kingdom. Recent research has emphasized the extent of housing deprivation in the province: in 1974 one in five dwellings was defined as unfit for human habitation compared with only 7% in England and Wales, and a further 33% required substantial remedial action. In one large area of Belfast as many as 47% of dwellings were unfit. [1] Health statistics too, reveal significant shortfalls: infant and perinatal mortality is considerably above the

---

* John Darby lectures in Social Administration at the New University of Ulster and is author of *Conflict in Northern Ireland* (1976).

Arthur Williamson lectures in Social Administration at the New University of Ulster.

levels for the other United Kingdom regions, and fewer children under five years of age attend child clinics. Thus, judged by every major indicator, Northern Ireland is the most socially disadvantaged region in the United Kingdom.

A more serious problem, however, is the lack of political consensus and the sectarian state which was associated with it. Birrell has demonstrated that the minority nationalist community in Northern Ireland perceives itself to be deprived and that there is evidence that its perceptions were accurate in terms of housing allocations and conditions, incomes, job opportunities and political representation. [2] The intercommunal disputes associated with these differences have often found violent expression and have led to a high degree of institutional segregation which, in turn, has created a number of specific difficulties for social service agencies. In the administration of primary and secondary education, for example, the maintenance of separate schooling for Roman Catholic and Protestant children has led to duplication of school buildings in areas which could not normally justify two schools. Sectarianism also imposes considerable administrative complications. Again, the minority community's identification of the police with the political establishment has effectively excluded law enforcement agencies from parts of the province and has undermined a number of attempts to reform the force. Some public and social services too, are forced to take sectarian differences into account when allocating their staffs.

Northern Ireland's disadvantages have assumed another and more dramatic dimension with the spread of violence since 1969. This has been most comprehensively demonstrated by the province's economic decline. Income from tourism, for example, fell from £28 million to £15 million between 1968 and 1972 and the two political strikes of 1972 and 1974 are estimated to have cost about £29 million in lost output. Between 1969–73 about 300 manufacturing firms were disrupted by violence and by the end of 1974 800 jobs had been lost in 16 firms which had closed permanently as a result of the troubles. Perhaps the most striking economic consequence of violence, however, is the cost of security operations and of compensation for damage to property and personal injury. Expenditure on police and prisons to the end of 1974 is estimated at £150 million and the cost of army operations in 1975 was reckoned to have been £60 million. In the early part of 1976 compensation claims were running at over £1 million per week. [3]

While these new strains on the economy are clearly serious, the real effect of the spread of violence is better demonstrated by the rise in the number of Northern Ireland's unsolved murders from two in 1968 to 900 in 1976. The monthly security figures, also produced by the Northern Ireland Office, provide a tally of the more easily measured indicators of violence, but only hint at its more subtle consequences. Nevertheless they detail a chronicle of destruction and death which is quite unique in the United Kingdom.

Table 1.1: Northern Ireland: Statistics on Security

	1970	1971	1972	1973	1974	1975
Shooting incidents	213	1,756	10,628	5,018	3,206	1,803
Armed robberies	—	437	1,931	1,215	1,254	1,201
Weight of explosives used (lb)	746	10,972	47,462	47,492	46,435	24,912
Deaths: (Security Forces and RUC)	2	59	146	79	50	31
Deaths: Civilians	23	114	322	171	166	216
Injuries	811	2,507	4,857	2,651	2,398	2,474

Violence and Communities

It is the more insidious effects of violence which are most difficult to portray. Many people live in conditions of endemic fear; social and public services are frequently disrupted and amenities eroded. However, the concentration of violence throughout Northern Ireland has been uneven, with parts of Belfast, Londonderry and South Armagh affected most often and other areas relatively untouched by overt violence, except in its psychological consequences. Furthermore, the manifestations of violence, even in the worst-affected areas, fluctuated considerably in their extent and effects; thus the inter-community rioting of 1969–71, the IRA bombing campaign, the activities of paramilitary groups and sectarian murders all affected different parts of the province and in different ways.

Nevertheless, all parts were affected to some degree and in the main people exhibited a remarkable ability to adjust to inconveniences—searches, security checks, interruptions of services, etc.—which would have been regarded as unacceptable a few years earlier. As the disruptions continued, people began increasingly to improvise and to look within the local community for human and material resources. The so-called 'People's Taxis' which started to operate on the Falls and Shankill Roads in Belfast, were reactions to the frequency with which bus services were withdrawn—itself a reaction to the violence. The unwillingness of housing repairmen to enter some districts led to the formation of repair squads within the local communities; these were eventually employed by the Northern Ireland Housing Executive. In a more general sense, the economic problems which accompanied the violence increased the popularity of self-help industrial co-operatives like Whiterock Industrial Estate in Belfast and the Tyrone Crystal Glass Company in Dungannon. This tendency for communities to rely increasingly on their own resources was particularly marked during the emergencies of 1969, 1971 and 1974. At these times of extreme crisis, rather than wait passively for outside relief, the communities worst affected by the violence set up evacuee centres, provided medical aid, supplied food and transport and generally took responsibility for relief operations.

The growth of community groups since 1969, and their character, have been intrinsically related to the violence. Many of the community leaders who had been active in the mid 1960s were replaced by men whose attitudes towards their communities and towards public bodies were radically different. An effect of violence has been, not so much to create new problems which in turn led to new forms of community action, but to sharpen existing grievances, to point to the ineffectiveness of old political structures, and to highlight deficiencies in housing, public and social services. More important, however, was the attitude of the new activists towards service agencies. After 1969 groups and their leaders were self-confident and aggressive; they demanded rights rather than asked for concessions. Even the paramilitary organizations should be regarded in this context of assertiveness. Rather than being a peculiar and deviant growth, the paramilitaries were a natural development of community action in a violent community. Communities now felt the need to protect themselves against attack. The conventional community groups were unable to provide for this need. But the formation of paramilitary organizations was not the only consequence of the growing violence for community action in Northern Ireland; many vigilante groups which had formed as a response to the early fear of invasion soon abandoned their overt military role and moved towards more normal community activities. Such groups provided the impetus for the expansion of community action in the early 1970s and, while abandoning violent tactics, were no longer prepared to play a passive role in their dealings with official bodies. [4]

Although some local government officials and provincial politicians regarded the emergence of confident and demanding community groups as a threat to their positions, many social service agencies were forced to reach an accommodation with them. This applied most obviously to public services which had been disrupted or excluded by paramilitary activities. In parts of the province it has not always been possible for gas, electricity or transport services to continue without the agreement of paramilitary groups. Bodies such as the Northern Ireland Housing Executive, local authority welfare offices and planning departments had to change their policies and modify operating procedures as a result of pressure from community groups and the need to secure their co-operation in implementing policy. When agencies appeared to be dilatory, as in the case of the Belfast city planners, groups combined forces to prevent proposed urban redevelopment and the building of an unpopular ring road, as well as to force the planners to democratize decision-making procedures. So the violence in Northern Ireland encouraged the development of a community movement which has demanded that communities should by right have a real part in making decisions affecting them, and which was often able to force agencies to concede this right.

Violence and Agencies

The spread of violence created greatly increased work loads for some agencies, and caused complex operational problems for them all. The prison and probation services, for example, had to react to a situation where Northern Ireland's prison population rose from 727 to 2,848 in the years from 1968 to 1974. But much more fundamental problems were raised when probation officers, who had long accepted as their normal brief the endeavour to modify criminals' behaviour, were expected to cope with large numbers of political prisoners; modification of their behaviour implied adopting a political stance, and social workers attached to the prison service objected strongly on professional grounds to carrying out traditional probation work with those convicted of political offences.

Within months of the outbreak of violence almost every agency found itself facing similar operational and ethical questions: how should social workers respond when a court order to take a child into care cannot be carried out because his parents live in a 'no-go' area which police may not enter? What are ambulance drivers to do when prevented by hostile crowds from reaching wounded and dying soldiers, civilians or policemen? Should transport executives treat with terrorist leaders in order to lessen the danger to staff and vehicles? What procedures are appropriate when hospital intensive-care departments have to accommodate not only the critically ill, but a round-the-clock roster of soldiers preventing the escape or 'rescue' of a wanted patient? How should teachers discipline children who are affiliated to illegal organizations, have access to guns and refuse to accept the authority of the school? Similar problems are encountered by housing managers when leaders of paramilitary organizations distribute the keys of vacant houses to members and sympathizers and when it becomes impossible to enforce sanctions when tenants refuse to pay rent.

The responses of different agencies to these new problems varied widely. Some services proved resilient and adaptive; others were characterized by inertia and inflexibility. In some morale remained high and clients needs were satisfied; in others staff became demoralized and services flagged. While some agencies, such as transport, ambulance and fire services, were more overtly affected by violence, the impact of social and political disturbance on schooling, personal social services and health services may have been more fundamental, but less easy to assess. Agencies with clear-cut and specific functions, such as fire and ambulance services, proved relatively easy to disrupt, but had a rapid recovery rate. Their staffs took pride in keeping the service going whatever the odds, and interruptions were short lived. Emergency medical services, and in particular casualty arrangements, became highly efficient and coped well with the extraordinary demands put upon them by the arrival of large numbers of injured within a very short time. But other sectors of health and personal social services coped less successfully with side-effects of violence. Social workers, for example, occasionally found that the recording of information about the circumstances of their clients had become a dangerous activity, particularly when the clients had allegiances to paramilitary organizations. Public health inspectors found it less easy to enforce statutory criteria when the usual sanctions could not be applied. In areas affected by violence, education welfare officers were unable to improve low school attendance figures; as a result, their attempts to do so in untroubled areas then brought accusations of partisanship and unfairness. Both in their professional roles and otherwise, health and social service staffs often found themselves in situations of stress and danger. This, in turn, affected staffing levels in some areas so that by 1973–4 numbers of staff were drifting from the more dangerous—and more socially needy—areas, and clustering in areas of Northern Ireland where violence was less endemic.

It is difficult to generalize about the reasons for the varying reactions of different agencies to violence, or why some responded more successfully than others, but Northern Ireland's experience since 1969 suggests a number of observations which would merit further investigation:

1. The structure of agencies, as well as their function, has an important relationship to responsiveness. Services with a high degree of specificity of function, like the fire service and medical casualty departments, often have a command structure characterized by considerable devolution of responsibility to senior officers on the ground, who possess undisputed authority to act. This was most often true of the uniformed agencies which had a clear service indentity, and their responses in emergency situations were usually speedy and effective.

A major determinant of an agency's ability to adjust to an emergency situation was the rigidity of its structures. Highly bureaucratized bodies, like civil service and some welfare departments, often found that their decision-making structures were too rigid to enable them to deal responsively with new circumstances. In particular, there was a marked tendency to approach the new problems from the standpoint of their own administrative difficulties rather than from their clients' needs. This did not arise from any lack of humanity, as is demonstrated by the constant efforts to improve the administration of services. Nevertheless, highly bureaucratized organizations were unable to make the radical shift in objectives and activities which the advent of violence demanded.

2. The public services which adjusted most capably to the demands of a situation of concentrated and sustained violence, such as has operated in Northern Ireland since 1969, were often those whose functions had involved them with the consequences of violence before the troubles. To doctors, firemen and policemen, for example, the post-1969 problems were not entirely new, although considerably more extensive and complex, and procedures and techniques were available to cope with them. It was the agencies to whom the problems were most novel which found it most difficult to solve them.

3. In a violent situation which is characterized by political disputes, the perceived neutrality of an agency is a major factor in determining its acceptability in communities. Even the fire service was sometimes rejected because its work was seen to hamper the objectives of politi-

cally motivated terrorism. Doctors were almost always accepted because of their high social status, their tradition of professional neutrality and confidentiality and the emergency nature of casualty work. Psychiatrists who worked in the internment and detention camps, on the other hand, were sometimes regarded with open suspicion. It is difficult to judge whether these political perceptions are a characteristic of community violence or a manifestation of the suspicion prevailing in a divided society.

Emergencies

The political crises which heightened Northern Ireland's troubles to near disaster levels created acute problems for social service agencies. They found little guidance in existing research. It is true that there is an extensive literature on the causes and consequences of civil violence. The United States *Report of the National Commission on the Causes and Prevention of Violence* (*see* J. H. Skolnick, *The Politics of Protest*, Simon & Schuster, New York: 1969) and investigations such as H. D. Graham and J. R. Gurr's *History of Violence in America* (Bantam Books, New York: 1969) present descriptions and analyses of riots and civil disorder. However there is no substantial treatment of their effects on social service agencies. There is a body of literature on disaster planning but this relates to natural catastrophes and accidents and does not discuss the peculiar social problems resulting from civil disturbances in a divided community. A. F. C. Wallace, writing about the 1953 tornado in Worcester, Massachusetts, developed a time-space model of disasters which has subsequently been adopted by, among others, Bates (1963) and Bennet, (1973). He postulated that there were seven phases in natural disasters: steady state; warning; impact; isolation; rescue; rehabilitation; irreversible change. This model, which is extremely useful in explaining the development of natural disasters, is not entirely appropriate to political emergencies such as those in Northern Ireland. Some of the problems encountered during natural catastrophies were not features of emergencies in the province; on the other hand, Northern Ireland experienced a number of particular difficulties which arose from her community divisions. For example, Wallace described the first emergency phase as 'steady state'. While this state of equilibrium might accurately describe many communities in Northern Ireland, it is scarcely an accurate description of the tense and unstable pre-emergency conditions which prevailed in the emergency-prone areas in Belfast. Again, natural as distinct from political emergencies usually result from a particular disaster—an earthquake, fire or flood—which has a relatively short and sharp impact, often followed by serious distress; political emergencies are less predictable and the ensuing social crisis may last for weeks and may change direction on a number of occasions. A further characteristic of political emergencies in a divided community is that relief agencies, which often perform the major role in natural disasters, may be regarded with suspicion or hostility and find it almost impossible to perform their functions. All these differences between natural and political emergencies, not to mention others such as the geographical concentration of the former and the tendency of the latter to be dispersed, are observable at every stage.

It is our proposal that emergencies which have their roots in community discord are qualitatively different from those arising from natural disasters, and require a different analysis. The first problem, however, is one of definition. One of the many difficulties facing social welfare agencies during periods of civil disorder lies in determining when the situation has reached emergency level and requires crisis procedures and processes. Using one set of criteria it could be argued that conditions in parts of Northern Ireland have amounted to an emergency since 1969. Even if one defines emergency as a period when distress reaches exceptionally high levels, it is very difficult in some cases to determine when it has started and when it ends. It is important, therefore, to clarify what is meant by 'emergency' in the context of this chapter. The term is used here to indicate a situation where latent community differences, sharpened by a heightening of tension and sparked off by a recognizable catalytic happening, lead to a concentration of social distress which is qualitatively and quantitatively different from and more serious than the background conflict from which it emerged. Three periods between 1969 and 1974 satisfy these criteria: parts of the months of August 1969 and August 1971, as well as the fourteen days of the Ulster Workers' Council's strike in May 1974. Each of these emergencies included four distinct stages which may be further broken down into eight characteristics:

1. A background of community conflict
2. Impact
3. Responses to the crisis
4. Aftermath

Table 1.2: Emergencies in Northern Ireland: A model

Stages	Characteristics of each stage
A. *Background*	1. Presence of a potential for violence 2. Prior heightening of tension 3. Catalytic happening which sparks off emergency
B. *Impact*	4. Primary impact: direct violence affects areas 5. Secondary impact: refugees from direct violence affect new areas
C. *Responses*	6. Immediate response by affected communities 7. Delayed response of agencies
D. *Aftermath*	8. Social recovery 9. Return to political instability and potential for violence

A. Background of political conflict

The first prerequisite of a political emergency is the presence in the community of a potential for violence. In Northern Ireland there are two self-acknowledged groups, marked by distinct political, economic, religious, social and cultural identities, which represent the main social characteristics of the region. Antagonism between the loyalist and nationalist communities, the former of which was associated with political hegemony until 1972, has been the major political character-istic of the area for 150 years and has periodically produced out-breaks of intercommunity violence. One consequence of these violent episodes was the segregation of urban working-class people into what the *Official Report* on the 1886 riots described as 'separate quarters, each of which is given up almost entirely to persons of one particular faith, and the boundaries of which are sharply defined'. These hostile communities with their distinct and separate identities offer a concrete and visible manifestation of community antagonisms, and greatly enhance the potential for inter-group violence. Without such segrega-tion political emergencies such as occurred in Belfast in 1969 and 1971 would have been impossible.

These differences are a constant feature of Northern Irish society. But the months preceding the political emergency invariably witness a heightening of the basic community tension. These periods are often characterized by political disputes, such as the Home Rule controversies of the 1880s and 1910s, which also preceded the most recent political emergencies. Thus the events of August 1969 followed months of violence and rioting in Belfast and Londonderry; the early months of 1971 saw loyalist demonstrations for the introduction of internment, escalation of the IRA bombing campaign and a considerable increase in the amount of intimidation in Belfast; in 1974 too the establishment of a power-sharing Executive led to protest marches, paramilitary activity and political unrest which culminated in the UWC strike and the political emergency which accompanied it. On all three occasions rumours of conspiracies and sell-outs abounded. All served to sharpen the latent hostilities in the community and increase the likelihood of a political emergency.

The third element which may convert serious social unrest into a political emergency is a specific catalytic happening, which is related to the central political division. The more dramatic the event, the more likely is violence to follow. In 1969 it was the invasion of the Falls Road, when 10 people were killed; in 1971 it was the introduction of internment; the political emergency of May 1974 was more gradual in its build-up, but the event which ultimately sparked off the emergency was the decision of the Ulster Workers' Council to enforce a strike.

It is important to note that on at least one other occasion all three background characteristics were present but no emergency followed. This was in the period immediately after the introduction of Direct Rule in March 1972, which was certainly catalytic to loyalists, and which followed intense political and paramilitary activity. The difference on that occasion was that loyalist politicians were able to take a speedy initiative and assume a leadership which satisfied their supporters. So the loyalist anger was canalized into such activities as token strikes, temporary barricades and political marches, which the government made no attempt to curtail. If this observation can be applied generally, the period immediately following catalytic political events may become violent, but may also be defused by convincing political leadership. It is also worth noting that, in March 1972, the build-up of tension before the introduction of Direct Rule was essentially political in character. On the other three occasions the build-up of tension was violent.

B. Impact

Two of Northern Ireland's recent political emergencies—those of

August 1969 and August 1971—were accompanied by extensive overt violence and a concentration of social distress: the third, resulting from the UWC strike of 1974, also produced a concentration of social distress, but a much lower level of violence. The two violent occasions followed very similar courses. At the beginning there was direct physical violence—shooting, intimidation, bombing, riots—and an attempt by communities to reach security from threat; families fled from hostile areas to the safety of their co-religionists, and barricades were erected against possible incursions. This, however, was only the first stage. A major feature of Northern Ireland's emergencies and the ensuing social crises, distinguishing them from the natural disasters described by Wallace and others, was their dynamic nature. While they often involved rioting, gun battles, intimidation, population movements and a curtailment of transport, they did not always contain all these elements, and not always in the same order. The immediate reaction to a political emergency was shooting and rioting; this was followed by an exodus of families from violent areas, often leaving the province; the inflow of intimidated families and the need to house them; the entry of security forces into the affected areas. Each aspect of the social crisis subtly altered the course of the political emergency and the response required to cope with it. Furthermore these changes in direction, which were almost impossible to anticipate accurately, took place over a period of weeks. The experience of the Northern Ireland Community Relations Commission emergency operation in 1971 demonstrated the need to monitor on a daily basis the dynamics of the emergency.

A necessary modification to Wallace's description of the impact phase is that Northern Ireland's emergencies have produced primary and secondary impact areas. The primary impact areas were the flashpoints which suffered in the first violence of the emergencies, and which were marked by rioting, shooting, damage to property, injuries or deaths. As a result, many inhabitants of these areas sought refuge in what they regarded as more secure districts. Their arrival created a secondary impact in the host areas, which was characterized by overcrowding, material shortages and the establishment of relief centres. The distinction between the primary and secondary impact areas was often blurred, since there were usually some primary characteristics in the secondary areas. The main practical difference was that the most serious effects of the emergency were experienced in the primary impact areas, and that most of the relief operations took place in the secondary impact areas.

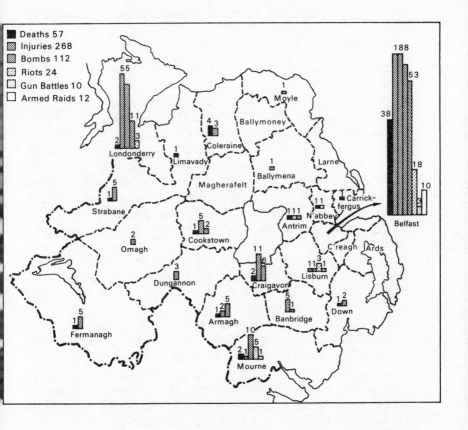

Map III   Northern Ireland: spatial distribution of types of violence.

This map is an attempt to illustrate the uneven distribution of violence across Northern Ireland. No official body in Northern Ireland publishes information showing the geographical distribution of violence, and this map was compiled from an analysis of violent incidents during an arbitrary sample period (the first fourteen days in October of each year from 1969–75). The main sources were R. Deutsch and Steve Magowan, *Northern Ireland: A Chronology of Events* (3 vols.) and a content analysis of *The Irish Times*. It is obvious that no firm conclusions should be drawn from an exercise such as this, although a number of interesting themes do emerge. The most remarkable feature is the concentration of violence in the urban areas of Belfast and Londonderry. During the periods of study 72% of deaths and 91% of injuries resulting from civil disorder took place in these areas (the figures for the urban preponderence of other violent activities were: bombs—55%; gun battles—33%; armed raids—83%). For the most part rural violence was concentrated in the areas bordering the Irish Republic and in the 'Murder triangle' around Craigavon. Many other parts of Northern Ireland were virtually unaffected by violence during the study periods.

The map does not demonstrate the considerable variations from year to year in the pattern of violence.

C. Responses

Efforts to relieve the distress resulting from the emergencies were severely hampered by the accompanying curtailment of communications between and within communities. Gun battles, riots, bombs and arson were features of the 1969 and 1971 emergencies, especially in Belfast, and movement was difficult and dangerous; in 1974 a network of barricades effectively prevented free access to some districts. Buses were withdrawn from the troubled areas; milk, food, petrol and medical supplies soon became scarce; relief agencies often found it difficult to enter those parts of the city where distress was greatest. This combination of acute distress and the absence of normal services caused people in the affected areas to fall back upon their own resources for immediate relief. Communities spontaneously threw up their own leaders, and the atmosphere of excitement which has been observed in natural disasters was also conspicuous in Belfast, where relief workers were sustained for much longer periods than would normally have been expected.

As a result of these factors, and a failure to adapt themselves effectively to new circumstances, the re-entry of the agencies into the troubled areas coincided with the final stages of the emergency rather than the period of acute distress in its first days. On those occasions when welfare authorities accepted the fact that their role in emergencies was a supportive rather than an executive one, as they began to do in Belfast in 1971 and to a much greater extent in 1974, their co-operation with local groups immediately produced improved performance.

D. Aftermath

A final and major difference between natural and political emergencies is their last phase. Wallace described the final stage of a disaster as 'recovery and reorganization', a period characterized by the construction of a new life by the victims of the emergency and the restoration of a stable community. No such stage can be easily recognized in a political emergency, since without a political settlement the likelihood of recurrence remains high. Naturally there is a return to a superficially more stable situation, but each emergency adds its contribution to community myths and community fears. Consequently, the last phase of a political emergency is not the restoration of stability. It is merely a return to the start of the cycle. The potential for violence within the community still remains. All that is required for another political emergency is renewed heightening of tension and another catalytic happening.

It is perhaps in relation to the effects of emergencies that Northern Ireland's experience of violence has most relevance to other countries. Since 1965 there have been more hospital disaster drills in the province than have occurred in all of Great Britain since 1951, and the Royal Victoria Hospital in Belfast has acquired a world-wide reputation for its emergency surgery and for its relief drills. However, it is much more difficult for social service agencies to draw up specific emergency plans. Types of medical casualties may vary with the changing patterns of violence but, when they enter the hospital, the situation is to some extent controlled. The social problems during emergencies, on the other hand, are more unpredictable in both their manifestations and their consequences. But while it is not possible to devise precise contingency plans, a number of general guidelines are apparent. It would be a useful development, for example, if social service agencies were to accept a number of tenets about emergencies: that they are unpredictable in terms of timing, extent and consequences, but that some districts are more vulnerable than others; that the key to the agencies' emergency role should be the provision of the basics of life—food, shelter, transport; that much of this provision can only be provided through community-based contacts. The search for such general principles in turn suggests particular strategies—decentralization of emergency supply depots to reduce access time; detailing of particularly vulnerable areas and priority of executive power for them. Improvements have been made in some of these directions, but generally the agencies have drawn back from accepting frankly the irrelevance of traditional models of relief provision in times of emergencies, and the need to redefine their roles. This redefinition must be firmly rooted in their acceptance that they have only very limited possibilities for direct action during emergencies. Consequently there is need for the establishment of firm and limited priorities—'at risk' families suggests itself as one possibility, the very young and very old as others—and for the temporary abandonment of conventional activities in the affected areas. These changes should be made frankly and publicly. In other words, on the outbreak of an emergency, the welfare authorities must immediately place themselves on an emergency basis in the disaster areas, adopt a supportive role to the community organizations in the provision of relief, and confine their executive functions to stated and clearly defined activities.

Another essential role for welfare agencies is that of supporting the establishment of a co-ordinated relief organization for statutory and voluntary agencies. In the United States civil defence is the joint responsibility of all three echelons of government—federal, state and local—under the Office of Civil Defence. This structure, which is primarily geared against hostile invasion, also comes into operation when disasters occur. Even when the disaster area is too small to have its own Civil Defence Organization the nearest organization assumes control, as happened in tornado-struck Cameron parish, Texas, in 1963. While it could not be argued that American civil defence procedures operate perfectly, the establishment of a similar structure in Northern Ireland would ease two of her outstanding emergency problems. In the first place, as well as including representatives from the army, police, welfare agencies and voluntary bodies, it would have the authority to declare when a state of emergency exists—a serious problem in Northern Ireland where, in the absence of any guidelines for such a definition, many agencies are reluctant to move on to an emergency footing until other agencies have done so. The other advantage of establishing a civil defence structure is that it would assume real and absolute executive powers during an emergency. It could give orders to member agencies, and its power would last until the emergency ended. Since the Ulster Workers' Council stoppage in May 1974, district officers have prepared local emergency plans for social work services with the encouragement of the Department of Health and Social Services. These demonstrate clearly the willingness of some agencies to build on past experience. Nevertheless, attempts by the main statutory and voluntary bodies involved in emergency relief to establish plans for co-ordination failed in 1972 and early 1974 because of the unwillingness of agencies to surrender voluntarily any of their functions to another body. Subsequent events have demonstrated more than ever their need to do so.

Notes

1 *Social and Economic Trends in Northern Ireland, 1975*, HMSO, 1976.
2 Birrell, D., 'Relative deprivation as a factor in conflict in Northern Ireland' in *Sociological Review*, **20**, 3, 1972, 317–44.

3   Davies, R. and McGurnaghan, M. A., 'Northern Ireland: the economics of adversity', in *Quarterly Review of the National Westminster Bank*, London: 1975, 56–68.
4   The assertiveness of community groups and their opposition to the proposed Belfast Urban Motorway is discussed in Weiner, R., *Rape and Plunder of the Shankill*, Belfast, privately published, 1975.
5   Wallace, A. F. C., *Tornado in Worcester: Disaster Study Number 3*, Washington, D.C.: National Academy of Sciences, 1956; Bates, F. L. *et al.*, *The Social and Psychological Consequences of a Natural Disaster: Disaster Study Number 18*, Washington, D.C.: National Academy of Sciences, 1963; Bennet, Glin, 'Community disaster in Britain' in Jones, Kathleen (ed.), *The Year Book of Social Policy in Britain*, London: Routledge and Kegan Paul, 1973.

Part A: Violence and Institutions

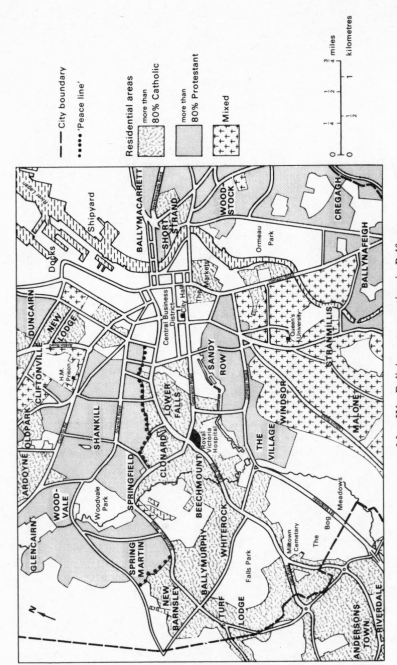

Map IV Religious segregation in Belfast

— City boundary
⋯ 'Peace line'

Residential areas

more than 80% Catholic

more than 80% Protestant

Mixed

2 Public Services

Barry White*

Introduction

Extremists on both sides in Northern Ireland have used attacks on the public services to harass the government of the day, disrupt commercial life and demoralize the community. Response to the emergency was slow, until the full seriousness was apparent, but it has improved in effectiveness with experience. Ways have been found to minimize disruption and live with terrorism, including irregular contacts with the terrorists themselves to try to determine the true cause or intention of any violence. Guerrilla warfare in Ulster could be a prelude to revolutionary attacks on similarly developed Western societies, and the main lesson learned has been that public services can cope with almost anything, by adapting to and anticipating trouble. People are still divided on the legitimacy of violence, but all have accepted the necessity for tight security at home, at work and on the streets. Although society has survived a prolonged period of violence at this level of intensity there could be no certainty that it would pull through without unlimited government assistance.

Background

The public services were a prime target for violence from the earliest days of Ulster's troubles for the traditional revolutionary reasons. They were vulnerable, they were identified with the establishment and attacks on them had a three-fold purpose. They impressed the population with the strength of the attackers, left people frustrated with government ineffectiveness and resulted in a stepping up of security which was often oppressive. The campaign against the public services

* Barry White is a leader writer with the *Belfast Telegraph*.

took various forms, direct and indirect, including bombing, robbery, hi-jacking, fraud, intimidation and non-payment of bills, under the guise of civil disobedience. It came from the two main directions, from the IRA, based in the Catholic population, whose aim is to drive British influence out of Northern Ireland, and from Protestant paramilitary forces, who have traditionally used force against both Catholic nationalists and the British to convince both of their capacity for civil war if any change in Ulster's constitutional position were contemplated.

The violence came in three different phases, overlapping each other to some extent. Phase I, from 1969 to 1972, was distinguished by politically motivated violence, through bombing or civil disobedience, to bring about short-term political change. Phase II, 1971 to 1974, was marked by economic violence, aimed at trying to weaken Britain's links with Ulster by burdening her with vast amounts of compensation for damage to the public services. Phase III, 1972 to the present, saw the stepping up of violence to finance the paramilitary organizations on both sides, through robbery, protection rackets and general gangsterism.

Phase I met with considerable success from the point of view of both the Protestant and Catholic extremists. Firstly, Protestant bombing—blamed on the IRA—helped right-wing Unionists to overthrow the liberal Prime Minister, Captain Terence (later Lord) O'Neill in April 1969. Then, following Protestant attacks on the Catholic Falls district of Belfast in August 1969, the IRA went on the offensive and eventually a weakened Stormont Government had to submit to direct rule from London in March 1972. Phase II was relatively unsuccessful, since Britain was easily able to withstand the economic bombing campaign of the IRA, and gradually the emphasis changed to attacks on military personnel. Phase III continues unchecked in 1977, preventing the public services from relaxing their security and making it difficult to pursue bad debts in areas where the police are unable to operate freely. It keeps the political situation on the boil, by reminding people of the Mafia-like power of the paramilitary organizations, both Protestant and Catholic, but presents comparatively little threat to the public services.

Violence and its Effects

The effects of violence have been felt in every public utility, both directly and indirectly. Electricity, gas and water services were all hit by bombs at installations around the country and at offices in the towns and cities. They also suffered severely from the effects of the civil disobedience campaign which was intended by its organizers to be limited to a rent and rates strike against internment, introduced in 1971, but was widened, unofficially, to include non-payment of bills from all the public services.

Protestant paramilitaries were the first to see the political potential in bomb attacks which damaged public confidence in the government, and their first strikes at electricity and water supply targets in March and April 1969 opened the first cracks in the Unionist monolith. Blame fell on the IRA, despite denials, and by the time the truth came out, six months later, republicans had taken over the campaign of violence.

Otherwise the bombing campaign against the public utilities was only moderately successful over the whole period of the troubles. The electricity service has a built-in capacity to absorb emergency demands, in case of breakdowns; gas was never seriously attacked, except for an unexplained premature blast in Belfast in October 1976, and water was never again hit as vitally as it had been in the opening offensive. The civil disobedience campaign probably had as great an effect as the actual bombs for it meant that large numbers of Catholics ceased paying all bills, including car tax, television licence fees and electricity and gas charges. The setting up of virtual no-go areas meant that the law could not operate effectively against defaulters, and service engineers and meter readers were *personae non gratae*. (Private debt collectors were also unwelcome, and companies had to write off thousands of pounds worth of hire purchase transactions.) Large deficits were built up in the public sector, totalling £17 million in July 1976, and regular payers on the Protestant side blamed increased charges on non-paying Catholics. Incidentally, the withdrawal of regular visits by personnel from the public services broke valuable contact with the powers-that-be and increased the sense of isolation in ghetto areas. Another factor which added to the difficulty of pursuing defaulters was the mass migration of Catholics from mixed areas to 'safe' districts of West and North Belfast, or to Britain, leaving no trace of their whereabouts.

The Post Office and telephone system also suffered greatly from the effects of terrorism, ranging from a concerted campaign to knock out provincial telephone exchanges to systematic hi-jacking and robbery of Post Office vans, especially in border areas. Many sub-post offices were raided regularly for money to be paid out in welfare benefits, but the service continued through it all, even if some payments had to be transferred temporarily to central offices, and the standard twice-daily postal deliveries were almost unaffected. The scale of the destruction was quite staggering: up to mid-1975, 172 vehicles had been stolen and destroyed and there had been 26 cases of severe damage to main post offices. Fourteen sub-post offices were destroyed and 25 badly damaged. Of 195 telephone exchanges, 29 were destroyed and 10 very badly damaged. The Post Office logged 125 terrorist or riot attacks on Post Office buildings, 554 armed robberies on post offices and 227 on vehicles. Eight employees had been killed—two of them on duty. IRA-inspired frauds cost the Giro service about £½m.

The fire service bore the brunt of the economic bombing campaign mostly conducted with incendiary devices in shops or with bombs with incendiary material attached. The service also continued non-stop, despite some initial difficulty convincing Catholics and Protestants of its political neutrality. In Belfast, one-fifth of fire calls during the period 1969 to 1973 were connected with civil disturbances and under the provincial Fire Authority, 1971–3, the ratio was one in seven. Ten fires, of which three were in Belfast, are estimated to have cost over £1m. each. The worst, at Belfast Co-operative's headquarters, cost £10m. Despite the fire service's involvement, only one man died in action associated with civil disturbance, shot by Protestants in mistake for a soldier, and four were seriously injured.

In the field of transport, bus services are particularly vulnerable, since routes are well known and drivers have no means of defence against marauding gunmen. No riot was complete, in the early days, without its burning bus or buses and, as well as the rallying effect of a blazing bonfire, the disruption proved the impotence of the authorities. The only weapon the bus companies have is to withdraw services after attacks have been made and although this has sometimes led to criticism of the authorities the paramilitary organizations have taken most of the blame. Attacks on bus stations were prevalent at one time but the bus companies proved they could operate satisfactorily without them. In Belfast bus depots were badly sited in mainly Republican areas and their occupation by soldiers helped to identify the city bus service with the government.

The cost of maintaining services, often beyond the point where some buses were bound to be lost to rioters, amounted to some 450 buses destroyed in the period 1969 to mid-1975, including 250 Ulsterbus and 200 Citybus (confined to the Belfast area). Sixteen bus employees were killed, 10 of them on duty.

Train services, limited to Belfast–Londonderry and Belfast–Dublin lines, with commuter services to North Down and South Antrim, were equally at risk and the concentration of IRA fugitives along the South Armagh–Louth border meant frequent disruption of the Belfast–Dublin line—63 times to mid-1976—with hi-jackings and real and hoax bombs placed in stationary trains. Stations were frequent targets and repeated bomb attacks on Belfast's three stations reduced them to little more than shells, although all remained operational. Because of a £4m. development plan completed in 1976, two of them did not need re-building. From 1972 to August 1976, Northern Ireland Railways had to cope with 97 genuine bombs, 145 hoaxes (where something was found, which was not a bomb), and 291 scares, an average of two a week. They reckoned they recovered slightly less than 50% of the damage in Government compensation. There was only one fatality—a woman killed by one of two bombs planted on a commuter train.

Air and sea routes were affected indirectly by the sudden reduction in tourist traffic and directly by occasional bombs, calculated to cause maximum alarm, but in no case lethal. Two shipping routes, Belfast–Heysham and Belfast–Ardrossan were axed, largely because of the drop in the tourist trade, but the airport slightly increased its traffic flow, from 1.1m. in 1971–2 to 1.3m. in 1973–4, with the help of soldiers travelling on and off duty. Since then the numbers have fallen steadily. There was a concentrated bombing campaign, from June to September 1973, directed against the airport, but the combination of strict security precautions and complete exclusion of non-travelling visitors from the airport buildings minimized the dangers.

The troubles obviously put an enormous strain on the media, both local and national, as they tried to paint a true picture of what was happening. The broadcasting media kept themselves strictly impartial, in accordance with their charters, but in general the press sided with the establishment, or one or other of the sectarian factions. This was partly for historical and ideological reasons, partly for self-preservation and partly for circulation advantage. The three Belfast newspaper offices suffered periodically from bomb damage, but publication was only interrupted briefly at the *Irish News*, and the *Belfast Telegraph* carried on with editions of reduced size after a bomb exploded inside the building in September 1976. The *Telegraph* also lost several vans, burned by extremists hostile to the paper's editorial line. The most spectacular interference with press freedom was the IRA's destruction of the £6m. *Daily Mirror* printing plant near Belfast, because of its allegedly pro-Army bias. BBC headquarters in Belfast was damaged four times by explosions, aimed at the building or at nearby showrooms, but only once was its nightly TV news bulletin forced off the air. There was one 'occupation' of the building by Protestants, demonstrating against conditions at the Maze prison. In addition, there were several bomb attacks on television transmitters in remote country areas.

Another aspect of the terrorists' attempt to disrupt the life of the community was a concerted bombing campaign, by explosive and incendiary devices, against town and city centres. This involved the systematic destruction or damage of shops, hotels, restaurants, public houses and places of public entertainment, like cinemas and theatres. Not only did this hit the commercial livelihood of cities like Belfast and Londonderry, which saw much of their trade depart to outlying centres, but it substantially lowered the quality of life for the inhabitants, and began a series of tit-for-tat bombings of public houses in particular which led to a substantial change in social habits. (By mid-1975 over 400 pubs had been damaged or destroyed.) People became reluctant to venture out at night to places of regular entertainment, or to public bars which were liable to attack, and alternatives were devised. Drinking clubs, legal and illegal, sprang up in all parts of Belfast, to replace bombed-out pubs and provide safer meeting places, with cabaret acts an additional attraction. Most were run by paramilitary bodies, the IRA, the UVF and the UDA—who themselves were responsible for bombing legitimate pubs—providing a valuable source of revenue and building up their standing in the community. Illegal clubs should have been unable to receive drink supplies, but the normal practice was for the paramilitary owners to buy through a licensed club or pub, a practice to which the authorities turned a blind eye. A brief attempt was made early in the troubles to restrict licensing hours to avoid late-night violence, but it was abandoned because of unenforcibility and complaints from the licensed trade. Cinema and theatre attendances, already decreasing, fell away sharply during the troubles, partly because of the early closure of public transport services. Belfast lost more than a dozen cinemas over the period, and two of its three regular theatres closed. Hotels and restaurants throughout the province came under heavy attack from terrorists and, over a six-year period, 1970–5, 24 were destroyed, 41 were damaged and seven closed undamaged. Tourist numbers decreased by 60% and revenue was down by one-third, from 1968 to 1974, with the result that the industry employed half as many staff as could otherwise have been expected. Sport too, suffered from diminishing gates and the fact that few nationals from outside Northern Ireland were willing to risk appearing on Ulster soil. Limitations on normal social intercourse may have been a factor behind the sudden, and for puritanical Ulster, surprising establishment of a flourishing massage parlour trade, which became a cover for prostitution. Some of these businesses were added to the paramilitaries' Mafia-type empires, which also included cut-price grocery stores, another means of establishing links with the people and promoting their aims. Government-registered co-operatives with strong paramilitary ties were formed in ghetto communities, buying over several retail outlets and securing valuable public housing contracts.

Responses of the Agencies

Until 1969, Northern Ireland had been a relatively law-abiding society, so it was natural for the public services, like other public agencies, to be cautious in their response to the violence. They did not know, nor did anyone, how much feeling there was behind the campaign, how long it would last in face of military pressures, and how it would develop. Their response was also affected by the radical reorganization of local government which took place in 1973, after years of preparation, meaning that public services which had been based on old nineteenth-century structures were centralized in province-wide authorities. This affected electricity, water and sewage, as well as housing, roads and buses. Different services responded in different ways, because some were more vulnerable to violence than others, but in general the decision was taken at an early stage—under the Northern Ireland administration—to carry on serving the public, come what may and not to be deterred by the political or financial cost. Some services, like electricity and gas, put the safety of their employees first and minimized risks by leaving it to the employees' discretion whether or not they should go into troubled areas. Others, like Ulsterbus, accepted that they had to take these risks to preserve the service, and no exceptions were made for employees' sensibilities. Most security-conscious of all was the electricity service, not only because the headquarters building was bombed early in the campaign, killing an employee, but because it was appreciated that while society could carry on without piped water, mail, or buses, it would grind rapidly to a halt if power were cut off. Extra security precautions at power stations cost £7m. and the continuing drain on resources was £1m. a year in 1976.

Tightening up security was the most obvious response, once the nature and scale of the violence were known. At the same time heads of several of the agencies decided, independently of the politicians, that some contact had to be made, however indirectly, with the terrorists. They needed to know which violence was planned and which was random, so that any apparent changes of course could be probed to avoid false conclusions being drawn. An example of this was Ulsterbus' reaction to an IRA murder of a bus driver in Londonderry which led to a face-to-face meeting between the two wings of the IRA and senior Ulsterbus executives to clear the air. 'Gentlemen's agreements' were worked out by means of which each side could predict with some accuracy what reaction would be provoked by any given action. Most contacts, however, took place at second-hand, through intermediaries like the clergy, or front organizations which spoke for the paramilitaries, and agreements were almost invariably honoured.

Often there was a stark choice for the public services, to carry on with their duties as laid down by statute, or to withdraw from the scene. The first risked the lives of employees, or at least the loss of hardware, like buses, trains or other vehicles, but the second, if embarked upon too soon, could set the population against the service, without bringing opprobrium upon the IRA or the UDA. When it was timed just right, as in the case of the buses, withdrawal of service was the most effective anti-terrorist device of all. People could see how the service had striven to keep going until finally being forced to protect itself. The result in such cases was that people recognized the attackers as the enemy, whereas, if the authorities' response were too sudden, resentment would build up against the service. An equally effective weapon, frequently used, was the spontaneous strike called whenever workers felt they had to register an instant protest against the killing of a colleague. In the case of organized disruption of traffic by bus hijacking, burning, etc., security forces generally stood clear, risking criticism, rather than allow themselves to be dragged into riots.

There were many cases of response being too slow, too fast, or simply inadequate, but in general public services adapted well to the unusual strains and received substantial backing, in terms of finance and morale, from the government, especially under direct rule from London, from 1972 onwards. Until then the public services had been inevitably associated with the Stormont administration, which to Republicans meant that they were part of the political structure which had to be destroyed. But under Westminster rule the Catholic population was better disposed to the administration, and this took some of the pressure off the public services. It did not, however, break habits of civil disobedience, and the limitations of the law meant that some services were supplied free, since workmen could not get into some areas to switch off supplies or empty meters.

Under constant attack, or threat of attack, the public utilities had to learn to live in a situation of permanent instability, which had several interesting by-products. They had to keep the public fully informed of what was happening and why they were unable to deliver their usual service, and this meant much more emphasis on public relations, and appearances on TV and radio. Public support was enlisted and cuts or interruptions in services were accepted as part of the natural order. In many cases this meant direct approaches to local community associations which helped give the public services a more human face.

The fire services, particularly in Belfast, took great pains from an early stage to establish themselves as a neutral party. Those who were lighting the fires wanted people in their area to think the firefighters were partial to the other side, and to repulse them, but the propaganda war was eventually won by the firemen, and they have since had free access everywhere. All the public services developed much more expertise in dealing with the media, which was in sharp contrast with their previous performances.

Throughout the public services, there was a corporate will to refuse to let the terrorist succeed; this helped staff morale through the worst periods when the normal reaction would have been to close down. Although staff was mixed, Protestants and Catholics, there was remarkably little friction between those working side by side. In the Post Office, for instance, Protestants and Catholics continued to work together in a sorting office in the Republican Lower Falls district, without interference. All the agencies claim that staff are chosen on merit, not religious or political affiliation, and although there were isolated allegations of collusion, voluntary or under pressure, with terrorist organizations in some areas of the public services, it is generally true that politics did not enter into staff relationships. Leadership was an important factor in maintaining good working relationships, both within the services and with the general population, and each of the utilities and transport undertakings was fortunate in having managements which were strong and yet sensitive enough to local conditions to maintain a high degree of confidence.

In the transport field, where the staff were particularly vulnerable to attack, since routes took them through troubled areas, good morale was crucial. The experience was that although the staff came from different backgrounds and represented the broad balance of the population in terms of religion and politics, the pressures of violence held them together as a team. In the same way, passengers were surprisingly tolerant of inadequacies in the service and ceased to complain about delays and diversions. This was particularly apparent in the case of air travel, where people put safety first, were prepared to accept checking-in an hour before departure, willingly enduring spartan conditions in temporary huts, if security could be guaranteed. Reaction to the concerted campaign against the airport in 1973 illustrated the different attitude to violence of those who have to live with it because Northern Ireland is their home, and pilots and crew from Great Britain who fly in and out. While the local population was soon reassured by the extra security at the airport, British Airways allowed aircrew to refuse to fly to Northern Ireland and did not leave aircraft at Aldergrove overnight in case of sabotage.

The media found they had to adopt new attitudes both to those who were causing violence and to their own staff. The press, local and national, unanimously condemned violence, but the newspapers had different ways of apportioning blame, according to their political or religious bias. For instance, the Catholic-owned *Irish News* would sometimes criticize the British Army for provocation, implying justification for Catholic reaction, while the *Daily Mirror* would often ignore this factor. National papers could adopt a more critical attitude to the troublemakers on both sides, because of their greater detachment, while local newspapers had to have more consideration for the attitudes of their readers, who had ambivalent feelings. Paramilitary organizations tended to be much more tolerant of criticism in the London and Dublin press, which they learned to expect, than in the local press. Of the Belfast morning papers, the *News Letter* was unashamedly attached to the Unionist and Protestant cause and the *Irish News* was equally committed to Irish nationalism and Catholic rights, while the only evening paper, the mass circulation *Belfast Telegraph* steered a middle-of-the-road, pro-reform, pro-British government course, which encountered occasional difficulties with its mixed readership. But although a boycott was attempted at one time by Protestant extremists hostile to the newspaper's liberal editorial policy, it had little effect. Meanwhile the only Sunday newspaper, the non-aligned *Sunday News*, thrived on a regular diet of weekend violence.

There was much heart-searching in the media about whether newsmen were helping to feed the troubles by reporting them in detail but it was generally decided that journalists should not try to play a political role and there was no radical change of direction. Staff were under great pressure and on occasions were threatened by the paramilitaries for their interpretation of the news. It was a difficult situation where leader columns were condemning violence while reporters were daily talking to the men who created it, but in time the paramilitaries and their supporters learned to appreciate the press' two functions, to tell the news and comment on it. They also learned to manipulate the press, making false claims, or inventing new paramilitary organizations as a cover for their more nefarious activities. The security forces also used their unique position, as purveyors of news from different parts of the province, to give stories a favourable slant at times, which the press, working within strict deadlines, was unable to challenge.

Generally speaking, the Protestant working class has been suspicious of, if not antagonistic to, all forms of journalism, since sections of the media identified themselves closely with the Catholic cause in the early days of civil rights. On the other hand, Catholics have welcomed media coverage of minority grievances and paramilitary spokesmen have been accessible and articulate. Journalists have rarely been attacked, but the fact that they sense Protestant hostility has often helped to reinforce their sympathy for the minority and affect their judgement of the majority's case.

In a situation where local communities feel imprisoned or threatened by violence, and confine themselves within well-defined areas, there is a need for a localized news and information service, which has been met by a flourishing fringe press. Some publications are duplicated sheets, circulated mainly for fund-raising purposes, while others are well printed and professionally presented. Nearly all have an extreme political bias, depending on whether they circulate among Protestants or Catholics, but some are mainly concerned with community issues or problems, while others openly encourage paramilitary activity. Organs like the Catholic *Andersonstown News* have developed into almost indispensable community information sources which should survive the troubles; others, like the Protestant *Loyalist News*, which went as far as to publish a detailed 'Know your weapon' series, will clearly lose their *raison d'être* if peace returns.

The most striking change brought about by the troubles in public transport has been the advent of two taxi systems, indirectly controlled by the paramilitary IRA and UDA, and serving the two main arteries of West Belfast, the Catholic Falls Road and the Protestant Shankill Road. The so-called 'People's Taxis' were introduced on the Falls to provide a cheap alternative service to buses at times of civil disturbance, but they are now an established feature on both sides of the peace line, with a fleet of about 300 London-type taxis, hitting seriously at bus revenue and jobs. They are illegal, in that they use unrecognized taxi stands and carry up to a dozen passengers, far beyond the legal limit, per trip, but they have virtual immunity, because of the power of the taxi operators to block roads in protest against harrassment. It is widely suspected that buses have been attacked, on occasion, in order to create demand for the taxis, and this is another reason why the bus companies, fearing more losses, do not seek confrontations. The cost to Citybus of the 'black taxis' was estimated in 1976 at £1m. a year.

Lessons Learned

In the utilities sector the emergency was regarded as a challenge to the ingenuity of professionals who have always prided themselves on being able to cope with any kind of breakdown. For every problem caused by violence or civil disobedience, a solution was invariably found, if the power of the law allowed. (The latter was, in fact, a very inhibiting factor. Even while in certain areas law could not be enforced, the administration still stuck strictly to the letter of the law. For example, when the Army wanted to use black paint on a street corner which had been whitewashed by the IRA to show up patrolling soldiers for its snipers, a permit had to be obtained under the Special Powers Act, requiring the signature of the Secretary of State.)

But although the electricity service proved during the Protestant strike of May 1974 that generators could be kept going, without damage even well below danger level, a decision was made that such risks should not be taken again. The equipment survived once, but, on reflection, the engineers believed the danger to the system was too great. Also, in the event of a political emergency, there is an unwritten rule that no attempt should be made to use the link between the systems North and South of the Irish border to supplement failing supplies in Northern Ireland. Such a move may have been anticipated by Protestant paramilitaries when, well before the 1974 strike, the cross-border link was blown up.

The fire brigade learned a lot about the deployment of men and resources in times of peak demand, and one of the results is that the number of appliances sent to any one fire has been reduced to a bare minimum, because of the danger of a series of alarms. The value of cash incentives, to overcome recruitment problems in the police, the prison service and the fire brigade—every fireman has a special allowance for making himself available for a call-out 24 hours a day, 7 days a week— has also been proved. But as violence continued police and firemen pressed for increased danger money payments and in September 1976 firemen staged a boycott of fires which were caused by terrorists and which did not endanger life. The importance of symbols, in such a divided society as Ulster's, has been appreciated at the highest levels, and care was taken to see that the badge of the Northern Ireland Fire Service formed from an amalgamation of the Fire Authority and Belfast Fire Service in 1973 was as neutral as possible.

There was also a practical response to a petrol bomb attack on a fire officer's car which was mistaken by Republican rioters in Belfast for a police car. Clearer identification was ordered, and there have been no further accidents. Another lesson learned in the early stages was not to approach fires from the direction of hostile territory, Protestant or Catholic, even if this was the quickest way of getting to the fire. Some crews did, and were instantly identified with the opposing faction. By arrangement with local paramilitary commanders, routes were agreed which minimized crowd resentment of 'invasions' by the statutory authorities.

The IRA bombing campaign against telephone exchanges helped to develop local expertise in the installation of temporary equipment, some of which has been used for years at a time, and in the building of new exchanges. The normal practice had been for British companies to fit the equipment, but because of the reluctance of skilled engineers to travel to Northern Ireland, local telephones employees have had to learn installation techniques. In Belfast, the letter slits on all post boxes were narrowed by the fitting of a steel plate after a rash of pillar-box bombs. But no solution was found to prevent vandalizing of phone boxes, which were methodically destroyed in some estates to prevent informers using the police confidential telephone.

Belfast bus operators soon learned to reserve their oldest and most expendable buses for riot areas like the Falls Road, and in this way Government compensation could be said to have helped to modernize the bus fleet. After repeated bomb attacks on bus depots, Ulsterbus decided that loss of windows was no reason for withdrawing buses from service, and experimented with perspex and hardboard, as well as glass-fibre, vandal-proof seats. Hardboard temporarily proved more popular than glass in some areas where stone-throwing was prevalent. As well as actual bombs placed in hi-jacked buses, there was also a high proportion of hoax bombs, especially during periods of Protestant activity, and after losing several buses to army bomb disposal methods—which could consist of firing anti-tank rockets—senior executives of Ulsterbus decided to intervene. They themselves undertook the examination and disposal of parcels when a hoax was suspected, and are credited with saving eighteen buses in this way. In addition to thwarting the terrorist and saving valuable hardware—buses cost £12,000 to replace—leadership from the top has a boosting effect on morale and damages the paramilitaries' standing.

The Belfast–Dublin train line was particularly vulnerable to hijacking and bomb hoaxes near the Irish border, and to by-pass suspected bombs on the track or in trains, a bus service ferried passengers between Portadown and Dundalk. Here, again, the disruptive effect was minimized, with the result that hi-jackings became less frequent.

At Belfast airport, security was gradually stepped up from a body search in the early stages to the closing of the airport to non-travellers and a thorough luggage check by security personnel. After the discovery of a bomb on a plane in July 1974, probably planted in London, catering services were withdrawn for a time and hand luggage banned. Belongings are packed in plastic bags by security men in London and collected, still sealed, in Belfast. The airlines remained responsive to the security question and to passengers' tolerance, and as soon as conditions allowed, normal services were restored. However, the security forces remained highly conscious of the airport's importance as a prestige target for terrorists and, after a remote-controlled mortar attack on the airport, roads under the flight path were sealed off and permanent checkpoints set up in July 1976.

Elsewhere, there was extensive use of sophisticated security devices, like closed-circuit television, to check for bombers, and the efficiency of shatter-resistant plastic film on windows was severely tested. The Government contributed to security consciousness by withholding full compensation for damage from firms which neglected to take adequate precautions, and by subsidizing the employment of guards, as well as by recruiting its own (about 400) male and female security officers who gradually replaced soldiers at city centre checkpoints. Firms with up to 10 employees received a grant of 75% of the salary of a security man—up to £1,200 a year—and there were proportionate grants for bigger companies. After seven years of the emergency it was estimated that the 'security industry' was worth at least £10m. annually, providing full-time jobs for more than 7,000 civilians, quite apart from members of the security forces.

The media maintained the closest and most continuous contact with the terrorists on all sides, and a system of code words was worked out with known and unknown telephone callers to ascertain that anonymous calls claiming responsibility for bombings or killings, or issuing warnings, were genuine. Doomsday plans were worked out to pool printing resources in the event of bomb attacks knocking out plant. Many new advertising campaigns were devised by the Government information services to break down public resistance to 'informing' on terrorist suspects and newspapers and TV were extensively used to put this message across, to the extent that Government advertising revenue was a considerable source of income in lean circulation times. The *Irish News* continued to run death notices and display advertising booked by illegal organizations, alongside Government advertising, but although this created some annoyance in official circles, the newspaper's difficulties were appreciated. Meanwhile, the *Belfast Telegraph* maintained a policy of refusing advertisements from unlawful paramilitary bodies. From its position of neutrality, it organized a disaster fund in 1969 to help victims of the August rioting, raising £66,000, to which the Northern Ireland Government added £250,000. Letters to the editors were carefully scrutinized for propaganda, by both the paramilitaries and security forces and, although all letters were authenticated, newspapers had to allow pseudonyms because of danger of retaliation.

Journalists whose work brought them into close contact with paramilitary sources were often privy to information which could have led to charges being made. But despite pressure from police, they invariably protected their sources or refused to give evidence in court for ethical as well as personal safety reasons and also because any breach could have threatened all pressmen. One BBC reporter was briefly imprisoned. Three journalists who fell foul of the IRA felt forced to leave the country. In appreciation of the extra strains, most broadcasting and newspaper staffs received an extra week's holiday and/or cash holiday bonuses.

Local newspaper circulations were buoyant during the early excitement of the troubles, but fell away by 15–20% as the violence palled and other factors, like higher prices and the general decline in newspaper readership, took effect. Street sales were hit by the reduction of city centre business.

The output of local BBC television increased greatly over the period, while BBC radio coverage doubled, leading to the establishment of Radio Ulster, based on BBC Belfast, in January 1975. An independent commercial station, Downtown, opened in 1976 with the facility for interrupting programmes for up-to-the-minute news. International interest in the troubles contributed to the rapid development of colour TV and Belfast became an important training ground for junior reporters and cameramen because of its unrivalled opportunities.

Broadcasting executives were particularly careful to ensure that coverage remained unbiased, and in the BBC the Northern Ireland controller retained the right to veto any item produced in Ulster, for local or national use, in case it should inflame the situation. Nevertheless, different standards could often be detected in news broadcasts for local and national consumption, with a tendency to play down criticism of the Army in national bulletins. Meanwhile the Dublin radio and TV network, RTE, tended to regard events from a Catholic viewpoint. On several occasions the Independent Broadcasting Authority, which monitors independent television and radio, judged that programmes which were shown in Britain were too controversial to be viewed in Ulster. There was considerable concern about the possibility that widespread news coverage of violence could contribute to further violence and, after some evidence that on-the-spot reporting of riots was having this effect, the media tended to wait until the all-clear was given before broadcasting.

Another broadcasting innovation in Ulster, at the height of the troubles in 1969 and 1971, was 'pirate' radio, set up in Catholic and then Protestant ghettoes, to provide a slanted local information source and create wartime camaraderie. These stations were soon located and put out of action by the Army, but already had proved their effectiveness in urban guerilla warfare by the speed with which they could bring people on to the streets in response to an emergency appeal. In broadcasting, as in the press, doomsday plans have been drawn up to ensure that a reliable information service will be available and, as a discouragement to Protestant extremists contemplating seizure of independence from Britain, the BBC controller announced in 1975 that £1½m. would be needed annually to maintain the service.

But the most effective contribution to the general security picture was the sealing off of large areas of downtown Belfast and Londonderry by security gates, manned in the first instance by soldiers and later by civilian search officers. There was a reluctance to concede that this was the only reliable way of preventing the terrorists bombing at will, from the point of view that it represented a partial victory for the IRA and greatly inconvenienced shoppers. But the development of the car bomb, and later the proxy bomb by which a driver under threat could be made to deliver a bomb himself, eventually forced it upon the authorities.

Pedestrianization of shopping streets, which had long been resisted by doubtful Belfast traders, was an instant success. Security was not foolproof, and bombs exploded occasionally inside the gates, but this did not destroy public confidence. At first there was no attempt to interfere with traffic along main city centre thoroughfares, but the explosion of more car bombs led to the banning of through-traffic, other than well-searched buses, and the complete sealing-off of the city centre by a series of security gates. Early fears were that this clamp-down, combined with limitations on parking, which meant that vehicles could not be left unattended, would ruin city centre trade and cause intolerable inconvenience. These, however, were not realized. Outside Belfast, almost every country town sealed off its centre in similar fashion as an effective counter to the car bomb menace.

The bombing campaign led directly to the introduction of a new twenty-four-hour public service, first under the Community Relations department and then the Department of the Environment, which was responsible for emergency repairs in the wake of explosions. As soon as news of a blast was received, men set out to board up windows and do emergency repairs, free of charge. Government compensation was paid for the repair or replacement of all bomb-damaged property, since there was no way for citizens or public services to insure themselves against civil disorder. This led to the payment, between 1968 and August 1976, of £24m. for personal injuries and £162m. for property. Outstanding claims were £18m. and £30m. respectively, making a total of more than £230m. in compensation. The Post Office alone has claimed more than £2m., and the cost of its security measures was estimated in 1975 at more than £2m.

Conclusions

The troubles have continued for longer than any previous period of political unrest in Northern Ireland and as long as any undeclared civil war in a developed Western society. Many students and executives in public services in Britain and elsewhere have visited the province to see how the authorities have coped. Some see events in Northern Ireland as a foretaste of urban guerrilla warfare around the world and are anxious to learn new techniques for possible future use. The Ulster Workers' Council strike in 1974 has been the subject of close scrutiny to deter-mine if or how a strike of this nature could be beaten in a humanitarian society unwilling to risk the death of unprotected citizens. There is a tacit acceptance that the Government's tactics were faulty, in that, against the advice of the local Executive, they shirked an early confron-tation with the strikers while continuing to subsidize the civil popu-lation without discrimination.

At a lower level, planners and managers who have to work in divided societies like Northern Ireland have been interested to see how public services continue to function, despite social unrest. A fire chief from South Africa has shown great interest in the way the Fire Service has been able to send crews of mixed religion into Catholic or Protestant areas without trouble. His experience was that only black crews were acceptable in black areas.

But the most obvious export resulting from the troubles has been the Ulster experience, over six years, of tight security in virtually every public place, affecting every public service. People have learned, in fact, to accept this as part of daily life and the more thorough it is, the more pleased they are. Standards of service have slipped, but the public accept this without serious complaint so long as they are presented with evidence of the cause of trouble. Certain management techniques have been evolved over the period which could be of use elsewhere should similar breakdowns in public order occur. This has prompted one Government-employed executive to suggest that he and his colleagues should be asked to give lectures in Britain, or wherever there is a possibility of civil stoppages, about the best means of handling emergency situations.

In any assessment of the performance of the public services under fire, it is necessary to put the terrorist threat in its proper perspective. Terrorism, including sectarian assassinations, was almost always related to the political situation and was used by the IRA to maintain an impetus for change or, in case of the Protestant paramilitaries, to prevent change. There is no evidence that either side ever intended, or was capable of, knocking out vital public services for any length of time, but they did want to put pressure on Government and, in this context, both sides can claim successes. The fact that the public services survived this kind of limited assault without any great difficulty does not suggest that they would automatically be able to survive a wider conflict, in which the Protestant and Catholic populations were more fully involved. Certainly the maintenance of public services has been greatly dependent on the fact that, to date, the paramilitary forces have been seeking only limited objectives and that the British government has offered total support, in terms of assistance for security, military protection and financial compensation. Without this, the story could have been very different.

3 Health Services

H. A. Lyons*

Introduction

The British National Health Service, since its inception in 1947, has never been asked to cope with a situation of severe and prolonged civil disturbance, and this chapter attempts to describe how the various branches of the health services in Northern Ireland have managed under these unusual conditions. The effect on general medical practice, the public health services, and general and specialized hospitals is outlined. The types of injury are described and there is a brief reference to how some of these have been treated. The psychological impact on the population generally is described and comparisons are made with other areas of conflict in the world. Special reference is made to the short- and long-term effect on children and teenagers. The Northern Ireland situation has created difficult ethical problems for doctors and others engaged in the health services, and some of these are discussed. Finally, an attempt is made to draw some general conclusions from the effects of six years of strife on the health of the population.

Background

Continuing violence in Northern Ireland since 1969 has cast considerably more work on the health services. Over 1,600 people have been killed and about 20,000 have been injured. Prior to 1832 civil disturbances were common in rural parts of Northern Ireland [1], but since that date, rioting has also been a feature of city life, occurring approximately each decade. Some of these disturbances have been studied in considerable detail by official Commissioners of Enquiry [2, 3]. Others

*H. A. Lyons is a consultant psychiatrist in Belfast and author of a number of publications relating to violence and psychiatric problems.

have been described by authors such as Henry [4], Boyd [5] and King [6]. The surgical aspects of the nineteenth-century riots were described by Foy [7] and Murney [8]. The authors record the frequency of head injury due to blunt instruments such as sticks, stones and bottles.

The reaction of a civilian population to a civil war was described by Du Saulle [9] at the time of the Franco-Prussian war; by Smith [10] during World War I; at the time of the Spanish civil war; and there were numerous reports during World War II on the effects of the air-raids on the population of various cities in Britain and other countries, (Lewis, [11]; Atkin, [12]; Harris, [13]; Hopkins, [14]).

The particular stresses operating in Northern Ireland, especially in urban areas, during the past six years, were not really comparable to war conditions as, during time of war, the people of the country are united and there is a strengthening of community ties and a lowering of social barriers. The stressful conditions in time of civil war approximate more to the Northern Irish situation, but in the case of civil war usually one geographically distinct part of the country rises against another. In a riot, however, people in the same or neighbouring streets are often the enemy, one's workmates become the intimidators, and one's customers the petrol bomb throwers. The community divides, but in the two sub-divisions there is increased solidarity, there being more social support and community spirit behind the barricades.

Public Health

The public health services have been put under stress mainly in urban areas of Northern Ireland, and in particular in the cities of Belfast and Derry. To a lesser extent some towns have been severely disrupted, such as Newry and Strabane. Due to the great movement of people resulting from intimidation and rioting, very considerable stress has been placed on the resources of community services.

The problems of Belfast have been described fully by Taggart [15], the former Medical Officer of Health for the city. The acute problems began after the severe rioting on the night of the 14 and 15 August 1969. About 4,000 people left their homes and 500 houses were suddenly made uninhabitable. Accommodation had to be found for these people. Initially reception centres were set up in schools and church halls. Health visitors, midwives, district nurses, together with welfare officers worked long hours to give what help they could in rehousing these people. These various workers were often in the front line. In spite of the great movement of people, often living in unsanitary and crowded conditions, there was no outbreak of an infectious disease.

The burden on the public health inspectors has greatly increased and this has led to some reduction in standards. It is difficult to get landlords to carry out abatement of sanitary nuisances when the occupants are squatters and no rent is being paid. Also for a long period there was a rent and rates strike, so there was little motivation on the part of landlords to carry out repairs. There is also the problem of inspectors, workmen and refuse collectors going into certain areas, and as a result of these various factors, there has been very considerable deterioration in the physical environment. Once houses have been damaged by explosions or simply vacated due to intimidation, vandals rapidly move in and large areas of housing have been destroyed as a result. The areas of Belfast and Derry affected have been areas of high density and low social status. These features become more marked in Belfast as the area approaching the city centre is reached, where, in addition, a large slum clearance programme is under way. Segregation in Belfast is related to socio-economic ranking, and very high segregation is found with low status and high density [16]. Some of the factors indicating a disintegrated society, namely poverty, recent history of disaster, extensive migration, rapid and widespread social change, cultural confusion and a high frequency of hostility, are in operation in this area. However, in working-class Belfast, common antipathies contribute towards integration within the groups involved, especially at times of maximum civil unrest.

Public health staff, especially midwives and home nurses, have often had to enter troubled areas at night. Some have had their cars hi-jacked, but fortunately there have been no serious casualties among staff. However, several workmen repairing damaged houses have been shot. Some unusual problems have arisen for public health inspectors, such as the control of the increased rat population. Because of deterioration of the physical environment, and in particular because of the large number of boarded up and bricked up houses and masses of decaying rubbish, the increase in the rat population has been large. Large amounts of food have had to be condemned as unfit, due to bomb damage. In spite of these difficulties, the routine work of health clinics has continued. Devotion to duty and morale of the staff have been high. Some community staff have, understandably, become emotionally involved in a way that hospital staff have not, the latter being able to remain rather more detached. Medical visitors to Belfast are often taken to see Cupar Street Clinic and Ashmore Street Hostel which sit astride the so called 'peace-line'. They are surrounded by an area of extreme destruction, yet the routine work of these places has continued during the past six years.

General Practice

In Northern Ireland there are 760 family doctors with an average number of 2,000 patients each on their list. There are few general practitioners who have not had some experience of the effects of the civil disturbances, as many of their patients have been injured or assassinated. This would be especially true of the general practitioners in Derry and West Belfast who, in addition to injured patients, have found that many of their patients have developed anxiety symptoms. They have also had their working routine disrupted to a major degree. The vast majority of general practitioners remain objective and treat all patients impartially. In Belfast and Derry there is an understandable tendency for some to identify with the political aspirations of the majority of their patients, but this does not influence their clinical judgement and treatment. A few feel it their duty to use their standing in the community, and their specialized knowledge, to speak out on such issues as internment, interrogation, alleged army brutality, and army guards in hospitals.

Doctors, like nurses and various para-medical staff, have had the advantage of integrated education at under-graduate and post-graduate level, and for this reason relationships between doctors have generally been excellent. They continue to meet regularly at various levels. There are very active Post-Graduate Medical Centres at hospitals throughout the province, and doctors meet at these centres regularly for lunch and educational meetings. There are several medical societies and doctors of all religious and political persuasions meet socially very frequently. Most doctors have the advantage of knowing each other personally, in contrast to a general war or other disaster zone where medical staff, often from different nationalities and cultures, may experience communication difficulties. This problem has not arisen in Northern Ireland.

The working life of the average family doctor has not altered. In certain areas of Belfast, Derry, Newry and Strabane, the physical environment has deteriorated, and some of the surgeries in these areas are surrounded by severely damaged properties. Surgeries are occasionally broken into. One of the more frustrating things doctors have had to cope with is the slowness of moving around cities and towns. Traffic is frequently held up by searches by security forces and, at other times, by demonstrations and strikes by a wide range of political groups. The large 'Doctor' sign on a car has been very useful and usually results in minimizing traffic delays. General practitioners have often been on the scene of explosions and shootings and rendered first aid, but usually the injured are rushed straight to hospital. Occasionally an injured gunman may not wish to go to hospital and if he goes to a general practitioner this may raise various ethical problems for the doctor.

In troubled areas family doctors treat fairly large numbers of people for minor emotional upsets. Most of these patients are put on tranquillizers or sedatives, and the consumption of tranquillizers in Northern Ireland has increased very sharply in recent years. The early and responsible use of sedatives by doctors may have prevented more serious psychological symptoms developing. It has been demonstrated by Sargant [17] that, under severe stress, sedation has a definite prophylactic value. Although prescribed drugs have increased greatly in consumption, there is little evidence of drug abuse. The use of cannabis is practically non-existent among the teenagers of the troubled areas. Among the reasons for this are that young people are finding excitement in their group activities and that leaders of the paramilitary organizations are very opposed to drug abuse and punish offenders and pushers alike by shooting them through the knee joint.

General Hospitals

Northern Ireland has one of the leading medical schools in the British Isles and has several first-rate teaching hospitals. Some new hospitals, equipped with modern facilities, have been built in the past two decades. Thus it is probably unique to have a civil war in the midst of such advanced medical services. There was no need for first aid posts or field hospitals as casualties could be rushed to a major hospital often in as little as ten minutes. This is certainly true of Belfast and Derry. Those severely injured near the border could be transported to Belfast by helicopter.

The Royal Victoria Hospital, Belfast, is situated right in the heart of the troubled area of West Belfast. From 1969 to 1973 very severe violence occurred in the vicinity of this hospital and gun battles frequently took place in the immediate environs of the hospital. Gun fire and explosions were obviously causing anxiety to staff and patients alike but the close proximity of this hospital to the battle zone meant that seriously ill people could be rushed into hospital and receive expert medical and surgical attention in a matter of minutes.

Attendances of patients in the various departments of the Royal Victoria Hospital have fallen slightly, especially in the follow-up clinics. This is partly due to the inherent dangers of travelling to and from the hospital, but also to the fact that a large new hospital, The Ulster Hospital was opened in the relatively peaceful eastern suburbs of the city shortly before the troubles began, and some diversion of patients was bound to occur. This new hospital dealt with many of the casualties from East Belfast. The Belfast City Hospital also coped with many casualties and, during the past five years, a major building programme has been in progress on this site. The army had a unit at Musgrave Park Hospital where some soldiers were treated. In addition, certain prisoners and internees were treated in a high-security unit at this hospital. The large post-war hospital at Altnagelvin, Co. Derry, coped with all the casualties from the city of Derry and the surrounding area. Smaller provincial hospitals had to deal episodically with large numbers of injured people when, for example, a bomb exploded in a crowded pub. These smaller provincial hospitals had a less highly developed disaster procedure than the major Belfast hospitals.

Since 1951 about 45 major disasters have occurred in Great Britain, but in the past few years, the Royal Victoria Hospital has had incidents requiring the use of the disaster drill on over 50 occasions; thus this hospital has had very exceptional experience. The disaster procedure and the lessons learned have been very fully described by Rutherford [18, 19]. He stresses the following points:

(i) The importance of setting up a command structure whose responsibility it is both to monitor the influx of casualties and to direct staff where to work; also to mobilize additional staff if necessary.

(ii) The importance of sorting out the injured as soon as they arrive, and very careful documentation of all patients arriving.

(iii) Co-operation with the news media and relatives; giving details of the numbers and state of the injured and dead. The presence of senior administrative, nursing and medical personnel during a disaster is essential.

There have been difficulties in maintaining sufficient numbers of nursing and medical staff in some hospitals. This is partly due to staff leaving the country and, in certain areas of Belfast, especially that around the Royal Victoria Hospital, due to dangers and difficulties of travelling in the area. To relieve some of the difficulties, a bus was privately hired for the benefit of out-patients and staff. This runs every half hour during the day from the city centre to the Royal Victoria Hospital and back again. As it is clearly marked 'Hospital', it can often get through various types of road blocks when other vehicles cannot. Another means of alleviating the stress on nursing staff was the introduction of recreational breaks of a few days' relaxation at a comfortable seaside hotel.

The Injured

It is not the function of this article to describe in detail the various surgical techniques and resuscitation measures used in the treatment of casualties. These have been written up in various medical journals, and only an outline of the types of injuries and some methods of dealing with them will be given.

Five main types of injury have occurred:

1 *Bullet wounds:* Initially low-velocity bullet wounds were common and the bullet was often found *in situ*. As the violence escalated, high-velocity bullets became more common. These pass through the body and cause massive destruction of tissue in their path. Rubber bullets used in riot control cause bruising and occasional severe facial and eye injuries.

2 *Blunt injuries:* From stones, bricks and other objects.

3 *Injuries produced by explosions:* These can be due to blast or flying missiles, such as parts of the container or car in which the bomb was positioned. Flying glass is especially liable to cause multiple lacerations. Explosions can also cause injuries by crushing people under falling walls and ceilings, etc.

4 *Burns:* These can result from petrol bombs, fire or the blast of explosives.

5 *CS Gas:* This was used principally in Derry. Those affected were treated mainly at first-aid stations set up in the local community and staffed by family doctors. Only a few came to general hospitals. The immediate effects were lachrymation, sneezing, acute chest pain and often vomiting. In healthy people there appeared to be no serious long-term effects but restraint is obviously required in its use [20].

In those coming to hospital after a bomb explosion the main finding is a multiplicity of wounds. Reference can be made to some common sites of injury.

A   *Ear injuries:* The ear is frequently injured by blast, and deafness, often only temporary, results. The tympanic membrane (ear drum) may be ruptured in both ears, or the inner hearing mechanism may be damaged.

B   *Ocular injuries:* Perforating injuries of the eye are fairly common and often result in blindness due to the severe force of the perforating object. The rubber bullet was a frequent cause of eye injury.

C   *Severe head wounds:* Bullets are the principal cause of head wounds, and the high-velocity bullet causes great destruction of brain tissue. The management of these cases has been described in detail by Crockard [21] and Gordon [22]. Immediate resuscitation and early operation increase the chances of survival very considerably. Tracheal intubation followed by controlled ventilation proved the best way to reduce intracranial pressure. Haemorrhage is often very severe in these wounds and immediate intravenous infusion, followed by early operation to stop the haemorrhage, is necessary. Therefore, delay in reaching an intensive care and neurosurgery unit often proves fatal. Many patients with severe head injury have made a remarkable recovery. The same cannot be said regarding wounds of the spinal cord where the damage tends to be permanent. Patients with bullet wounds of the head do not travel well and it is much better if they can be taken directly and quickly to the neurosurgical unit. Prior to transportation, resuscitation is essential and an anaesthetist should accompany the patient from the peripheral hospital to the main accident centre.

D   *Knee injuries:* Limbs are fairly often injured by bullets and the severity depends mainly on the velocity of the bullet. 'Knee-capping' is a frequent punishment or disciplinary measure used by paramilitary groups and is probably unique to Northern Ireland. There are various degrees of this particular punishment. For the less serious offenders a low-velocity bullet is shot through the soft tissue above the knee: the second degree is shooting the patella (knee cap) and the third is a bullet right through the knee joint, which often results in a permanently stiff knee. The recipients of these injuries may have been suspected of being informers, or their offence may have been of an entirely different nature, such as selling drugs or committing some sex crime.

E *Chest injuries:* Severe chest injuries and blast injuries of the lung do better than was the case in World War II. This is due to the availability of intensive care units which are well staffed and equipped to give continuous attention, including prolonged controlled respiration [23].

The ambulance service has been under considerable stress since the troubles began. Drivers and attendants have frequently had to deal with the dead, the dying and the very seriously injured. At other times they have picked up casualties in the middle of a gun battle. Following some of the bomb explosions up to a dozen ambulances have had to go to the site. A mobile ambulance control unit is also sent, and the base hospital is informed of the number and type of casualties. Many slightly injured and shocked people arrive at the hospital almost simultaneously. The very seriously injured may arrive later due to the time required to extricate them from the rubble. Doctors are not usually present at the disaster site and it has been suggested by Rutherford (*see* [19]) that a senior medical officer would be useful at the site to advise the police, firemen and ambulance about the sorting out of casualties, and to report back to the base hospitals.

Another unusual aspect of the casualties in Northern Ireland due to the civil disturbances, is the question of compensation. Under the Criminal Injuries to Persons (Compensation) Act (Northern Ireland) 1968, people injured either physically or psychologically, are entitled to financial compensation. Generally speaking the awards have been fair. In other 'war zones' this provision does not exist. It raises the question of 'compensation neurosis'. In comparison to civilian road traffic and industrial accidents, the compensation cases resulting from the civil disturbances are settled reasonably quickly and, in the author's experience, the question of financial gain is not a major motivating factor. The one area where compensation awards seemed to be rather unfair was in the case of awards to widows of members of the security forces who had been killed and considerable hardship resulted from inadequate awards in these cases.

From the psychological point of view, most of those who had been in an explosion developed a post-traumatic effective disturbance, especially an anxiety phobic reaction [24]. There was a significant relationship between age, severity of illness and rate of improvement, the younger patients being less severely disturbed and improving more rapidly. There was no significant relationship between previous psychiatric illness, physical injury, death or severe injury to others in the explosion, type of explosion and the severity of symptoms or rate of improvement.

Child Health

The effects of the civil disturbances on children and teenagers are worthy of special mention. Many children have been injured and some killed in bomb explosions, and a large proportion of assassination victims has been teenagers. One finds that injured children are remarkably resilient and generally recover much more rapidly than adults.

Psychological effects on children have been documented [25, 26]. In the short term many children seem to find the disturbances an exciting, and novel experience. Over the past years the children of Ulster have had little need of vicarious reduction of aggression and anger. Their catharsis comes from performing actual acts of violence either actively or passively, directly or indirectly. Such acts become manifest at home, at school, and in the streets, in the form of disobedience, vandalism and crime. There is, in fact, a lack of respect for law, order and authority of any kind. General moral standards appear to have fallen. There has, for example, been an increase in cases of rape in the province, often involving teenage boys carrying out the rape as a group activity, sometimes with very young girls.

The media have covered the effects on children very fully and have often tried to suggest that large numbers of children are psychologically disturbed. For example, a well-known international weekly in 1971 published photographs of children in Belfast playing with toy guns. Various films have also been produced which attempt to show disturbed children, but the only real sign of any disturbance is in their anti-social group behaviour. A few children have developed anxiety symptoms, but one usually finds that their parents have had the same symptoms either previously or concurrently, and the anxiety has been communicated from parent to child.

Long-term effects on young people are very much more disturbing. Violence has become part of life for many children. They have become conditioned to it, and it has become a major part of their learning experience at a very formative time in their lives and, once this lesson is learnt, it is a very difficult one to eradicate. Pre-1969 Ireland tended to be a moralistic, regimented community in which the young were firmly kept in line by home, church and school training, but this process has broken down. Violence and various types of anti-social behaviour are no longer ostracized and, in fact, are often actively encouraged in certain parts of our towns and cities.

But what will happen when political settlement is eventually reached and young people no longer have licence to commit anti-social acts? It is only to be expected that acts of violence and anti-social behaviour will continue because of the conditioning of previous years. Vandalism and crime are likely to increase and become major problems. A remarkable feature of the civil disturbances has been the extent to which teenagers and younger children have been utilized by the militant organizations, and have played a very active part in the troubles. If they can be used in this way, surely it is conceivable that such potential could be harnessed for the betterment of the community? Some acceptable way of providing an element of excitement in the lives of the young must be provided. One of the tragic aspects of the situation is that the children and teenagers, as well as being conditioned to violence as an acceptable way of life, are also being taught to hate those of a different religious group, and another generation of bigots is appearing on the Northern Irish scene.

Psychological Effects

The situation in Northern Ireland in the past six years has provided an unusual opportunity to study people under conditions of severe and prolonged stress. In recent years there has been a considerable interest in the reaction of people to extreme environmental stress, such as is experienced in war or natural disasters. There is now extensive literature on military psychiatry; for example Lewis and Engle [27] collected over 1,000 papers on the subject and, more recently, studies have come from Vietnam [28]. The various names used to describe combat reaction have changed from 'nostalgia' [29], through 'shell-shock' and 'war neurosis' to 'combat fatigue' and 'combat exhaustion', reflecting the changing attitudes towards the concept of the condition. The reaction of soldiers differs from that of civilians in many ways. The soldier serving in Northern Ireland is usually separated from his home and family. He has little freedom of independent action and he might not clearly understand the conflict in which he is involved. No studies have so far been published describing the psychological reactions of troops in Northern Ireland, but various papers have described the civilian reactions. Fraser [30] did a survey in Belfast following the severe rioting in the late summer of 1969. He looked at the figures for Belfast generally, and divided the city into 'peaceful' and 'riot' areas. He found no increase in the number of patients referred to psychiatrists or admitted to psychiatric wards from areas directly involved in rioting, although there was a significant increase in the number of prescriptions given for tranquillizers. There was a slight increase in psychiatric referrals from the 'peaceful' areas.

The author carried out various studies. The first of these was a study of patients in three general practices in West Belfast following a period of very severe rioting [31]. It was found that the young and elderly were more at risk, and that social isolation was not an aetiological factor. Patients who had been referred to psychiatric out-patient clinics, day hospitals and mental hospitals were also reviewed. It was found that there was a slight reduction in referral and admissions during 1969 and 1970. There was no increase in acute psychotic illness. A few patients were readmitted as a preventive measure to mental hospitals during the severe rioting because they were vulnerable in the situation, e.g. chronic alcoholics and some residual psychotics (schizophrenics). Similar findings have been reported from various countries during wartime. It would seem that when people have a role to play, and feel more involvement in their community, life has more purpose and satisfaction; this protects them, at least in the short term, from developing psychiatric illness. As the incidence of depressive illness in both these studies appeared to be low, it was decided to carry out a more detailed analysis of the incidence of depression and the suicide rate [32]. The number of patients with depressive illness was obtained from central records for each year from 1963 to 1970. It was found that there was a highly significant decrease in the incidence of depressive illness during 1969 and 1970 in Belfast. This reduction was more pronounced in males, especially males in social groups IV and V. This reduction in male depressives was found in all areas of Belfast but was more significant in areas of severest rioting. In contrast, the results from the relatively peaceful County Down show a sharp increase for male depressives.

The suicide rate fell by about 50% in 1970 and the homicide rate rose very sharply. This trend has continued. Suicidal attempts, which are different phenomena from actual suicide, have increased fairly rapidly in the United Kingdom and two studies carried out in Belfast in recent years show a similar trend, namely, a rising suicide attempt rate [32, 33]. This different phenomenon does not seem to be related to the civil disturbances and a similar fall in actual suicides has been reported from all European countries actively involved in World War II.

One explanation for these findings is based on the hypothesis that depressive illness is caused by the inhibition of aggressive responses to frustration. It appears that depressive illness is high in communities in which there is a strong inhibition of aggressive action, and conversely a low incidence of depression has been reported from communities where aggression can be more readily expressed, as in various primitive societies. Certainly in recent years there has been ample opportunity for the people of Northern Ireland to show aggression, and many of the usual inhibitions imposed on society in the Western world have largely broken down. It has been impossible for the inhabitants of many of the towns and cities of the province not to become involved to some extent. Many do not actively participate physically, but the aggressive acts which occur in the city become the main topic of conversation which has a strong emotional content with a strong cathartic role. Many people do develop symptoms of anxiety such as insomnia, loss of appetite, restlessness, irritability and general nervousness but these symptoms are appropriate to the dangers of the situation in their area. It would be more indicative of mental illness if people in situations of danger did not develop anxiety symptoms. This 'epidemic of anxiety' has been well controlled by the use of simple tranquillizers, and psychiatrists have not seen many chronic anxiety states as a result of the severe environmental stress.

So far, one can state that the psychiatric services have been able to cope with the civil disturbance in Northern Ireland, and the existing psychiatric facilities, namely in-patient beds, out-patient clinics and day hospitals, have proved adequate. There has been a slight shortage of staff partly in common with the psychiatric services in other parts of the United Kingdom, but also due to the tendency for some doctors and other para-medical staff to leave the province. There may well be an increase in psychiatric referrals once peace returns to the province.

Ethical Considerations

The vast majority of doctors, nurses and other para-medical staff in Northern Ireland have remained objective in their treatment of patients and, as stated in the Declaration of Geneva, 1948, have 'not permitted considerations of religion, nationality, race, party politics or social standing to intervene between duty and patient'. Understandably some doctors, although retaining their objectivity in the treatment of patients, have identified with certain political groupings and aspirations.

One strongly emotive occurrence was the introduction of internment in August 1971. Many people found this procedure morally offensive, and some doctors were faced with the dilemma of what to do when they were asked by the authorities to see internees. In most cases, where the problem was an acute medical or surgical one, the doctor's duty was clearly to 'give emergency care as a humanitarian duty unless he is assured that others are willing and able to give such care' (International Code of Medical Ethics, 1949). The difficulties arose when the authorities requested a psychiatric opinion. If a psychiatrist carried out an examination and prepared a report, it was possible that this report would be used as the basis for making a political decision, viz. whether to continue detention or release the internee. If psychiatrists had fallen into this trap they could have found themselves in a similar situation to Russian psychiatrists, whose reports on political dissenters can lead them to be incarcerated in mental institutions for years, and to be discredited in the eyes of the community. One possible way around this difficulty is for the consultant psychiatrist only to see the internee at the request of his own family doctor, only to visit in cases of real emergency, and only to give advice verbally to the family doctor. If hospital admission is necessary, which should be a rare occurrence, the psychiatrist involved should insist that release from internment be a prerequisite to hospital admission.

The admission of acute surgical or medical cases from the ranks of internees raises fewer problems, the main one being the question of armed security forces guarding internees in a general hospital setting. Generally this is unacceptable, and if it is done, the hospital could be accused of supporting the system. Government and security forces would argue that if no security arrangements exist escape is likely, and, in fact, has occurred on a few occasions. As was stated by Williamson [34], relationships among both patients and staff in hospitals have been excellent. By a mutual and unspoken consent the topics of politics and religion are not usually discussed, and when they are, arguments put forward deftly avoid any impasse.

Another dilemma facing doctors in Northern Ireland, is the conflict between the secrecy of the hippocratic Oath and the Northern Ireland Civil Law Act of 1967, which states that it is the duty of every citizen, including doctor, lawyer and priest, to report any serious crime of which he has knowledge. Thus if men with gunshot wounds are sent to hospital, are the security forces to be notified? The large hospital may get over this difficulty by passing the responsibility of issuing lists of injured to senior lay administrators, but the individual doctor still has to attempt to resolve this difficult conflict.

A third problem may arise in the area of interrogation of suspects or prisoners. This has been the subject of various reports [35]. It has occasionally been suggested that the presence of a doctor might prevent excesses, but practically all doctors would find this highly objectionable and would want no part in it.

Conclusions

The main difference in casualties treated in Ulster due to the civil disturbances and those in other war zones, is the very rapid evacuation to fully staffed and equipped hospitals. This is due to the small size of the province, together with the excellent hospitals that exist in it. As a result, many severely wounded people have survived who would probably have died if wounded in other 'war zones'. Severe infection of wounds which was a major problem in World War I and World War II is relatively rare.

Many people in the province have felt considerable anxiety, but this could be regarded as a normal physiological reaction to danger. The incidence of mental illness and suicide has dropped and this would be in keeping with other countries during war-time. The disturbing psychological aspect is the general lowering of standards of behaviour, and in particular the fact that children and teenagers are being taught that violence is an acceptable way of achieving aims. Group hatred, as Hitler illustrated in the Nazi youth movement, is a very powerful force and, unfortunately, the younger generation is being taught to hate.

When one compares casualties in Northern Ireland with other areas such as Vietnam, it is fairly obvious that generally the medical, nursing and ancillary services have coped well. The scale and numbers are different, but the main factor is the already existing excellent medical facilities which have shown no sign of breaking down under the additional stress of many thousands of seriously injured people.

The conflict has raised certain ethical problems. This type of problem has already attracted the attention of world medical opinion in countries such as South Africa, Russia and South America and the Ulster situation only raises the same dilemma in a slightly different disguise.

Notes

1   Broeker, G., *Rural Disorder and Police Reform in Ireland, 1812–36*, London, Routledge and Kegan Paul, 1970.
2   *Report of the Commissioners of Inquiry, 1857*, Dublin: HMSO, 1857.
3   *Report of the Belfast Riots Commissioners, 1886*, Dublin: HMSO, 1886.

4   Henry, T., *History of the Belfast Riots*, London: Hamilton and Adams, 1864.
5   Boyd, A., *Holy War in Belfast*, Belfast: Anvil Press, 1969.
6   King, G., *The Orange and the Green*, London: MacDonald, 1965.
7   Foy, G., *Surgical Reports on the Belfast Riots*, Dublin, 1886.
8   Murney, H., *Statistical Report on the Injuries sustained during the riots in Belfast from 8th August to 22nd August, 1864*, Belfast, 1864.
9   Du Saulle, L. H., 'De l'état mental des habitants de Paris pendant les événments de 1870–71', *Annales Medico-Psychologiques*, **2**, 222–41, 1871.
10 Smith, R. P., 'Mental Disorders in civilians, arising in connection with the war', *Proceedings of the Royal Society of Medicine, Section of Psychiatry*, **10**, 1916. 1–20.
11 Lewis, A., 'Incidence of Neurosis in England under war conditions', *Lancet*, **2**, 175–83, 1942.
12 Atkin, J., 'Air-raid strain in mental hospital admissions', *Lancet*, **2**, 72–4, 1941.
13 Harris, A., 'Psychiatric reactions of civilians in war time', *Lancet*, **ii**, 152–5, 1941.
14 Hopkins, F., 'Decrease in admissions to mental observation wards during the war', *British Medical Journal*, **1**, 358, 1943.
15 Taggart, J. McA., 'Community Health Services under Stress', *Public Health*, **87**, 6, 1973, 225–31.
16 Jones, E., *The Social Geography of Belfast*, London: Oxford University Press, 1960.
17 Sargant, W., 'Physical treatment of acute war neurosis', *British Medical Journal*, **1**, 1942, 574–6.
18 Rutherford, W. H., 'The Accident and Emergency Department in the Surgery of Civil Violence', *Recent Advances in Surgery*, Harlow: Churchill Livingstone, 1973.
19 Rutherford, W. H., 'Disaster Procedures', *British Medical Journal*, **1**, 1975, 443–5.
20 MacDonald, N., 'C.S. Gas in Northern Ireland', *Proceedings of the Medical Association for the prevention of War*, **2**, 1970, 10–12.
21 Crockard, H. A., 'Gun Shot Wounds of the Head', *Recent Advances in Surgery*, Harlow: Churchill Livingstone, 1973.
22 Gordon, D. S., 'Missile Wounds of the Head and Spine', *British Medical Journal*, **1**, 614–16, 1975.
23 Rodgers, H. W., 'Surgery of Civil Violence', *Recent Advances in Surgery*, Harlow: Churchill Livingstone, 1973.
24 Lyons, H. A., 'Terrorists' Bombing and the Psychological Sequelae', *Journal of the Irish Medical Association*, **67**, 1, 1974, 15–19.
25 Fraser, R. M., *Children in Conflict*, London: Secker and Warburg, 1973.
26 Lyons, H. A., 'The Psychological Effects of the Civil Disturbances on Children', *The Northern Teacher*, 1973.

27 Lewis, M. and Engle B., *Wartime Psychiatry*, New York: Oxford University Press, 1954.

28 Bourne, P. G., 'Military Psychiatry and the Vietnam War', *The Psychology and Physiology of Stress*, New York: Academic Press, 1969.

29 Hammond, W. A., *A Treatise on Insanity in its Medical Relations*, London: Lewis, 1883.

30 Fraser, R. M., 'The Cost of Commotion', *The British Journal of Psychiatry*, **118**, 257, 1971.

31 Lyons, H. A., 'Psychiatric Sequelae of the Belfast Riots', *British Journal of Psychiatry*, **118**, 1971, 265.

32 O'Malley, P. P., 'Attempted Suicide', *Journal of the Irish Medical Association*, **65**, 5, 1972, 109.

33 Lyons, H. A., 'Attempted Suicide by Self-Poisoning', *Journal of the Irish Medical Association*, **65**, 17, 1972, 435.

34 Williamson, F., 'Day Hospital in a Troubled Community', *The Nursing Times*, 1972, 1638–41.

35 *Parker Report*, Belfast, 1972.

4 Education

Michael McKeown*

Introduction

Any survey of the impact of the civil disturbances in Northern Ireland in the years between 1969 and 1975 has to take account of two crucial factors which make it difficult to make bold statements about their effects on educational provision. The first consideration is that the duration of the disturbances has encompassed several generations of pupils in either primary or secondary cycles and the pattern of disorder has altered within the duration of any one cycle. The second consideration is that the incidence of disturbance was not evenly distributed throughout the region of Northern Ireland. Since the violence tended to be concentrated in specific areas, it is likely that schools in those areas encountered problems of a different order from those encountered by schools in less disturbed areas. This chapter attempts to identify the manner in which some schools have been severely affected and the nature of the difficulties facing such schools. It also seeks to outline the more generalized difficulties imposed upon the whole education system as a result of the disturbances and the manner in which the system has been forced to modify itself to take account of the problems created by the disturbances.

To do this it is necessary to sketch briefly administrative provisions for school management in Northern Ireland. Although most of the developments examined here are matters of public record, in some cases the material used has been acquired on the basis of confidentiality and in such circumstances the schools concerned have not been identified.

Observers both within and without Northern Ireland examining the social structures of the area have frequently remarked upon the exis-

---

* Michael McKeown is a tutor with the Open University and an official of the Irish National Teachers' Organization.

tence of a clearly defined system of dual educational provision. The dualism is crudely presented in terms of a Catholic/Protestant or Voluntary Control/State Control dichotomy. Such distinctions in fact find no place within the statutory instruments regulating educational provision within Northern Ireland, [1] but they serve to highlight the reality of education in the area. This reality is that, within the compulsory school attendance age range, Protestant and Roman Catholic pupils attend schools whose enrolment is almost exclusively composed of children in the same religious grouping. Essentially, Protestant school children attend what are statutorily called Controlled Schools while Catholic school children attend what are statutorily called Voluntary and Maintained Schools.* A measure of the distribution between the two systems is afforded by reference to the enrolment figures of non-selective primary and secondary schools as of January 1974 [2].

Table 4.1: Schools and Pupils in Northern Ireland, January 1975

Schools and Pupils		Controlled	Voluntary and Maintained
Primary:	Schools	587	536
	Pupils	111,825	100,685
Secondary:	Schools	90	90
	Pupils	53,687	47,731

While it would not be legitimate to assume that all the Protestant pupils were enrolled in Controlled Schools and all the Catholic pupils in Voluntary and Maintained Schools, nevertheless this does afford a rough guide to the numbers of children in each religious grouping. This guide is supported by an estimate made in 1969 by the Irish National Teachers' Organization that the percentage of Catholic pupils in the total enrolment at that time was 'over 44 per cent'[3]. This figure has not been challenged by any source.

Apart from allowing for the existence of a *de facto* system of religious segregation, educational legislation in Northern Ireland also provides for a high measure of devolution within the system. Management of

* Controlled schools are those owned and directly administered by the five Education Area Boards which took over the functions of the eight former Local Education Authorities in October 1973. Since such schools were formerly called County schools the two terms are used interchangeably in this account. Although the great bulk of Voluntary and Maintained Schools are those under Catholic control there is a small number of Voluntary Grammar Schools which are Protestant foundations.

schools is exercised by local committees responsible to the school owners who, in the case of Controlled Schools are Area Education Boards, in the case of Voluntary Schools are the school trustees and, in the case of Maintained Schools, comprise representatives from both these bodies.

These factors combine to create a situation where areas of responsibility impinge upon each other and demarcation lines between respective spheres of responsibility can, within the managerial context, become blurred. While the Department of Education, representing central government, takes overall responsibility for determining general policy and establishing academic and physical standards, it devolves authority to school owners who in turn devolve it through management committees to school principals and staff.

This principle of devolution has probably proved one of the great strengths of the system in enabling it to respond flexibly to the pressures to which it has been subjected since 1969. These pressures can be classified under four heads, the first two of which were specific to schools in those areas which experienced the highest measure of civil disturbance; the other two were common to schools throughout Northern Ireland. The spread of disturbances is discussed in a report in the *Northern Teacher* of Winter 1973, [4] which shows that of 159 secondary schools responding to a survey of the effects of the civil disturbances, 26 (16.4%) indicated that they had suffered severe disturbance. It is valid to assume that this percentage can be projected onto the primary schools. Pressures experienced by schools were of four types:

(*a*) the impact on school holdings and facilities
(*b*) the effect on school enrolment figures
(*c*) the implications for internal discipline and administration
(*d*) the social demands imposed on the education system.

School Buildings

The most immediate impact which the violence has had upon a small number of schools has been the temporary loss of part or all of the school premises. This loss has arisen from two causes: requisition or physical damage. Schools have been requisitioned for two purposes. In circumstances of intercommunal violence of the sort some areas of Belfast suffered in the summers of 1969 and 1971, neighbourhood schools have been used as relief centres to house evacuees fleeing from the scene of the rioting.

Such schools were generally sited in Catholic districts in North and West Belfast and were usually Voluntary or Maintained schools (i.e. under the management of a committee on which the local Catholic parochial authorities enjoyed a majority voting position). The immediate decision to open them and place their facilities at the disposal of the refugees could be, and was, made by the Chairman of the local management committee, and in most cases the refugees were his parishioners. The schools were used for dormitory, cooking and sanitary purposes and their use for these purposes was never challenged.

Since these periods occurred within the school holiday period, initially the educational role of the school was not impaired but in some instances when the school resumed at the beginning of term, school staffs found that part of the school accommodation was in use by refugees. Teachers tended to be tolerant of this situation while gradually building up a degree of pressure upon the school committee to impress upon the refugees that they must seek alternative accommodation. As relief measures became co-ordinated and central facilities established, this in fact happened and, after an initial disturbance of a few weeks, the half dozen schools concerned were able to revert to their normal routine.

A more serious threat to some schools arose from their occupation by the military for billeting purposes. In some cases the occupation was negotiated with the Local Education Authority, the forerunners of the Area Boards, but of course they could only offer the facilities of their own schools. Two Controlled schools were occupied for a considerable period, Finiston Primary School in North Belfast for four years and Vere Foster Primary School in West Belfast for three years. Since both of these schools had lost considerable numbers of pupils because of the disturbances, there was a surplus of accommodation and the loss of space did not seriously disrupt the smooth operation of the schools. The presence of the military of course had direct educational consequences as the school buildings themselves became targets for subversive attacks.

Maintained schools were also occupied and it would appear that in regard to these schools the initial occupation was made under the Special Powers Act; the continuing occupation was then retrospectively formalized through negotiations with Catholic clerical authorities. The schools affected were primary or secondary schools in West Belfast and Derry city and the presence of military units in such sensitive areas raised difficult issues of principle for the clerical authorities. While they had to take account of a degree of antagonism from the local population and the likelihood that the security of the schools was being put at risk by the military occupation, they had to balance this against identifying the Catholic authorities with an anti-army stance, especially since they were dependent upon the goodwill of the Army for the protection of other Catholic schools in more exposed areas.

The occupied schools did indeed come under attacks. The gymnasium of the De La Salle secondary school was destroyed in a rocket attack upon the building in August 1972 and, when shots were directed at the Army post in St Peter's secondary school on 21 September 1972, staff there took strike action. Strike action was also threatened in another occupied school, Blessed Oliver Plunkett Primary School, where the Army presence had seriously curtailed the accommodation available. Only after emergency conferences involving the teacher union concerned, the Department of Education, the Belfast Education Authority, the Army and the school management, were the difficulties resolved by an accelerated Army evacuation, but not before St Peter's secondary school pupils had been for several months dispersed around various other buildings within a two-mile radius.

Although it has already been suggested that the degree of devolution within the Northern Ireland education system had generally a beneficial effect, it does appear that in the case of schools occupied by the Army against the wishes of school staffs, the consequence of this devolution made it difficult to secure a quick resolution. Each of the official agencies involved seemed unwilling to accept the obligations of their respective spheres of responsibility. The implications of the occupation for the safety of the staff and pupils and for the educational work of the school were largely ignored and were in fact eventually only taken into account when the strike action of the teachers focused public attention upon the issue.

One hazard arising from military occupation was the threat of mortar or rocket attack upon the school premises. Although several schools suffered such attacks, the greatest risk of physical damage arose from malicious attacks upon school property or from incidental damage arising from explosions near the school, especially in the case of parochial schools sited near Catholic churches. The malicious damage could arise from the random vandalism accompanying general disorder and the absence of effective policing in an area, or from a premeditated act of destruction with a sectarian content. Sectarian attacks tended to cause more severe structural damage and entailed more serious disruption of school work. In the area embracing Antrim, Down and Belfast at least thirteen schools suffered such attacks and in several cases were totally destroyed. Outside Belfast, several schools in Derry city have been attacked as well as schools in Tyrone and South Derry. In the weekend of 27 February/1 March 1976, six schools were attacked and suffered varying degrees of damage. Four of the six were in Belfast and included both Controlled and Maintained schools [5].

Our Lady of Mercy secondary school in North Belfast was on several occasions the target of both bomb and arson attacks, in which a whole wing of the school was destroyed, as well as mobile classrooms. Its primary supplying school on the Crumlin Road was also the target of a bomb attack in which a wing was destroyed. Ballymacward Primary School and Tir na N'og Primary School in Co. Antrim were among other schools destroyed by bomb attacks. In such cases the Maintained School Management Committees had to seek the good offices of the area boards concerned to supply them with temporary mobile class-rooms from their existing stock. It would appear that in such cases the Board Authorities offered full co-operation to the Maintained Schools Committees.

The longer-term problem of physical replacement was more compli-cated in that the school committees had to follow through the Malicious Damages procedure to recover the costs necessary for replacement. However, in most cases committees found their insurers willing to make an interim settlement while the insurance company pursued the issue through the courts.

A much wider band of schools experienced minor damage of a non-structural sort through proximity to a bomb explosion or through the increased level of vandalism which was a direct consequence of the disturbances. In the survey referred to earlier, it was revealed that 72 out of 159 (45.3%) schools responding had experienced a rise in van-dalism after school hours and 12 (7.5%) of these schools considered it of a serious order. Vandalism was of such a nature, e.g. forced doors, burned classrooms and destroyed apparatus, as to make certain sections of the school temporarily unusable, necessitating short-term closures or time-table alterations. For such schools the problem tended to be the difficulty of keeping the school building secure and getting necessary running repairs done. Both for Controlled and Maintained schools this was the direct responsibility of the Area Boards. Boards appear to have responded as best they could both in getting work done and in taking preventive measures, such as appointing security men to guard the school premises. However, difficulties of interpretation could arise in determining whether certain projects were capital projects and thus the responsibility of the school owners, or maintenance projects and thus the responsibility of the Area Board. Even where these problems were resolved, the difficulty of persuading contractors and workers to undertake work in certain sensitive areas meant that for many schools necessary repair work was left undone for considerable period.

Enrolment Figures

Probably the most visible and dramatic impact the disturbances have had upon the population within the Belfast conurbation has been on the location of population. Traditionally working-class areas in Belfast had tended to be identified with one particular denominational group. The reasons for this have been both historical and social. Barritt and Carter, [6] using the 1951 census figures, demonstrated that in Belfast city wards like Smithfield and Falls, where Catholic populations constituted 91.2% and 92.8% respectively, there was a very high degree of religious segregation. Within smaller units the segregation was even more rigid. Boal and Robinson, looking at the Springfield/Shankill area of West Belfast in 1968, discovered 'two very distinct territories' [7].

This degree of separateness did not prevail to the same extreme extent in post-war housing developments on the North, South and West of Belfast and it was from the newer housing areas that the great exodus of population occurred between 1969 and 1973. In mixed areas like Rathcoole, Upper Springfield and Twinbrook, members of whichever religious group found itself in a minority moved out to what they considered safer territory in what has been described as 'the largest forced population movement in Western Europe since the Second World War' [8]. This movement had two distinctive features; the great majority of those moving were Catholics moving from a variety of districts into the West Belfast area: a smaller number of Protestants were displaced as a result of intimidation in the West and North Belfast areas as well as by the institutionalizing and strengthening of the informal boundary lines at the interface between traditional enclaves in the inner city.

Although the main movements were within these areas, 18.9% of the schools responding in the *Northern Teacher* survey reported that their enrolment had risen significantly as a result of population movement, while 26.4% reported that their enrolments had significantly fallen. For most schools affected by population movement problems created tended to be educational rather than administrative; although the school size was not significantly affected, there was a considerable movement of pupils into and out of the school. In one girls' Maintained primary school in North Belfast the enrolment figures suggest a relatively stable condition over the period in question [9]:

Table 4.2: Enrolment: A North Belfast Girls' Maintained School, 1968–74

1968	– 452	1972	– 514
1969	– 499	1973	– 467
1970	– 495	1974	– 456
1971	– 507		

This relatively stable picture conceals the transfer of individual pupils which was regular and sustained throughout those years. A measure of this is suggested by the fact that during the 1969–70 period a total of 147 families withdrew children from the school and left the district. Although there are really no devices to assess the educational impact of such disruption upon the children concerned, it would be most surprising if the pupils' educational progress were not impaired by the difficulties of adjustment to different schools with different curricula and teaching methods.

Schools which encountered administrative as well as educational problems were those which experienced a net loss in pupil enrolment. The nature and extent of their problem is illustrated by the four examples listed below [10].

Because of the differences in the systems of management which we have already noticed the position of a teacher in a Maintained school experiencing a significant loss of numbers was radically different from that of a teacher in a Controlled school. Since a teacher in a Controlled school was an employee of an Area Board which owned all the other Controlled schools in its area, such a teacher was confronted, not by a threat of redundancy, but by the possibility of a transfer to another school. It would appear in such situations the teachers affected were offered considerable latitude of choice among the vacancies occurring within the board area.

Teachers in a Maintained school, however, were not in such a fortunate position since they were employed by a school committee which generally had no other vacancies at its disposal. In a Maintained school with falling numbers teachers were as a consequence forced to find alternative employment for themselves. Their difficulties in this

Table 4.3: Pupil Enrolment: Four Belfast schools, 1969–75

School	Type	Area	Year	Pupil Enrolment	Staff Employed
A	Controlled Primary	N. Belfast	1969	500	15
			1975	138	7
B	Maintained Primary	S. Antrim	1971	992	34
			1975	238	10
C	Maintained Boys' Primary	E. Belfast	1971	241	8
			1975	73	4
D	Maintained Girls' Primary	E. Belfast	1971	160	8
			1975	67	4

respect were eased by two factors. The first was that the Department of Education adopted a very flexible staffing policy towards both Maintained and Controlled schools in such a situation and by a series of *ad hoc* strategies permitted them over the years to retain a higher number of staff than their numbers warranted. In the Ministry of Education report for 1972 the justification for this is explained: 'In the interest of maintaining as much continuity of staffing as is possible in the circumstances, teachers have been kept in post as a rule, even when enrolments have been depleted and a number of schools in the most deprived and distressed areas have been allowed staff in excess of what in normal terms would have been their entitlement.' [11]. Scrutiny of the figures listed above will clearly illustrate this. For those teachers who had to move, the financial impact of the change was modified in that Northern Ireland's salary regulations provided for a promoted teacher retaining the promoted scale no matter what his position in the new school, so long as the move was occasioned by redundancy.

Apart from these administrative concerns such developments clearly had unfortunate educational implications for the schools concerned. School organization was disrupted, teacher morale sagged as a result of uncertainty about the future and the quality of teaching was severely impaired. Flexibility was reduced since teachers with specialist qualifications had to be employed as class teachers and in some cases, such as schools C and D listed above, the one-form class units had to be combined to make a two-form class unit. Corporate enterprises like school concerts and competitions by school teams had to be abandoned since the spread within any age range had become too narrow to permit such activities. As against this, it must be observed that some class teachers, especially within the Inner Belfast area, detected a rise in literacy and numeracy standards subsequent upon the fall in class numbers.

Finally another feature of the consequences of the population movement should be noted at this point. In several areas the nature of educational provision was totally altered. In the Twinbrook area on the south-west periphery of Belfast the development plan had envisaged the provision of both a Maintained school and a Controlled school to cater for the children of what was conceived as a mixed area. In the event, by the time the Controlled school premises were available the outflow of Protestants from the area and the influx of Catholics had totally altered the nature of the community and as a result the then Antrim Education Authority, which had been building the Controlled school, sold it to the local Catholic authorities to be administered as a Maintained school. A similar exchange was negotiated in Belfast when a Controlled school in North Belfast became depleted and its facilities were transferred to the local Maintained School Committee.

In West Belfast a Controlled Primary School, Vere Foster, sited in the New Barnsley district, lost its Protestant enrolment when the Protestant community moved to other areas. As the school numbers ran down, most of the existing staff were transferred to other Controlled schools. Then as children of the new Catholic arrivals began to enrol in the school the Area Board adopted the policy of appointing Catholic staff as the numbers again built up. This school is now nearly the antithesis of the provision envisaged in the Education Order in that in what to all intents and purposes is a Catholic school, i.e. one attended by Catholic pupils and staffed in the main by Catholic teachers, the management is in the Controlled category rather than in the Voluntary or Maintained categories.

Internal Discipline and Administration

A feature of the violence in Northern Ireland which has frequently been commented upon by observers has been the extreme youth of many of those involved. This applies as much to the premeditated violence of the saboteur and gunman as to the random violence accompanying street demonstrations and rioting. Inevitably many of those who were directly involved in violent action were in attendance at school and the presence of such elements in the schools presented teachers with problems of a nature never before encountered in their professional careers. Not unnaturally, it was the tragic and bizarre episodes which tended to attract the attention of the news media; the killing of a grammar school pupil on his way to school in North Belfast: a teacher shot dead by intruders in his school in Fermanagh: the occupation of a school and intimidation of the staff by a political group in West Belfast: a gun attack on pupils engaged in games at a school in South Belfast: an assault by military personnel on members of a school staff in a secondary school in Derry. Such incidents were the most extreme illustrations of a level of strain which was imposed upon a much broader band of schools and which compelled the schools in some respects to modify their practices and expectations.

In a society where political demonstrations, street rioting, gunfights and urban terrorism had become such regular features of life it was unlikely that school organization and administration could remain unmodified. The areas of organization most immediately affected were attendance levels, school openings, the obligation of parental care, and discipline. The fall in attendance levels was associated with three developments, each of them directly associated with the disturbances. Frequently parents withheld children from attending school on days on which demonstrations or disturbances were anticipated or following nights where the level of violence had destroyed the peace of an area. There was also an element within the school population which absented itself deliberately because of the prospect of the excitement afforded outside the school. Finally, the general atmosphere prevailing in some areas prevented corrective action being taken against this very group. In the *Northern Teacher* secondary school survey, 30 of the responding schools (18.9%) indicated that their average attendance had fallen to under 85%. Figures issued in 1975 showed that, whereas in 1968/69 the average attendance in Controlled Secondary Schools in the Belfast area had been 88.9% and in Maintained Secondary Schools 88.2%, by 1973 these figures had fallen to 80.9 and 79.6 % respectively. Just how difficult the situation had become in certain areas of Belfast is illustrated by the figures of absenteeism observed in five large secondary schools in disadvantaged areas of Belfast during the calendar year 1974 [12].

Table 4.4: Absenteeism: Five Secondary schools in Belfast, 1974

School V	School W	School X	School Y	School Z
32%	28.3%	26.0%	23.2%	27.9%

The difficulties arising from attempts to improve these attendance levels is illustrated in the *Northern Teacher* report which indicated that 31 of the respondent schools considered that fear of intimidation was preventing education welfare officers (the group responsible for enforcing school attendance) from performing their duties in those school areas. It is known that, in at least one Education Board Area, welfare officers were given instructions that they were not to put themselves at risk and that they should exercise their own discretion in carrying out home visits and the subsequent legal back-up procedure. It must be recognized that a high level of truancy is a common factor in the education of deprived urban communities and that in the Northern Ireland context the level of truancy was probably heightened by the impact of raising the school leaving age in 1973/4. Nevertheless the level of absenteeism amongst older pupils in certain areas of Northern Ireland reached such a high level that it seems fair to agree with the Report of the Working Party on Home-School links that 'it must be largely attributable to the abnormal political condition of the last few years when education welfare officers have had to contend with unprecedented difficulties—even physical danger—in visiting homes in many areas' [13].

While parents naturally felt apprehensive about letting their children out into a disturbed area, school staffs experienced the same apprehension once the pupils arrived in the school and so legally passed into the care of the school principal and staff. The particular risks to which school children were exposed in travelling to and from schools were confrontations with school groups from hostile areas, closure of roads and withdrawal of public transport. In considering these possibilities schools had to make decisions about their commencement and closing times and, at particular times, whether they should open at all or whether they should remain open. Fifty-five of the respondent schools in the *Northern Teacher* report (34.6%) indicated that their pupils had been harassed on the way to school by pupils from other schools; eleven (6.9%) reported that they had adjusted school hours in order to prevent rival school groups confronting each other on their way to and from school. Where groups of pupils did perforce meet on their way to school, security patrols, nicknamed in the media as 'the lollipop patrols', were employed to keep the groups apart. Eventually, to relieve this drain on manpower, the practice of 'busing' was introduced in some areas.

Once the children were within the school, teachers might have difficult decisions to make about retaining them in the event of a report of disturbance. If they retained them there was a danger that external violence would develop to a point where eventually pupils might be released into a very dangerous situation where there was no safe way for them to reach home. To close early, on the other hand, might contribute to a heightening of a crisis atmosphere as well as release into a conflict a pool of potential participants. These were difficult situations for school principals and, although they might receive guidance from various quarters, the final on-the-spot decision had to be made by the individual concerned on the basis of sensitivity to local feeling. The general good judgement might perhaps be perceived in the manner in which the 'hoax call' practice was abandoned. In 1971/2 as the wave of bombings reached an unprecedented level many schools were inundated by hoax warning calls, presumably coming from the pupils. After an initial period of automatic clearances and subsequent disruption, schools became more guarded in their response and hoax callers, confronted with failure, gradually abandoned this tactic.

This minor trial was one experienced by schools in tranquil areas just as much as by those in disturbed areas. Another experience universal through all areas was the manner in which schools had to limit extra-mural activities such as educational visits and inter-school competitions. The unsettled conditions of the time made schools unwilling to accept the risks entailed in transporting children through potential danger areas. Eighty two (51.6%) of the *Northern Teacher* schools indicated that their activities of this nature had been curtailed to some extent, while (11.3%) reported that there had been a large curtailment.

A particularly sensitive problem for teachers in some areas concerned relations between their pupils and the security forces. Because of the situation where school children were engaging in subversive and criminal activities it was inevitable that, as a group, they should come under the surveillance of the security forces. A measure of the degree of juvenile involvement is afforded by the report of the Deputy Chief Constable of the RUC on 9 March 1976 that, in the fourteen months since the beginning of 1975, 175 children and young people had been charged with serious crimes and of this number 11 had been charged with murder [14]. Problems for teachers arose when the security forces attempted to take into custody and question pupils under their legal care, i.e. in the school or in the vicinity of the school during school hours. In both Derry and West Belfast teachers became aware of occasions when school children were being approached and questioned by soldiers during times when the pupils might have been considered to be under the school's care [15]. This led to the lodging of official protests by *ad hoc* teacher groups in both areas and, in reply to one of these, the Home Office in London acknowledged that 'On December 3rd, 1971, eleven boys between the ages of 13 and 16 were arrested in Belfast' [16]. Teachers believed that such actions ignored both the provisions of the Children and Young Persons Act (1968) and the common law duty of care imposed upon the teachers. However, a legal opinion offered on this matter in January 1975 pointed out that the Emergency Provisions Act specifically overrode the Children and Young Persons Act and that the entitlement of teachers to act as intermediaries or even to remain present while pupils were being questioned on school premises was 'arguable'.

The degree of disruption demonstrated here, allied to the general mood of violence in the community at large, might support a snap judgement about 'blackboard jungle' conditions in the schools. Such a view is not in fact supported by evidence. Although in the survey 78 schools (40%) reported a growing lack of respect for the authority of the teacher and 79 (49.7%) claimed that the pupils were less amenable to the ordinary discipline of the school, such comments do not support a picture of classroom anarchy and are in fact quite consistent with the suggestions of similar trends in both Britain and North America. This suggests that, in so far as the traditional roles have become modified, this owes more to the common characteristics of western urban society than to the circumstances peculiar to Northern Ireland.

If reasons are sought for the continued stability of the teacher/pupil relationship during the disturbances they might be found to be associated with two considerations. Firstly the depleted attendance levels which have been noted may well have represented the absence from the schools of those very elements which would have found the school atmosphere and discipline uncongenial and who might, if they had been in regular attendance, have acted as a disruptive minority within the school. The second factor can perhaps be found in the homogeneous nature of the school units. The very fact that in large measure they mirror social and religious segregation within the wider community meant that they were one of the few examples of social institutions which did not embrace the divisions of the wider community. An educational structure which at post-primary level was composed of the four quadrants illustrated ensured that the community divisions were replicated in the school management but not within the population of each school:

The divisions of the wider community were also not reflected in school staffrooms either. Judging by the political participation and identifi-

Table 4.5: Post-primary divisions in school populations

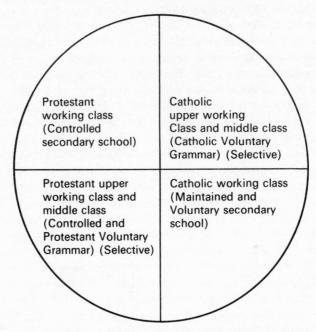

Protestant
working class
(Controlled
secondary school)

Catholic
upper working
Class and middle class
(Catholic Voluntary
Grammar) (Selective)

Protestant upper
working class and
middle class
(Controlled and
Protestant Voluntary
Grammar) (Selective)

Catholic working class
(Maintained and
Voluntary secondary
school)

cation of teachers to be observed in the composition of political groups in Northern Ireland it is probable that teachers share to a high degree the political values and attitudes of the pupils they teach and of the parents of those pupils. This high degree of agreement both within the school enrolment and between staff and pupils probably helped to minimize any adverse effects the disturbances had upon the disciplinary standards of the schools.

The Social Demands on the Schools

If it is correct that the separateness of the two school systems helped to reduce internal friction within the schools this must be considered as a rather negative virtue and would not impress those who perceive educational goals as reconstructionist. The reconstructionist view of education holds that the educational agencies of a community should be directed towards securing rapid social change within that community. Faced as it is with a high level of social disorder it might have been expected that there would have been some evidence of an increased interest in the reconstructionist view of education within Northern Ireland. It is true that there is some evidence of this, but it does not appear to be of a particularly high order.

Interest has tended to focus upon four areas of educational development. These have been compensatory education, curricular reform, structural reform and community education. Advocates of a compensatory programme who claim that an education programme should endeavour to compensate for the economic, cultural and social deprivation experienced by children from lower income groups could point to the association to be observed between the spatial distribution of social problems in the Belfast area and the incidence of violence in areas of the city [17]. Of necessity, however, the constraints upon a compensatory programme are very stringent. One of the constraints is the difficulty of developing a sufficiently sensitive measure to use in identifying areas most in need of a compensatory programme. Those areas in Great Britain such as parts of Liverpool and the West Riding of Yorkshire which have been identified as Educational Priority Areas have been so identified by reference to social criteria which would not be sufficiently discriminating for use in Northern Ireland.

A further constraint is the financial arrangement which links levels of public spending in Northern Ireland to a proportionate level to the rest of the United Kingdom. This of necessity limits the freedom of initiative enjoyed by the Northern Ireland Department of Education. It is however significant that, following the cuts foreshadowed by the Chancellor of the Exchequer in the 1975 Public Expenditure White Paper, the Northern Ireland Secretary of State indicated that 'in Northern Ireland priority had been given to maintaining levels of expenditure on education services' [18]. The social considerations underlying this political decision can perhaps be inferred by reference to the criteria offered to schools which were seeking to take on extra staff for the school year 1976/7. Two of the four areas of work which the Department identified were: the expansion of measures such as home/school links designed to further the educational welfare of pupils and the development of evening activities in secondary schools in deprived urban areas. Clearly there was a compensatory interest in such decisions.

Apart from an improved staffing ratio the other contributions to a compensatory programme have been out-of-school enterprises. In an effort to integrate schools with their local communities, summer play schemes were introduced in urban areas. Using the local school as a centre, paid supervisors were appointed to organize indoor and outdoor activities for the school children during the summer holidays. In Belfast alone over 10,000 children were in daily attendance at these centres during the first week of July 1975 [19]. Forty centres were in use, as well as privately owned sports and recreational facilities. Although the early experiments in this field led to complaints about considerable damage to school property, as experience was gained this became less of a problem. In 1975 the Belfast scheme became more ambitious in fostering exchange visits between the children attending different centres.

It is probably not unfair to suggest that initially at any rate these schemes were envisaged as 'fire brigade' exercises designed to reduce the risk of sectarian clashes arising from the holiday boredom of urban children. More purposeful in intent were the activities of various voluntary groups which looked to the educational possibilities of permitting school children to learn about the life of less divided communities. Largely through the initiative of community groups outside Northern Ireland, mixed groups of school children from Northern Ireland were given the opportunity to travel to centres throughout the British Isles, Holland and North America and live for some time in selected homes in these areas. As this practice developed the local sponsoring groups formed themselves into a Holiday Co-ordination Committee which received a grant from the Community Relations Department to meet its administrative costs. This Department, which in 1974 was taken over by the Department of Education, also helped with travel costs within the British Isles provided that the groups assisted were drawn from the 'urban areas of special social need' and could be described as 'mixed groups' [20]. Over 600 children participated in this scheme during the summer of 1975 but it is probable, from the evidence available from individual schools, that at least an equal number travelled under different auspices to areas outside the British Isles.

While such schemes clearly had an integrative intent they have been criticized on several grounds. The first is that the costs involved restricted the benefits of the scheme to a very limited number. An equivalent expenditure on integrated holiday schemes wholly within Northern Ireland would have permitted a much greater number of children to benefit. It is also suggested that lack of follow-up quickly erodes any gains deriving from the interdenominational associations formed abroad. Some teachers have also complained that the holiday schemes have flourished at the expense of the school-sponsored educational visits which have become less attractive to the pupils.

If an improved staffing ratio and these limited examples of out-of-school activity seem to be merely gestures towards the concept of a compensatory programme the reason does not lie wholly in the financial constraints. There were those who did not regard the notion of compensatory education as useful in devising an educational response to Northern Ireland's problem. A member of the Queen's University Institute of Education, John Malone, has suggested that, 'if we view Northern Ireland politically as an Education Priority Area, what is required is not, to paraphrase Bernstein, a compensatory programme of education in "community relations" but simply appropriate education' [21]. Under the direction of Mr Malone, the Queen's Institute established in 1973 a Schools Curriculum Project 'to discover to what extent the school's curriculum influences community relations and how far schools may contribute to the improvement of community relations in Northern Ireland' [22]. Seven post-primary schools in Belfast and nine post-primary schools in Counties Tyrone and Fermanagh are involved in the project which is essentially a curriculum development and assessment programme. A similar type of programme has been initiated in the Schools Cultural Studies Project based in the New University of Ulster. In this project, in which seven Controlled and six Voluntary secondary schools are participating, the purpose is to develop a programme which might encourage:

1   the development of creative experimental approaches in schooling and curriculum, and
2   the cultivation of modes of sensitivity, tolerance and mutual understanding in personal and social relationships among secondary-school pupils in Northern Ireland. [23].

Together these two projects represent the most significant responses to the disturbances to be observed in the field of curriculum development in Northern Ireland. Another project however is worth noting here, even though it is still in a formative stage. This is an attempt sponsored jointly by the Institute of Education in Queen's University and the Rupert Stanley College of Further Education to develop a medium of community education which would provide learning opportunities for housewives within their neighbourhoods. The scheme started with a week-long summer school in Belfast in 1975 and has been continuing with two groups located in a primary school in West Belfast and one in North Belfast [24]. Although still in an experimental stage it represents further evidence of the manner in which the degree of civil unrest has focused attention upon the search for new educational strategies.

There remains, however, a school of thought which, while accepting that such strategies might have some ameliorative effect, believes that education can make no significant contribution to the emergence of a more ordered community in Northern Ireland so long as the dual system prevails. There have been two levels to this argument: the first sees in the existence of a dual system a major contributory factor to the present situation; the second position has been that, while the dual system may only have been a reflection of prevailing community divisions, its elimination would remove one obstacle to the emergence of a more cohesive community. The integrated schools issue has of course been a staple of educational debate in Ireland for over a century and a half but undoubtedly the subject came to be more hotly contested in the second half of the 1960s. In 1966, the then Northern Ireland Prime Minister, Captain Terence O'Neill, commented that 'a major cause of division arises from the *de facto* segregation of education along religious lines . . . Many people have questioned, however, whether the maintenance of two distinct educational systems side by side is not wasteful of human and financial resources and a major barrier to any attempt at communal assimilation'.[25]

Supporters of the concept of integration within Northern Ireland could point to the patterns in Queen's University, Belfast, the New University of Ulster in Coleraine and the Colleges of Further Education as examples of integrated education which could serve as models for integrated systems for the lower age ranges. As the debate became more lively in the search for social solutions, individual members of the Catholic clergy spoke approvingly of the desirability of shared-site schools and common facilities at sixth-form level. In 1971 the Presbyterian General Assembly passed a resolution declaring that 'integrated education would best serve the social, economic and educational needs of the community.' A pressure group calling itself 'All Children Together' came into being to lobby for and encourage integrated education. In the absence of any concrete proposals and in the heightened political tensions of the time the integration debate tended to be a sterile repetitious exchange. It was not until the 'power sharing' Northern Ireland Executive was established in 1974 that the Department of Education presented outline proposals for a system of 'shared schools' which could operate alongside the existing systems and would offer the opportunity for mixed education to those families which wished to avail of it. The proposals announced by Mr Basil McIvor, the

Executive member responsible for education, on 30 April 1974, received a qualified welcome from church bodies, teachers' unions and other interested groups but before they could be discussed any further the Northern Ireland Executive quit office and direct rule from Westminster was reintroduced. The new administration did not proceed with the proposals and Mr Roland Moyle, the Minister of State responsible for education, stated that because 'there was not a substantial degree of agreement in favour of the idea', the Government has decided not to pursue the McIvor initiative [26].

Possibly the only concrete benefit to emerge from the debate has been the encouragement of educationalists to explore the relationship between the values of the school and those of the wider community and it is possible that, because of the work of the Curriculum Projects and individual researchers in both QUB and NUU, the debate when it resumes will be more informed and purposeful than it has been in the past.

Conclusion

The political unrest which has convulsed Northern Ireland has obviously touched some individuals and institutions more directly than others. Its impact upon the schools system has, as we have seen, been varied. A relatively small proportion of schools have had to modify their school programmes because of external circumstances. A significantly high number of pupils have had their schooling disrupted because of transfers and school closures and some appear to have dropped out of the system altogether. It is impossible to make any assessment of the impact of these developments upon attainment levels but, if it has not been deleterious, then many of our assumptions about education must be wrong. For the teachers in the schools the disturbances have raised questions about job security, have forced them to modify their practices and in some cases to scrutinize their rationale. In this scrutiny they have been joined by other interests, including parental groups, who are asking whether more should not be demanded of the educative process.

One side of the coin, then, offers a picture of considerable disruption, tactics of adaptation and a mood of unease. The other side, however, shows a system offering a measure of certitude and stability in stark contrast to the external violence. The schools still provide an environment where moral values are defended and propagated and where the prospect of a better future is seen as an attainable goal.

That this should be so is a favourable comment upon the flexibility of the system, and the efforts of administrators, school managers and teachers who have in the main co-operated exceedingly well in an attempt to preserve a form of stability. Perhaps above all it is a comment upon the faith of the great majority of parents who continue to see in the schools the prospect of a better future for their children.

Notes

1   *The Education and Libraries (Northern Ireland) Order*, Belfast: HMSO, 1972.
2   *Northern Ireland: Education Statistics*, Belfast: HMSO, February 1974.
3   Irish National Teachers Organization, *Educational Administration in Northern Ireland*, Northern Committee, 1969.
4   McKeown, M., 'Civil Unrest: Secondary Schools Survey', *The Northern Teacher*, Winter 1973.
5   News Report, *Belfast Telegraph*, 1 March 1976.
6   Barritt, D. P. and Carter, C. F., *The Northern Ireland Problem*, London: Oxford University Press, 1962.
7   Boal, Fred and Robinson Alan, 'Close Together and Far Apart', *Community Forum*, **2**, 3, 1972.
8   Darby, John and Morris, Geoffrey, *Intimidation in Housing: a research paper*, Belfast: N.I. Community Relations Commission, 1974.
9   Interviews by author.
10 Interviews by author.
11 *Education in Northern Ireland in 1972*, Belfast: HMSO.
12 *Home–School Links*, Belfast: HMSO, 1976.
13 ibid.
14 News Report, *Belfast Telegraph*, 9 March 1976.
15 'Derry: from Conflict to Co-existence', *New Society*, 23 January 1975.
16 Letter in author's possession.
17 Boal, F. W., Doherty P. and Pringle, D. G., *The Spatial Distribution of some Social Problems in the Belfast Urban Area*, Belfast: N.I. Community Relations Commission, 1973.
18 *1975 Public Expenditure White Paper: Department of Educational Services*: Circular, March 1976.
19 *Interim Report of the Summer Education Scheme 1975*: Circular issued by Youth Service Sub-Committee, Belfast Education and Library Board, 19 August 1975.
20 *Circular: Summer Holiday Scheme*, Belfast: Department of Community Relations, 1975.
21 Malone, John, 'Schools and Community Relations', *The Northern Teacher*, Winter 1973.

22 Institute of Education, *Schools Curriculum Project 2*, Queen's University of Belfast, 1976.
23 Schools Cultural Studies Project, *Social and Cultural Studies*, The New University of Ulster, February 1976.
24 Rowlands, D. and Heggard, J., 'A Summer School for Housewives', *Adult Education*, March 1976.
25 O'Neill, Terence, *Autobiography*, London: Rupert Hart Davis, 1972.
26 News Report, *The Education Times*, 25 September 1975.

5 Social Welfare Services

Arthur Williamson and John Darby*

The foundation for the development of personal social services in Northern Ireland was laid by the Welfare Services Act of 1947. This established education, public health and personal social services as local authority responsibilities, and statutory committees in the six counties and county boroughs of Belfast and Londonderry discharged these functions until 1973 when, following the reorganization of local government, area boards took them over. Social work in Northern Ireland had developed in a much more integrated way than in other parts of the United Kingdom: Services for children had, since 1947, been the responsibility of the eight welfare (social services) departments, anticipating by two decades the Seebohm reorganization in Great Britain. The mentally handicapped had been the responsibility of the Special Care Service, a division of the province-wide Hospitals Authority, and under this service continuity and co-ordination of care was possible across the province.

The reorganization of local government services in 1973 resulted in personal social services being placed, together with all health services, under four Area Boards for Health and Social Services. These areas are in turn divided into seventeen districts and delivery of social, medical and nursing services is co-ordinated at district level by an executive team comprising the district heads of each of the services in addition to a district administrative officer and a representative of the District Medical Advisory Committee. This pattern is replicated at area level where chief officers comprise an Area Executive Team. The position of personal social services *vis à vis* health services is guaranteed by the provision of a special budget for social service growth. The Department

* John Darby and Arthur Williamson lecture in Social Administration at the New University of Ulster. John Darby is the author of *Conflict in Northern Ireland* (1976).

(formerly the Ministry) of Health and Social Services combines the functions of a regional authority and those of a government department. Each district has a district committee which has the responsibility of representing clients' views to professional officers and to the board. Members of district committees are appointed by area boards from nominations by district councils and voluntary organizations.

Like other aspects of social provision, personal social services in Northern Ireland are guaranteed parity of provision with Britain. However, just as levels of provision in Great Britain vary greatly between different areas, so in Northern Ireland historical accident, political priority and professional preference have combined to produce a pattern of manpower and facility provision which is inequitable; the eastern counties are considerably over-provided by comparison with the west, where unemployment, poor housing and infant mortality levels are among the highest in the EEC. This pattern of uneven distribution of provision with regard to need is also seen markedly in Belfast where the most deprived parts of north and west Belfast (including the Falls Road, Shankill Road, Ballymurphy, Andersonstown) suffer from an extraordinarily high tally of need and, in addition, have borne the brunt of sectarian violence. These areas, which form the administrative district of North and West Belfast, and which are the home of half of Belfast's population, are tightly segregated into a patchwork of Protestant and Roman Catholic housing estates and streets where many aspects of life are controlled by paramilitary organizations thrown up and sustained by sectarian violence.

Personal social services in Northern Ireland saw very rapid growth in the decade 1966–76. In 1966 there were only 250 social workers (17 per 100,000 of the population), and by 1974 this figure had more than doubled, though it should be noted that the distribution was uneven (26 per 100,000 in North and West Belfast compared with over 41 per 100,000 in Down) [1]. Numbers of staff with professional qualifications are somewhat lower than in Great Britain (N.I.—33.5%; G.B.— 41% in 1971) and through an ambitious training programme involving the province's two universities and its polytechnic, the Department of Health and Social Services is committed to a major increase in numbers of professional staff by 1980.

In many respects social work practice in Northern Ireland has paralleled developments in Great Britain, and regular and close contacts through the professional associations, training institutions, the National Institute for Social Work and the Central Council for Education and Training in Social Work, have encouraged and maintained similar development for social work in Northern Ireland. There are many important respects in which this pattern of development does not work either for the best interests of the public in Northern Ireland, or indeed for the profession. The arena in which social work operates in Northern Ireland is very different from the situation elsewhere in the United Kingdom. Firstly integration at delivery and planning levels between health and personal social services presents a range of opportunities, and difficulties, not present in Great Britain. More important, however, is the response which is demanded of the services by the extent of social deprivation. Family poverty unparalleled almost anywhere in the United Kingdom, widescale housing deprivation and an unemployment rate double that of other regions contribute to present a situation in which it is appropriate to ask if social work in Northern Ireland can remain content to follow passively in the wake of professional models geared to conditions of political stability, comparative affluence and more extensive social provision.

The chequered history of community work in the province points to the uniqueness of the Northern Ireland experience. Northern Ireland's first community workers were employed by the quasi-independent Community Relations Commission in 1970 and it was partly governmental alarm at the remarkable growth and aggressiveness of community action groups which led to its abolition in 1974. After much delay, responsibility for community work was divided between district councils and area boards. It appears from recent research that, within area boards at any rate, the integration of social and community workers has had the effect of shunting the latter towards a minor and supporting role.

A further feature of life in Northern Ireland which has important implications for social work is the security situation and the fact that in some areas effective power rests, not with the state, but with unelected paramilitary leaders. During political emergencies the implications of this become strikingly clear, when social distress makes the conventional emphasis on case work irrelevant. There have been three such periods since the outbreak of disturbances—in August 1969, August 1971 and May 1974—and during them social work services were presented with new and frightening demands. In 1969 and 1971 they had to take on the responsibility of housing thousands of refugees who had left their homes owing to intimidation; in 1974 they were faced with a situation in which large urban populations were without the public services on which many aspects of modern life depend. In each of these crises social service departments attempted to take on wide-ranging social welfare responsibilities for which they were poorly equipped and which were completely different from their conventional activities. In the absence of a functioning civil defence organization social workers in some places were the first and last line in the state's defences against social disaster and found new duties thrust upon them as government sought, under the floodlight of the world's press, to respond to a rapidly changing situation of widespread distress and hardship. Social work went by the board; emergency relief became the order of the day.

Government, Politics and Social Work

New complexities in the relationship between government, violence and social work were demonstrated almost from the start of the troubles, during the August 1969 emergency. At that time county boundaries delineated the territories of social service departments, and Counties Antrim and Down shared responsibility for part of the Greater Belfast area with the Belfast Welfare Department, the welfare arm of the Belfast Corporation. The response of the three agencies to widespread social distress pointed to differences in their perception of agency roles in a crisis. Counties Antrim and Down responded in whole-hearted and flexible manner, and their staffs worked virtually around the clock to relieve distress. The Belfast Welfare Authority, on the other hand, maintained normal routine and refused to accept that social upheavals generated by political turmoil were within its remit until it was compelled by government to introduce special measures to cope with at least some aspects of the crisis. Antrim Welfare Department opened an emergency social services office in the heart of troubled Andersonstown; its senior staff lived there and co-ordinated a special team of social workers drafted in from other parts of the province. Antrim provided bedding, food and heating and supervised the distribution of cash to needy families in addition to conducting a door-to-door enquiry into the extent of social need. Under an agreement between the Ministry of Health and Social Services and the Ministry of Finance, the former was given authority to grant-aid at the rate of 100% any additional expenditure incurred in respect of an emergency. An additional procedure permitted the Ministry of Health and Social Services to take over the functions of local authority (welfare) departments during an emergency. This power was not exercised; whether because the Ministry of Health and Social Services was reluctant to provoke a controversy with the powerful Belfast Corporation, or for some other reason, it is difficult to judge.

While it is clear that social workers everywhere work within restraints imposed by political structures, the security situation in Northern

Ireland has created extra problems. During the UWC strike in 1974 the recommendation by the Department of Health and Social Services concerning the suspension of Section 164 of the Children and Young Persons Act (1968), which permitted discretionary expenditure in special financial difficulties, caused distress in some parts of the province. Some social workers believe that this advice was dictated by a political wish to defeat the strike, rather than by genuine social welfare criteria. The Department, in strongly denying this, claimed that Section 164 was unsuitable for the sort of large-scale disaster which was anticipated, and exceptional social security measures already introduced were more appropriate to the circumstances.

Political tensions were also reflected within the social work profession itself. There is an inherent conflict between the professional detachment towards which social workers aspire and the cultural identification which is the inheritance of all Ulster people. On at least two occasions issues became public which revealed deep divisions within the profession. In 1972 some members of the social work profession stressed the link between the general political situation and their own work by reference to internment as 'the legislated creation of a population of one parent families' [2]. Again in 1976 differences within the profession erupted into public controversy about the effects of the Payment of Debt Act. This act permitted the government to withdraw at source from publicly allocated money—supplementary benefits, maternity and other grants, salaries *et al.*—for repayment of housing debts. This extraordinary act was introduced as a counter to the rent and rates strike which followed the introduction of internment in 1971, but was also used for debts unrelated to this strike. A public claim by social workers in one Belfast district that its effects were minimal, and that many people actually preferred to have their finances organized in this way, produced strong opposition from other social workers and community leaders, and revealed wide perceptual and conceptual differences within the profession [3]. These divisions have also provided opportunities. After some years of hoping that violence and its problems would go away, there have recently been signs that the social work profession is preparing to adjust to the peculiarities of its situation.

Direct Violence and Paramilitary Organizations

There are two problems in assessing the effects of direct violence on social work. The first is the striking variation between different localities; the second is the difficulty of evaluating an abundant body of evidence which may often appear melodramatic. Several social workers with voluntary organizations have been shot and killed and, in the words of one man in the district of North and West Belfast, 'the potential for personal danger is present in every case.' No branch of social work is immune from this danger, though it has affected community work more than other types of social work. Threats and intimidation are common and there are records of incidents where social workers' cars have been damaged and where particular cases have had to be dropped following threats. Though these represent only a fractional proportion of cases, even in the most troubled areas, the element of personal risk is one which must weigh with social workers. Near Belfast a social enquiry was interrupted by men with guns who demanded to know why information was being obtained. A social worker married to an army officer in a provincial town found that community leaders, who were also officers in a paramilitary group, possessed detailed information about her husband and were not reluctant to use it to influence her intervention on a case. Some community workers report that they sometimes drop their car keys after leaving a meeting; this enables them to look unobtrusively under the car to search for booby-trap bombs.

In areas where suspicion runs at a high level social workers are particularly on their guard and are careful to ensure that they are not suspected of being plain-clothes police or army intelligence agents. Some staff have been issued with large identification discs for their cars and in some districts it has become necessary to mark buses clearly *Handicapped People* in order to avoid confusion with workmen's buses which could be ambushed.

A particularly sensitive area of social work concerns taking children into care and many incidents of threat and violence are recorded, including one where a social worker's car was shot at and another where the car was stoned. In another case a child was removed from a children's home by his father, armed with a hand gun. The sequel to this last case illustrates an interesting aspect of the liaison of statutory agencies with paramilitary groups: within a few hours the child was returned to the home by members of a paramilitary group who warned the father that further interference with the child would be punished by kneecapping (shooting through the knee). In this case senior social services officers contacted paramilitary leaders, and explained the nature of the case and the reasons for taking the child into care.

Standby duty presents acute problems in some districts where violence is common. Policy varies widely between districts. In South

Armagh decisions whether or not to go out at night have to be referred by social workers to their District Social Services Officer (DSSO). In other districts senior staff operate on standby and are highly selective about the type of cases to which they respond; in one district, for example, mental health cases are normally answered, but children's cases must wait until daylight. In view of the risks involved, one senior female social worker is accompanied by her husband when on standby duty. Problems which are normal by day take on a new and frightening aspect in the early hours of the morning, particularly if a Protestant social worker is called to a Catholic area, or *vice versa*.

As in virtually all offices, shops and factories in Northern Ireland, security precautions are normally in force in social service offices. Precautions include in some parts of the province handbag searches by security officials, high wire fences around offices and electronic door-opening devices; in other parts there are no precautions whatever. Some district social service offices are located in the administrative blocks of hospitals where security precautions are normally minimal or non-existent, owing to the fact that hospitals have usually been regarded as neutral territory. Staff notice boards carry circular letters entitled *How to deal with letter bombs* and *Procedure for evacuation of the building*. Bombing of offices, however, is comparatively rare since the role and importance of social work in the community are normally recognized by paramilitary leaders. Indeed tacit agreements have been worked out to give immunity to social service offices and personnel. In one provincial town a social worker was hi-jacked and held for four hours while his car was used on a bombing raid; it later transpired that this action was in breach of agreements with a paramilitary organization, and undertakings were given that similar incidents would not recur.

Co-operation with paramilitary groups is a matter in which normal professional criteria and standards of conduct have had to be reconsidered. While few social workers any longer hold the view that there should be no contact with paramilitaries, the most significant differences within the profession are between those who are concerned about the political implications of such a liaison and those who see the issue purely in pragmatic terms. For example, many social workers are in contact with community groups which are closely linked with paramilitary groups. The Official and Provisional IRAs are involved in this way, and the UDA inspired the formation of the federated Ulster Community Action Group. In many districts paramilitary groups have a genuine welfare role, use their influence in matters such as representations to the housing authority and operate advice centres which provide a real service, although handicapped through lack of expertise and resources. In many places there is continuous co-operation between statutory social work services and these centres, and referrals are made from one to the other. Most agencies discriminate between violent and non-violent organizations and will maintain an 'acceptable level of co-operation' with less violent groups. Senior officers are concerned about the implications of extending recognition to such groups and often the paramilitary organizations are anxious to enhance their credibility and standing through co-operation with statutory bodies. Nevertheless, pragmatism is almost invariably the determining factor. During the Ulster Worker's Council strike in May 1974 effective control was exercised in many areas by paramilitary groups and social service agencies could not have performed any useful role had they not co-operated with them. Thus the Protestant Ulster Defence Association took over a meals-on-wheels service in one district with the support of the social service staff. Another illustration of co-operation was when, following threats to workers building an old people's home, the UDA put up a sign warning that social services property must not be damaged. Again, a divisional social services office which had been repeatedly robbed and vandalized was 'protected' by members of a Catholic paramilitary organization after arrangements had been worked out by senior social services staff.

During the early years of the troubles some social workers were very reluctant to negotiate with or recognize paramilitary groups. The UWC strike was a watershed in this respect. Since then most social service administrators have accommodated to what they see as the new realities and to the very real power exercised by these groups. Considerations of service to those in need have tended to take precedence over the niceties of protocol and decorum.

The Effect of Violence on Case Work

Most social workers in Northern Ireland are strongly orientated towards a case work approach and regard their primary task as dealing with families, children, old people and other groups with particular problems. Few of these categories have remained unaffected by violence, although its effects have varied throughout the province.

Nowhere have the effects of violence on traditional models of social work been more starkly illustrated than with social workers employed by the probation service. Probation work involves attempting to alter or modify the behaviour of clients which led to their being arrested.

In Northern Ireland, however, a large proportion of offenders are charged with political offences and conventional probation work would involve social workers in the task of attempting to alter their clients' political views. This prospect was so alarming to probation officers that in 1975 the profession categorically refused to work with clients who had been charged with scheduled offences—those involving political charges, although a number of probation officers maintain contact with their clients on a voluntary basis.

Violence has also left its mark in other aspects of social case work. Some social workers have observed a relationship between general violence in the community and a higher level of family violence. Its effect on family problems, however, is quite specific. The rise in Northern Ireland's prison population from 727 to 2,848 between 1968 and 1974, more than 1,600 deaths and an unknown number of men on the run have all left in their wake a considerable increase in the number of one-parent families in the province. In the social services districts close to the border, for example, there are social work cases resulting from fathers hiding out in the Irish Republic. One District Social Services Officer calculates that between 10% and 15% of the one-parent families in his district were directly attributable to the troubles.

The involvement of the very young in the excitement of rioting and disorder has attracted the interest of the media since the beginning of the troubles. The social worker usually comes into official contact with these young people at a secondary rather than a primary stage—when the youth has been brought to court or committed to a training school or borstal. At a younger age level there has also been growing concern about the number of children at risk. The main professional problem for social workers, however, is not so much their increased case loads as the greater likelihood that cases will be accompanied by threats of violence. Many of the extra cases involving children and one-parent families stem directly from violence, so the threats are not taken casually by social workers. Few are prepared to request police protection in view of its political connotations, and the fact that this could compromise their relationship with clients.

The main influence of violence on case work has been to swell work loads and highlight issues which previously were underrated. For example, population movements from Belfast to such towns as Craigavon, Lisburn and Antrim have added to the number of one-parent families, physically handicapped and psychologically disturbed people in those districts, since many of the new arrivals were victims of, and evacuees from, Belfast's violence.

The effects of violence on psychiatric social work has been extremely complex. Research has indicated that the psychiatric effects of violence are substantially different for different age groups and for different parts of the province [4]. There has been an increased incidence of suicide among the under-30s and marked increases in anxiety, attempted suicide and general depression have been observed, not in the areas suffering from overt violence, but in peripheral districts like North Down. The need to monitor this sort of change and the lack of resources and expertise with which to do it is an obvious but often unacknowledged problem.

There is a curious reluctance on the part of many social work staff to recognize the connection between violence and their work. It is misleading to claim, as some social workers have done, that the fact that more people have been killed on the roads in Northern Ireland than by terrorists means that political violence does not make extraordinary demands on the time, expertise and courage of social workers. Violence has produced 1,600 deaths, thousands of imprisonments and detentions and these developments have pushed many young people towards random vandalism or into the regimented violence of the paramilitary organizations. Old people and the mentally handicapped are often at the mercy of youths who—in the absence of effective policing —maintain a reign of terror in their neighbourhoods. While it is true that the number of cases which are directly attributable to violence is limited, its cumulative effect is much more serious and has attracted no research and very little public or professional discussion. In the main social case work in Northern Ireland continues along its traditional path and violence is regarded as an additional irritant rather than a catalyst.

Staffing

It is virtually impossible to determine the extent to which social work staffing levels have been affected by violence. While it is true that the most violent areas have the poorest staffing ratios, it must also be recognized that there is always a strong correlation between violence and social deprivation, and also that areas of high social deprivation normally find it difficult to attract staff. It is not easy to estimate the relative importance of these two factors, but it is generally acknowledged that a social worker's credibility and acceptance depend far more on competence and impartiality than on religion. There are, however, some exceptions to this generalization. For instance, it has proved dangerous for staff to move backwards and forwards across the peace line from Protestant to Catholic housing estates; where this is necessary staff are anxious to establish their *bona fides* as social workers to allay suspicions that they might be plain-clothes army or police personnel engaged on surveillance. This atmosphere of nervousness and suspicion has also served to reduce the number of social workers recruited in the Irish Republic and Great Britain for employment in Northern Ireland, and has increased the tendency for social work staff to seek employment in their home areas. One result has been a greater feeling of insularity, which in turn creates new professional problems.

Social Workers and Other Agencies

Problems have also been generated for social work by other agencies. For example, in some parts squatting is so widespread that the Northern Ireland Housing Executive 'pre-allocates' houses—assigns them to tenants before they are completed—in the expectation that the tenants will prevent illegal occupation. Since the houses at this stage often lack basic services, heat, light, water, and their residents are therefore technically homeless, social service departments are obliged to provide basic facilities such as cookers and heaters. Work of this type provides very little job satisfaction, and social workers resent being required to cope with problems which arise from the administrative difficulties of other public bodies.

The tendency for social workers to inherit difficulties created by other agencies is not confined to public and social welfare bodies. Since 1969 there has been a proliferation in the number of organizations carrying out quasi-social work. These range from paramilitary organizations involved in illegal housing allocations to the community relations work which the police assumed following the reorganization in the wake of the Hunt Report. The army also has a community relations department which engages in social welfare activities mainly through the provision of facilities and transport for community groups. Relations between these agencies and social service departments are often strained, particularly in view of the fact that social work staff in republican areas are anxious to have an identity which is untainted by contact with the British Army or the police. Army intelligence is well aware of the extensive knowledge of personalities and organizations possessed by social workers and in particular by community development workers. Some social workers accuse the army of regarding them as a 'confidential telephone service' and strongly resent army attempts to obtain information from them.

Other officials with a quasi-welfare role are the civil representatives employed by the Department of Education but attached to the army and responsible for liaison with the civilian population. They have access to army equipment and transport and have budgets which enable them to subsidize selected community activities on a modest scale. Because of their army affiliation Catholic communities are considerably less willing to work with civil representatives than groups in Protestant communities and view their activities with suspicion, fearing a covert military intelligence role.

North and West Belfast

A major difficulty in assessing the effects of violence on Northern Ireland's personal social services is the wide variation in different parts of the province. Some districts experience a level of violence so much higher than the average that it constitutes a qualitative rather than a purely quantitative difference. The outstanding example of such a district is North and West Belfast.

North and West Belfast is one of five districts which comprise the Eastern Health and Social Services Board. With a population of 240,000 it is larger than two of Northern Ireland's four Area Boards. The district includes the parts of the city which have been most affected by violence and holds a total of 26 flashpoints including, among others, Andersonstown, Turf Lodge, Ballymurphy, Lenadoon, 'The Bone', Ardoyne and the Falls and Shankill Roads, and Tiger Bay; during 1976 there were 50 killings in the district. As a result of the violence, North and West Belfast is deprived of many normal social amenities—buses are frequently called off, road ramps abound and some public service workers are reluctant to enter parts of the district.

The social problems accompanying these conditions are immense. A 1974 study of social malaise in Belfast found that the most serious areas of multiple deprivation were concentrated in the northern and western parts of the city; two earlier investigations in 1972 revealed unemployment rates of 38% and 14% in two West Belfast estates [5], and in 1975 the British Association of Social Workers found more than 1,000 mentally handicapped people and 400 children in care in the district. Until late 1976 it did not possess one purpose-built day centre for the elderly, and had an estimated shortage of 360 beds in residential accommodation. This combination of lack of provision and widespread social need became the responsibility of the Eastern Area Board, North and West Belfast District, in October 1973. Formerly much of the district had been within the territory covered by Belfast Welfare Authority, and the social services section of Belfast Corporation. The problems of West Belfast result in large part from neglect by Belfast Corporation in the last two decades reflecting its anti-working class policies, the seriously underdeveloped state of social work in the 1950s and 60s and, some social workers believe, political bias.

The work of social workers in North and West Belfast has been fundamentally affected by the violence endemic in the district since 1969. Damage to cars by vandals is commonplace; intimidation is widespread; the sub-district office in North Belfast has twice been bombed, and on the second occasion the evacuating staff had to jump over the live bomb to reach safety. The professional activities of social workers in the district are accompanied with increasing frequency by threats of injury or death. This most often happens when children are being taken into care; a senior social worker estimated that 10% of the child care problems in his office were accompanied by threats or violence. To call upon police or army for support would so compromise the acceptance of social workers as to constitute professional suicide.

Contact between social workers and paramilitaries is frequent. The Provisional IRA in Andersonstown often refer cases to the social service office and the UDA have been approached on a number of occasions to guarantee safety of access to cases in North Belfast, to stop intimidation, or to rehouse families. Such negotiations are usually carried out by senior social service staff, and are justified on the pragmatic grounds that the paramilitaries exercise control over what happens in many areas.

There is general awareness that the paramilitaries gain some credibility from such co-operation, but the moral obligation to provide social services usually prevails over ethical worries about working with men of violence. The pill is also sweetened by the fact that paramilitary leaders are often also members of community associations, and the professional niceties are preserved by maintaining contact with them under this other hat. Indeed, far from regarding the paramilitaries as a menace, social workers in the district believe that a dangerous development has been the growing dominance of North Belfast by teenage 'cowboys', who cannot be controlled by the paramilitary leaders. In this highly violent and volatile situation the paramilitaries are no longer able to offer social workers the protection which they could guarantee until 1975.

The administration of social work services in the district has clearly been affected by these developments, but more mundane considerations have also depressed morale. Working conditions have been poor; two teams of social workers worked until late 1976 from the Clifton Street Office, which was outdated, overcrowded and without interviewing facilities. Administrative services have been unwieldy, inefficient and inadequate. As a result it became difficult to attract staff to the district office, which operated at 50% below its establihsment during the first four years following its creation. Even more important, since the prospect of promotion has in large measure failed to attract qualified social workers into the district, internal promotions have prematurely elevated inexperienced staff to middle and senior positions. The effects of these shortages are cumulative. A combination of growing case loads and staff shortages has lead to overwork and to social workers being unable to pursue specialist interests; trainee social workers and social work assistants have not only been inadequately supervised, but have accepted responsibilities far beyond what is expected in other districts. Student placement opportunities are restricted and this further reduces the district's recruitment opportunities, thus completing the cycle of disadvantage.

Social workers in North and West Belfast react to these circumstances with some ambivalence. Despite a high level of staff loyalty and cohesion, they express frustration and anger at what they see as lack of sympathy for the peculiar and extraordinary difficulties of the district. Most of this resentment is directed against the Eastern Area Board and the Department of Health and Social Services, and the reaction of these bodies to the district's problems have certainly been less than perceptive. In January 1975 a report was produced following a conjoint exercise by the Department and the Area Board 'to identify the difficulties being experienced in the provision of personal social services in the North-West Belfast division, and to make recommendations to try to resolve these difficulties as a matter of urgency'. The investigating group, which contained no representatives from the district itself, analysed the problems in bureaucratic and administrative terms, attributing them to such factors as misunderstanding of administrative functions, lack of adequate supervision, and poor back-up facilities. There is nothing in the 3,000-word report to indicate awareness that the district's problems arose from its unusual social and political circumstances and the high level of violence. In the analysis of the area's background characteristics there is no mention of paramilitary organizations, and violence is dismissed in a two-line reference. This failure to appreciate the problems created by extraordinary levels of social deprivation and compounded by violence led to some remarkably poor analysis and inadequate recommendations. For example, despite the size and the peculiarities of the district, there is no mention of the need for positive discrimination policies, for incentives in pay and conditions, or for the establishment of a research unit to monitor the level of need and provision in the district.

North and West Belfast is the social services district in Northern Ireland where violence is most concentrated, and where its influence on the provision of social services is most marked; it is also the Belfast district which suffers most from multiple social deprivation. It may be that this very combination of violence and social need and its contrast to the relative normality of the rest of the province, has led social workers in other districts to underrate the effects which violence has had on their work. This would be unfortunate. The disease may be most obviously present in North and West Belfast, but the symptoms are everywhere.

Assessment

Many difficulties obstruct attempts to assess the effects of violence on social work in Northern Ireland, and some conditions must qualify any generalization on the subject. The first qualification to be made, and one which is rarely recognized, is that even a small area like Northern Ireland, comparable in size to Yorkshire and in population to Birmingham and Manchester, holds a wide variety of conditions. District Social Service Officers in many of the seventeen districts see their jobs in the same terms as their administrative counterparts in Kent or Cumberland; in North and West Belfast, on the other hand, violence has overshadowed normal working problems, depressed morale and created serious problems for social workers. Even to make this contrast, however, is to risk oversimplification. The pattern of violence is not the white of North Antrim or the black of North Belfast, but a spectrum of varying shades of grey.

A second major problem in assessing the situation is the variety of perceptions of violence found within the relatively close-knit ranks of social service administration. The general blandness of Department of Health and Social Services officials contrasts with the intermittent fears of social workers in different districts. District Social Services Officers are administratively the fulcrum of the service, but their knowledge of the day-to-day activities of social workers—whom violence effects most directly—is superficial and often inaccurate. A first generalization is that a social worker's perceptions of the impact of violence on the conduct of social work varies in directly inverse proportion to his rank. The closer he is to cases on the ground, the more is his work affected by violence. Even senior social workers, only one step away from the field, admit to a tendency to forget the hazards of field work. One senior in North Belfast who was asked by a subordinate to help deal with two difficult cases was assaulted twice in one day, and rudely reminded of reality.

Cases of direct assault, however, are relatively rare, and the more substantial effects of violence on social work are felt at secondary level. Violence produces a number of social problems which eventually find their way into the social worker's casebook. The marked rise in vandalism and teenage violence has not only increased the number of young people in jail, detention centres and borstals, but has created fears and apprehensions among old people and, in turn, affected the professional concern and workload of the social worker. Again, there is a direct relationship between community conflict and the growth of community organizations in the province, and this development demands new concepts of social work and a new understanding of the relationship of the profession to the community.

These pressures have led to a measure of confusion and defensiveness in the social work profession, a condition which is considerably worsened by a fundamental conflict about the relationship of its social case work and social welfare roles. There is no civil defence organization in Northern Ireland to adopt a co-ordinating welfare function during emergencies. Its absence was scarcely noticed until the outbreak of community violence in 1969. Since then there have been many emergencies, ranging from the widespread distress of August 1969 and May 1974 to hundreds of localized and short-lived crises resulting from bomb threats or explosions. In the absence of any appropriate organization to arrange evacuations and to provide temporary heating, shelter and food, these responsibilities fell upon the social work agencies. Some leading social workers believe that this role should have been rejected in an attempt to force the authorities to create suitable 'social defence' machinery. However, it was accepted, and social workers found themselves burdened with a general welfare role during emergencies which they were not only unsuited by training and experience to discharge, but which seriously hampered their normal case work. Since emergencies held the threat of community collapse, relief work was considered to have priority over the individual cases with which social workers would otherwise be dealing. Individual intervention continued of course, and indeed became even more necessary as violence increased; but the reality was that during emergencies neither function was properly carried out, and that social workers sometimes became disgruntled and confused about their work. It has become a theoretical and practical dilemma for the profession in 1969, and one which is no closer to resolution today than it was then.

This conceptual problem and the more practical difficulties presented to the social work profession by Northern Ireland's community conflict, suggest a number of essential changes for the operation of social work services. These refer in particular to social work training, social work practice and research.

There are probably no social work courses in the British Isles which are geared to the issues discussed in this chapter, which are now commonplace in some parts of Northern Ireland. The training institutions in Northern Ireland have been slow to recognize that their work setting is essentially different from the politically consensual and comparatively more affluent world of mainland United Kingdom. Trainees on social work field placements sometimes find themselves unprepared for the realities of social work practice and point to a serious hiatus between classroom and work in the field. Senior staff have accommodated, albeit tentatively and gradually, to the changing working environment. Preoccupation with practical and bureaucratic problems generated by the integration of personal social services with health services in 1973 has tended to disguise the extent to which professional and public perceptions of social work have altered since the troubles began. The recent great expansion in numbers of professional staff has meant that only a small proportion have had any experience of social work in a non-violent context.

These changes impose practical, political and ethical demands on social work courses. The political nature of social work involvement is often either unrecognized or misunderstood. It is virtually impossible for any field worker to maintain a consistently non-political stance. In the face of subjects such as internment or Payment of Debt legislation, the social worker's diagnosis of a client's situation and his attitude to it will be strongly conditioned by his perceptions of the legitimacy of the administration. His approach is likely to be dictated as much by his religio-political outlook as by an objective and professional analysis of the issues involved. The political nature of these issues is often ignored and staff of mixed religions may avoid discussing them in order to minimize the likelihood of sectarian tensions within the profession. Sensitivity towards such matters within the profession may also prevent it from acting as an effective pressure group to lobby government on social deprivation issues; there is strong but unacknowledged tension between effective representation of the needs of clients living in areas of great social need and the fact that action on some of these topics would inevitably bring polarization and dissensus within the professional association. Nevertheless in late 1976 the British Association of Social Workers, at both local and national levels, strongly expressed its opposition to the contentious issue of Payment of Debts legislation.

The ethical problems facing the profession also include such questions as co-operation with proscribed organizations, disclosure of confidential information under threat, or the resolution of conflicts which arise when a social worker comes to possess information which could lead to the arrest of people accused of serious crimes, including murder. Similarly the question of how to relate to other statutory agencies, including the police and the army, is one which has clear implications for social work courses.

The changing nature of the social work task is scarcely reflected in training. The widespread phenomenon of community action since the start of the troubles obviously deserves much greater attention. The psychiatric implications of violence also call for an increase in the community mental health component in the curriculum. Changes in probation work present new opportunities for family therapy. Courses should innovatively explore ways of using these new situations to develop and extend social skills.

If social service departments are to continue to discharge a civil defence role in emergency situations a number of training issues follow: most staff have had no preparation or training for the variety of tasks which they are called on to assume and their lack of expertise has led to frustration and confusion. For as long as social service departments are central to the state's intervention in respect of social distress in emergency situations their staffs must receive special training in the use of emergency equipment and procedure. There is a clear and obvious case for training in the range of tasks involved in implementing the emergency plans which now exist in every district.

A conference in January 1977 saw the first formal attempt to evaluate the effect of violence on social work teaching—after seven years of civil strife. Clearly there is a need for further discussions between social work teaching institutions and social workers themselves to seek appropriate methods of teaching social workers in a conflict situation. But if seven years seems a long time for teachers of social work to arrange their first conference on the implications of violence for social work training it is more remarkable that civil disorder has not yet been the subject of any conference of social workers. It is true that many social workers do not regard violence as any more important than other variables such as drunkenness or drug addiction. These, however, are dangerous analogies. The fact that violence and its effects are often evaluated exclusively in specific terms—its effect on case work with children, or old people, etc. which in some districts may indeed be slight—ignores the fundamentally pervasive nature of violence. While particular aspects of case work may apparently have been only slightly affected, the interaction between these may amount to a less obvious, and therefore potentially more dangerous, problem. There is a strong *prima facie* case that social work in Northern Ireland has been affected by violence. This merits serious and urgent investigation by both the profession and social work agencies.

In one instance, however, the case is even stronger. North and West Belfast, in addition to its socio–economic deprivation has been cursed with a worse concentration of violent acts than any other part of the province, and cannot attract the staff to deal with it. There is a case for formal recognition of the district as one of extraordinary social need, applying positive discrimination in its favour, and attempting to attract workers there by allocation of better resources and facilities.

One of the curious characteristics which distinguish social work from other professions in Northern Ireland has been its failure to attract the interest of researchers. Not only is there no tradition of academic research, but social work practitioners, most of whom have studied social research methods as an element of their training, rarely apply them to their work. The usual reason offered for this situation—that social workers are overworked—has obvious relevance, but no more so than in medicine, education or housing administration. In a dynamic and volatile situation research assumes, or should assume, an added importance. The fact that only one person is employed by social work agencies in Northern Ireland for a specific research function appears to result from a general disregard in the profession for both theoretical and operational research. The onus rests on academics to emphasize that social work training requires a critical understanding of broader social issues as well as the transmission of skills, and to demonstrate the relevance of social research skills to social work practice.

The fundamental problem posed by violence for social workers remains the profession's failure to acknowledge the peculiarities created by it, and especially the way in which it has confused the social worker's role. Whether or not social work in Northern Ireland should continue

to embrace a residual social welfare function in addition to its traditional roles has far-reaching implications for the profession and presents
a central question about the nature of social work in a conflict. The
recognition and resolution of this dilemma is our main recommendation.

Notes

1   Evason, E., Darby, J. and Pearson, M., *Social Need and Social Provision
    in Northern Ireland*, Coleraine, New University of Ulster, Occasional
    Papers in Social Administration, 1976, 156, 7.
2   Letter signed by 23 social workers, *Irish News*, 15 March 1972.
3   Letter signed by social workers, *Belfast Telegraph*, 23 December 1976, and
    correspondence following.
4   *See*, for example, Fraser, R. M., *Children in conflict*, London: Secker &
    Warburg, 1973 and Lyons, H. A., 'The psychiatric sequelae of the
    Belfast riots', in *British Journal of Psychiatry*, **118**, March 1971.
5   Boal, F. W., Doherty, P. and Pringle, D., *The Spatial Distribution of Some
    Social Problems in the Belfast Urban Area*, Belfast: Northern Ireland
    Community Relations Commission, Research Paper, 1974. The two sur-
    veys are described by Nial Duff in *Community Forum*, **3**, 1, 1973. The situ-
    ation described in these projects is further endorsed by a government
    paper published in March 1977, *Report of Study Group on Areas of Special
    Need*, Belfast: HMSO, 1977.

6 Housing

Susan Kennedy and Derek Birrell*

Introduction

This chapter outlines the main effects of violence in Northern Ireland on housing in terms of policies, objectives, procedures and administrative structures. It examines the establishment of the Northern Ireland Housing Executive, the ways in which violence has affected the housing programme, the response of government and housing authorities by amending policies and objectives and by the introduction of new policies and programmes to meet special problems. It also considers the response of the people of Northern Ireland through increased community participation and interest in housing problems. Clearly there are difficulties in establishing which effects are directly due to violence and which to other factors. It must be borne in mind that some effects noted may be only partially attributed to the disturbances and might well have occurred anyway; others ultimately owe more to sectarianism which has always been present within the society than to the violence since 1968.

While violence and civil disturbances have had an important effect on many aspects of housing, particularly in the Belfast area, perhaps the major connection between housing and violence lies in the significance of housing issues in the events of 1968/9, including the outbreak of disturbances. The first Civil Rights march in 1968 took place in protest against housing allocations by a local authority, reflecting dissatisfaction in the Catholic community with the administration of housing by some councils. At that time county boroughs, borough councils, urban district and rural district councils had responsibility

* Susan Kennedy was a researcher with the Northern Ireland Housing Executive.

Derek Birrel is a lecturer in Social Administration at the New University of Ulster, and has been involved in housing research projects for a number of years.

for the building, allocation and management of their housing stock. In addition there was a centralized housing agency, the Northern Ireland Housing Trust, which provided houses on a large scale throughout the province to complement the efforts of local authorities.

The Cameron Commission, set up in 1969 to investigate the disturbances, listed three complaints on housing as the first general cause of the disorders in 1968. 'A rising sense of continuing injustice and grievance among large sections of the Catholic population in particular in Londonderry and Dungannon in respect of (I) the inadequacy of housing provision by certain local authorities; (II) unfair methods of allocation of houses built and let by such authorities, in particular refusals and omissions to adopt a points system and (III) misuse in certain cases of discretionary powers of allocation of houses in order to perpetuate Unionist control of the local authority.' [1]. Eventually, the British government came to accept that housing conditions had not only produced the dissatisfaction which helped create the Civil Rights Movement but that there was an association between areas with poor housing and social conditions and the occurrence of violence [2].

Housing conditions in Northern Ireland are very poor compared to Great Britain. In 1974 20% of the housing stock in Northern Ireland was statutorily unfit compared to 7% in England and Wales; in all 35% of the total stock required some form of remedial housing action compared to 24 % in Britain; 172,000 dwellings were deficient in one way or another; about 600,000 people were living in inadequate housing. In the central and inner western areas of Belfast 50% of the dwellings were statutorily unfit for human habitation and only 15% of dwellings were sound [3].

The Establishment of the Northern Ireland Housing Executive

When the British Government intervened directly to influence and subsequently take over government in Northern Ireland, the amelioration of housing conditions became a primary objective of government policy. It represented an essential feature of a social reform programme towards the elimination of grievances and of a strategy that might help remove the underlying factors behind violence and ensure future viability and well-being. The violence can be said to have been an important factor in many initiatives in housing policy of which the decision in 1969 to establish the Northern Ireland Housing Executive was the most radical. The disorders of August 1969 had led to a meeting of representatives of the United Kingdom and Northern Ireland governments. Joint Working Parties of officials of both governments were established to examine certain problem areas, including housing. Following the reports of these bodies the decision to create a centralized housing authority was announced. A communiqué by the Westminster and Stormont governments stated that 'the governments have concluded that this is an emergency situation requiring emergency procedures'. It continued, 'they have, therefore, decided reluctantly that local authorities are not geared—and cannot be geared—to handle such a task and that the best hope of success lies in the creation of a single-purpose, efficient and streamlined central housing authority.' This authority was to take over responsibility for the building, management and allocation of all public housing from the local authorities, the Housing Trust and the Development Commissions. It was also decided at that time to introduce immediately a fair allocation policy. In June 1969 the Ministry of Development issued its guidelines on principles of allocation and a model points system which was then adopted by the Housing Trust, the three Development Commissions and a majority of councils.

The Housing Executive came into operation in October 1971 and, by July 1973, had taken over full responsibility for one third of the total housing stock in Northern Ireland, about 155,000 dwellings. The Housing Executive was not a totally radical innovation; the Northern Ireland Housing Trust had existed since 1945 as a centralized housing agency supplementing the activity of local authorities. In some years the Housing Trust had built as many houses as all local authorities and the private sector together. The Housing Executive structure is somewhat similar to the Housing Trust, with a nominated board as the central decision-making body, although three out of nine members are nominated by a Housing Council, an advisory body consisting of representatives of the new district councils.

The establishment of the Housing Executive was a recognition of the fact that the administration of housing policy in Northern Ireland did not inspire confidence throughout the community [4], and also of the poor house-building record of many local authorities [5]. The main benefits that were hoped for from its establishment were an increase in the number of houses built and a fair allocation scheme which would remove all allegations of sectarian discrimination in housing. However, the realization of these objectives has proved difficult in the last few years due, in part, to the continuing disturbances.

The Effects of Violence on Housing Provision

Violence has affected in varying degrees the normal operation of major aspects of the housing system.

1 The effect on house-building

House-building has slumped dramatically in the period 1969 to 1975 in comparison both to previous figures and to the government's housing targets for the period 1970–5.

Table 6.1: House Building in Northern Ireland, 1968–75

	Public Authority Housing	Private Enterprise	Other Agencies	Total
1968	7,924	4,075	121	13,120
1969	7,176	4,213	142	11,531
1970	7,692	4,038	104	11,831
1971	9,102	4,701	113	13,916
1972	7,203	4,298	149	11,650
1973	5,966	4,452	139	10,557
1974	5,412	4,312	349	10,073
1975	4,885	3,776	258	8,919

The drop in building has been most noticeable since 1973 in the public sector. The Development Programme 1970–5 [6] calculated that a total of 75,000 houses should be built between 1970 and 1975 to cope with new households formation (31,000), to meet existing shortages reflected mainly in overcrowding and involuntarily shared accommodation (20,000) and to allow a start to be made on the estimated 100,000 dwellings that were unfit and required clearance and replacement.

A study written in 1971 considered these figures an underestimate and recommended a building programme of 100,000 in this period [7]. The government accepted a housing target figure of 73,500 [8] and was able to announce that extra finance had been made available by the Westminster government to increase output. The annual level of completions was to be 17,000 by 1975. It was anticipated that about one third of this number would be privately built and public authority building would make up the remainder. However, the number of houses built has fallen far below these targets, particularly in the public sector where little more than half the target has been met.

The rate of building, particularly in the Belfast area, has undoubtedly been affected by violence and disturbances but it is not easy to isolate the effects of violence from other factors which have also contributed to the decline in building figures. The process of reorganization too has contributed to the decline. Transfer of responsibilities caused major problems and many local authorities let their housing programmes run down as soon as they knew they were to be taken over. Centralization of ancillary services to house-building—water, sewerage and roads—was an additional complication. As well as all this, rapidly increasing costs of home construction have had a significant effect as have high interest rates and higher standards of construction. But it is clear that violence has contributed to considerable delays in the completion of Housing Executive dwellings. There have been difficulties in getting contractors to tender in specially troubled areas, causing delays in site starts. Further problems related to violence include shortages of particular materials, vandalism and theft on new sites, labour shortages and sectarian problems. Supplies are more difficult to obtain in the province with suppliers carrying smaller stocks; violence has inhibited labour mobility with workmen being reluctant to travel to different areas to work. The fact that various trades, e.g. bricklayers, tend to be predominantly of one religion adds a further dimension to labour difficulties. In addition there has been a marked emigration of skilled building tradesmen to other parts of the United Kingdom. The Housing Executive's efforts to recruit professional and technical staff have also been affected by the reluctance on the part of skilled manpower to move to Northern Ireland during the present disturbances.

Much Housing Executive activity has been directed at redevelopment work and the problem of moving people from redevelopment areas and catering for overspill has been considerably aggravated by the disturbances. Religious differences and increasing segregation have affected public attitudes to redevelopment and rehousing. Bearing in mind that in the period 1975–80 it is planned to start work on 130 redevelopment areas around the province affecting 30,000 dwellings and up to 100,000 people, the significance of this problem becomes clear. Since the speed of redevelopment depends on the availability of acceptable sites for new housing for overspill, religious polarization will obviously increasingly affect the redevelopment programme in the future. The general problem of finding areas acceptable and secure for Catholics in Belfast is particularly significant in this respect. Surveys of occupancy rates in Belfast redevelopment areas carried out in December 1973 and 1974 showed that Catholic redevelopment areas have very low vacancy rates, while Protestant redevelopment areas have high vacancy rates, underlining the difficulty of providing acceptable alternative housing for Catholics in the Belfast area.

Clearly these difficulties do not exist throughout the province. Since 1969 there have been large-scale building programmes in Londonderry. In 1969, following the disturbances in Londonderry, a Development Commission was established to take over the functions of the old council which had had a very poor house-building record. The crash housing programme resulted in the completion of 3,062 houses between April 1969 and March 1973, 1,634 by the Commission and 1,428 by the Housing Trust. The Executive completed a further 1,349 between March 1973 and March 1976.

It is also worth noting that building in the private sector has not slumped dramatically in the period 1970–5 (*see* Table 1). The figures have remained very consistent, although the private sector has not expanded at the rate that it might otherwise have, had there been no violence. This consistency is probably due in part to the greater flexibility of private house construction as compared to the public sector, in its comparative diversity, its freedom from public accountability and its ability to cut corners. However, problems with shortage of materials and unavailability of labour for certain areas also have affected private house building. The difficulties have been acute and one large private builder has decided to cease operations altogether in Northern Ireland.

The size and nature of the Housing Executive have made it more subject to constraints than the private sector in its efforts to effect economies and make adjustments to ease the difficulties in house building. As it becomes established building should increase and its plans to start on 9,000 houses in 1976 were a marked improvement over recent years.

2 Housing allocation policy

One of the main benefits expected from the Housing Executive was the implementation of a fair allocations policy. The Housing Executive declared its intention 'to cater for all public housing applications in a fair and equitable manner'. A housing allocation scheme based on need has been applied throughout the province since January 1974. However the successful implementation of this scheme has been hindered by some consequences of violence.

In the years prior to 1969 integration of Catholic and Protestant communities had been increasing. The major parts of Belfast including new housing estates had a mixed population of Catholics and Protestants and there were relatively few completely segregated public housing estates in the rest of the province. But violence, intimidation and fear have resulted in the splitting of mixed communities and the expulsion of minorities. The pattern of movement has differed for each denomination. In Belfast, Catholic families have moved out of more areas and concentrated in fewer where they could feel secure, mainly in parts of West Belfast. In contrast, Protestant families have moved out of fewer zones and have dispersed about the city. This has resulted in the development of greater segregation in formerly mixed areas and the abandonment of mixed areas by both sides, often followed by the destruction of dwellings with the creation of one-demoninational areas by the eviction of the minority. The consequence has been that housing has become resegregated in such a way as to undermine the possibility of non-sectarian housing policies. The principle of allocation strictly according to priority in need is clearly difficult if not impossible to implement in this situation.

Another serious problem regarding housing allocation has been the high level of illegal occupations. Squatting is an accompanying problem to intimidation and mass population movement. Many families have moved into available empty accommodation or accommodation evacuated by intimidated families and have sometimes moved into new or partially completed Housing Executive dwellings. Squatting has also taken place in empty or evacuated private properties; unfortunately the only statistics available are for the public sector. In 1972 the total number of squatters was 2,000 but this increased to 5,000 by March 1973 and from 1973 to 1975 remained at an average of 5,500. In the early period squatting resulted from communal violence and, because of deep fear, families seized houses temporarily vacant or at an advanced stage of construction. In later years squatting escalated and the Housing Executive claimed that 'many who had not been threatened were only too ready to take advantage of the situation to find a better house or to live rent free' [9].

Squatting has been a problem mainly in Belfast with about 4,000 cases (80%) in the Belfast area. The breakdown of law enforcement is a factor in the prevalence of squatting and in some areas public authorities have been unable to take any action against squatters. Obviously squatting involves families jumping the housing queue and cheating the most needy. It has in some areas inhibited a rational programme of redevelopment and rehabilitation.

A more serious development and one which has arisen from squatting has been the virtual loss of control over the allocation of public housing in some areas by the Housing Executive with control passing to paramilitary groups. In parts of Belfast the allocation of empty or new dwellings had been determined by local paramilitary or political groups. R. Weiner has given an account of the involvement of paramilitary groups in housing allocation in the Shankill Road area and of the creation of the West Belfast Housing Association which dealt with allocations although it eventually worked in co-operation with the Housing Executive [10]. In July 1972 a street clash with the Army following an attempt by the IRA to extend its control over housing allocation in the then mixed Lenadoon estate aroused such intense feelings that it led to the breakdown of an IRA ceasefire. So it happened that in certain areas there was no authority which could support the Housing Executive in allocating dwellings in an orderly and equitable manner.

3 Homelessness

Most housing authorities in the United Kingdom have to cope with a relatively small number of homeless families, very few if the liberal definition is adopted (a family left without any kind of accommodation). In Northern Ireland thousands of people have found themselves in this situation as a result of intimidation, fear of intimidation, damage to their homes, or living close to areas of violence.

A survey of residential displacement in Belfast in the summer of 1969 found that 3,570 families had been forced to move, 82.7% of which were Roman Catholics [11]. Following the introduction of internment in 1971 some 2,069 families were found to have left their homes, 60% of which were Catholics [12]. Research by Darby and Morris [13] estimated a total of 13,000 families displaced between 1969 and 1973, representing some 50,000 people. Although there appears to have been less intimidation in recent years the total number of people displaced may now have passed the 60,000 mark. The movement of people has been concentrated in the greater Belfast area but there has been intimidation and displacement in other areas such as Portadown and Larne. The majority of families fleeing their homes took up temporary accommodation or moved in with relatives before eventually being rehoused or occupying empty property. This is obviously an acute form of homelessness especially when one considers that the definition of homelessness in Great Britain has been extended to include those who, because of the physical housing conditions in which they are forced to live, cannot have a normal family life [14]. Public authorities have thus been confronted with a major problem. Their responsibility to rehouse families has been complicated by the fact that many homeless families were formerly owner-occupiers or renters of private accommodation. Another consequence was overcrowding, since probably a majority of intimidated families moved in the short term to stay with relatives. This is particularly clear in relation to the large number of Catholic families moving to the Catholic areas of West Belfast.

4 The rate of obsolescence

Northern Ireland has a very high level of housing obsolescence. In 1974 35% of the total stock of housing required some form of remedial action, 50% of the houses in Belfast. Violence has again had a contributory effect: a total of 25,000 dwellings is estimated to have been affected by explosions in Belfast since 1969 resulting in varying degrees of damage. Large numbers of dwellings have been evacuated by their owners and have fallen into disuse, been broken up or vandalized. The total number of vandalized and bricked-up dwellings was 9,000 at the end of April 1975, some 7,000 of these being private rented or owner-occupied accommodation. A survey by J. Russell on vandalism in dwellings has shown that the majority of schoolboys who approved of the destruction or defacement of houses had straightforward politico-religious justifications.

Much of the housing in the inner parts of Belfast consists of privately rented dwellings but there has been a dramatic drop in the number of these dwellings in recent years. The 1971 census recorded 71,000 privately rented unfurnished dwellings in Northern Ireland, while by October 1973 this had declined by 11,000. There has been a loss of 8,666 dwellings in Belfast and in 1974 14,600 privately rented unfurnished dwellings out of a total of 25,800 in Belfast were identified as suitable for redevelopment [15]. It is impossible to quantify the direct influence of violence on this rapid decline but it has undoubtedly had some impact. The loss of these dwellings has also put more pressure on the Housing Executive waiting lists.

The effect of violence on the obsolescence rate can be seen particularly well in some places where, prior to the violence, housing was considered to be mainly of a satisfactory standard and the area had not been scheduled for clearance and redevelopment. One such area is the

Roden Street area situated between Catholic and Protestant sectors of West Belfast. This was not included in the Belfast Redevelopment Programme covering the period up to 1962. It was badly affected by the disturbances in 1971–2 and consequently the whole area has had to be redeveloped and 995 families rehoused. It is fair to conclude, therefore, that the problem of housing obsolescence in Belfast has been aggravated by the political disturbances.

5 Housing Finance

In 1971 a campaign of civil disobedience was launched in protest against internment, involving a rent and rates strike. At its peak there were 25,800 Housing Executive tenants on rent and rates strike although this number declined with the phasing out of internment. Although by 1976 there were only about 2,000 tenants still on strike and the Civil Rights Association advised the ending of the strike, nevertheless it has presented a problem of serious loss of revenue.

Although the rent and rates strike was itself a temporary phenomenon a steadily increasing number of people have fallen into rent arrears to the Housing Executive. In 1976 the total amount was estimated at £5 million, involving some 30,000 tenants. The number of Executive tenants not paying rent has been further increased by rent strike campaigns organized by local tenants' associations in protest against increases in rent.

Although no figures are available it is also likely that rent arrears have been building up in the private rented sector. Violence has created extra costs particularly for repairs and for making good damage caused by vandalism and squatting on new sites. It is very difficult to estimate the effect of the disturbances on the private market. It has been claimed that building societies have become reluctant to grant mortgages on properties in troubled or potentially troubled areas, that lending was stopped in high-risk areas and, more generally, that building societies in Northern Ireland which are almost wholly branches of British companies have become less willing to lend money in Northern Ireland. In 1970 the societies operating in the province lent out some 75% of their net receipts but this proportion declined steadily to 59% in 1974 [16]. This may however reflect a reduction in availability of property or reduced demand because of the troubles.

6   Official reaction to the effects of the violence on housing

The Housing Executive as a comprehensive housing body was a most convenient instrument for action on the problems which arose as a result of violence. It enabled the government to introduce uniform policies and to have co-ordinated procedures for different parts of the housing system.

On many major items of policy violence has had no, or only marginal, influence. For example, rent policy, the points system for allocation and improvement grants have been relatively unaffected. On other matters violence has brought clear consequences. Official reaction can be classified under three headings: firstly, the acceptance of the new realities of the housing situation in certain areas and the abandonment (temporarily at least) of existing policies still prevalent in more peaceful areas of Northern Ireland: secondly, the modification of existing policies to cover exigencies caused by violence; thirdly, the introduction of new policies to meet the novel problems thrown up by the violence.

(a)   Acceptance of realities

The Housing Executive has had to accept increasing segregation and the failure of allocation schemes to produce integrated estates in many areas. It has declared that 'forced integration is no more desirable than deliberate segregation [17]. Mr Harry Simpson, the first Director General of the Housing Executive, has stated 'I don't think it is possible for us, because of our ideas, to try to force people into living where they don't feel safe.' [18].

The impact of segregation is most clearly seen in the large movement of Catholic families into the 'safe' area of West Belfast with resultant overcrowding. These families are obviously unwilling to move to available accommodation in other parts of the city or the province. Thus, in order to provide housing for these families, it has been necessary for the government to advise breaking the Matthew stopline, a principle initiated in 1964 to limit the growth of Belfast by creating a green belt around the city and moving the overspill to growth centres.

The Housing Executive has also had to accept that the consequences of segregation and polarization for its redevelopment areas had been aggravated by the disturbances, by the impact of religious differences upon people's attitudes to redevelopment and rehousing. The Executive has had to accept that it would be unrealistic to ignore the fears and aggressions brought to the fore by the prolonged period of violence and has had to acknowledge that violence has reinforced opposition to change in the structure of the population, as well as limiting people's choice as far as consideration of other housing estates is concerned. The Executive has had to slow down the clearance of redevelopment areas until acceptable alternative accommodation can be found for families and it has begun experiments with timber-framed dwellings in an attempt to reduce the time taken to construct new homes.

The authorities have found it difficult to deal with the problem of squatting. In 1972 it was decided that genuine cases of families forced to flee their homes would be accepted as legal tenants and the Housing Executive attempted to establish contact with community groups and tenants' groups to enlist their support for an end to squatting. In 1973 it was announced that the cases of illegal occupants would be reviewed in those estates where control over allocations had been regained for a six-month period and where intimidation had ceased. This has meant in practice that many squatters have eventually been given a rent book and have become legal tenants. There may be little alternative to these policies in housing estates where decrees for possession cannot be enforced. The Executive has stated that it can do little without the support of society itself to bring to an end the violence and disorder with which squatting is linked [19].

(b) The modification of policies

Several modifications to existing policies have been made as a response to the consequences of violence. These may be illustrated firstly by reference to policies on redevelopment and slum clearance. House conditions in the inner Belfast area have become such a problem that the Housing Executive has had to revise considerably its redevelopment programme. It was decided to place more emphasis on the rehabilitation of existing dwellings rather than on the clearance and redevelopment of old dwellings or on new building. In 1975 the Government announced plans to speed up the purchase of dwellings for improvement in Belfast and to carry out repairs to some 12,000 houses to prevent their further deterioration and make them usable for the period up to their eventual replacement. The Government later introduced further proposals through legislation to give new life to old houses. There were four major proposals in the Draft Housing (N.I.) Order 1976. First, the Housing Executive was given special powers to take control of unoccupied homes in advance of acquisition and to require owners to secure or demolish unoccupied premises. Second, the Executive was to be empowered to declare housing action areas in which concerted action would be taken over five years to preserve and improve housing and living conditions. Third, a new structure of grants was proposed to encourage the repair and improvement of older houses; grants would be payable at 75% rising to 90% in cases of special hardship in housing action areas. Fourth, housing associations would be encouraged to take part in rehabilitation work.

The dwellings to be taken over are both privately rented and owner-occupied and a large-scale process of municipalization is planned. In the words of the Minister responsible for housing, 'The Housing Executive will become the largest slum landlord in Europe.' It is hoped that this approach may deal more adequately with the rapid rate of obsolescence of dwellings currently in the privately rented category.

Another example of modification of policies caused by the violence has been the Home Loans Scheme. This scheme was introduced in 1972 to help those who had difficulty raising finance for home purchase through the usual lending agencies, and was similar to local authority schemes in Britain. But it became clear that its importance by enabling people to purchase properties in areas where building societies were not keen to make advances and bringing into use dwellings which otherwise would have fallen into decay. In addition, some priority was given to applications from those on the Housing Executive Emergency Housing List. When scheme funds were cut back in 1975 home loans were restricted to those who were permanently displaced as a result of civil disturbance, those forced to move through redevelopment and those purchasing homes which qualified for improvement grants.

(c) *New policies*

The Emergency Housing Scheme was a new policy evolved to meet new circumstances. This policy was initiated by Belfast Corporation and continued by the Housing Executive. The purpose of the scheme is to rehouse in suitable accommodation those who have been made home-less by bomb damage or intimidation or who are in imminent danger of being made homeless. Since 1969 there has been an average of 600 families on the Emergency Housing List at any one time and in that period the scheme has dealt with 8,233 cases, including 7,432 in the Belfast area, although 30% of these managed to find their own alter-native accommodation. The need for emergency housing is met from two sources; from existing stock and from a register of individually purchased properties. Housing from existing stock is comparatively easy provided the applicant is willing to widen the geographical area of choice, but since the majority of applicants are Roman Catholics and are more restricted than Protestants in the areas open to them, delays are inevitable. This has become one of the most intractable housing problems in the province. 'The basic problem is not a lack of compassion, but a lack of housing in areas where victims of intimidation are prepared to live!' [20].

The operation of the Emergency Scheme has been subject to criticism, particularly concerning the procedure adopted by the Housing Executive of asking families for certification of intimidation by the police before they can be admitted to the Emergency List. There have been variations in the definition of intimidation by different police stations and the police have not always had evidence of it. Originally the Housing Executive also imposed a proviso that no one still resident in his home could be placed on the Emergency List, although this ruling has since been changed. There have also been criticisms of the difficulty in contacting the Emergency Housing Service [21].

Not all displaced families have used this emergency scheme: many have simply moved in with relatives or have been looked after by voluntary organizations. The Belfast Housing Aid Society has played an important role in emergency rehousing and in providing financial aid. Darby and Morris in their evaluation of the Emergency Housing Scheme concluded that there was a lack of willingness to apply sufficient resources to tackling the problem [22].

By 1975 the number of families on the emergency list had declined to 243 although a sudden increase in displacement and intimidation remained a recurrent possibility. One of the consequences of the Emergency Housing Scheme has been to move families from the private to the public sector. A study of housing movement throughout Northern Ireland in 1972 [23] shows, with reference to intimidated households (8% of all moves), 86% had moved into the public sector, 10% had bought houses and 4% moved to privately rented dwellings. These figures compare with a distribution among tenures before moving of 61% public rented, 19% owner-occupied and 19% private rented.

Evacuated Dwellings Policy applies to perfectly good houses in otherwise desirable areas, often being bought under building society mortgage schemes, which owners have had to abandon because of fear of active intimidation. Since its formation the Executive has attempted to help the large number of owner-occupiers who have had to abandon their homes because of the political disturbances and have been unable to sell them. Thus, in response, it introduced in March 1973 a scheme for the public purchase of evacuated dwellings with a view to their being brought back into use at the earliest opportunity, either by letting or sale, but particularly for persons on the Emergency Housing List. Between 1973 and 1976, 1,076 properties had been purchased under this scheme.

The success and public acceptability of this intervention by the Executive in the private sector has led to further intervention with the purpose of helping prevent decay in certain areas and reducing housing waiting lists. The Housing Executive has bought occupied as well as vacant dwellings. A new policy has been initiated of allowing home-hunters to indicate to the Housing Executive a dwelling which was bricked-up or on the property market but in need of renovation. Such a house could be taken into public ownership and given to the prospective tenant. A £5,000 ceiling has been put on each house, and dwellings must be in areas where decay has already set in.

The Housing Executive has also accepted responsibility for repairing bomb-damaged property, including emergency repairs to private dwellings. During the period 1972–3 a total of 14,000 homes were damaged. This repair service represents yet another drain on manpower and finances. Also during 1972 it meant that in Belfast regular maintenance inspection had to be suspended due to the extent of bomb damage on private dwellings.

During 1971–2 there were over 22,000 tenants in the public sector on rent and rates strike as part of the campaign of civil disobedience introduced as a protest against internment without trial. In 1971 the government introduced the Payment of Debt (Emergency Provisions) Act to counteract this. This legislation enabled deductions to be made from a wide range of social security benefits in lieu of rent. In 1972 out of 17,183 tenants on strike 13,299 were paying current rent and a contribution towards arrears deducted from social security benefits or from public salaries and wages. This Act necessitated the establishment of a new Benefits Allocation Branch of the Department of Health and Social Services. The Act has been criticized as leading to excessive deductions particularly since there is no right of appeal against the amounts deducted. It appeared also that those on rent strike and in receipt of supplementary benefits were no longer entitled to exceptional needs benefits.

Since 1972 there have been periods of amnesty when it has been possible for tenants to come off rent strike and reach an agreement with the Executive to pay off arrears over a two-year period. By 1976 the civil disobedience campaign had declined to a couple of thousand participants. But at the same time the number of tenants in rent arrears had increased alarmingly and arrears totalled some five million pounds. In consequence, in 1976 the government announced the extension of the Payment of Debts provisions to all those in rent arrears irrespective of whether or not they were participating in a campaign of civil disobedience.

This exceptional measure is clearly a breach of parity, the principle that Northern Ireland's social security legislation should be uniform with Britain's. There is no similar legislation in Britain despite large rent arrears in many areas. It does appear to undermine the traditional status of national insurance benefits, such as pensions or sickness benefit, as rights secured by virtue of contributions paid over many years. Also families in rent arrears are not entitled to rent rebates in regard to amounts deducted and there is an additional collection penalty to pay. The extension of the policy is a clear example of how exceptional measures introduced to counteract a civil disobedience campaign can subsequently become part of normal policy.

While the reaction of the Housing Executive to the emergency situation has been assisted by its comprehensive role, this has hindered its effectiveness in other directions. For example, this has necessitated the adoption of overall policies where different approaches appropriate to different areas could have been more effective: it is easier to take a strong position against squatters and rent strikers in areas where the security forces have a relatively high degree of control than where this control is absent. Also its commitment to housing according to need, its monopoly of public rented accommodation and its responsibility for all housing problems have caused the Executive additional difficulties: to evict the squatters might only add to the number on the housing waiting list, for example. In addition, in some difficult areas robberies and intimidation of Housing Managers on their door-to-door rounds have made it impossible to continue with this system of rent collection and the Housing Executive has responded by substituting an arrangement by which tenants pay their rent unobtrusively and safely through Post Office Giro. But as the one province-wide authority the Executive has felt obliged to operate the new system universally and the result has been a serious loss of contact between Housing Manager and tenant, not only on rent but on all aspects of housing, even in areas which are not disturbed and in which door-to-door visits with all their many advantages would still be perfectly possible.

Community Participation

Since 1968 there has been a remarkable upsurge in the formation and activity of tenants' associations and community groups. These groups have grown up for a number of reasons including the need for communities to organize mutual assistance following disturbances, the partial breakdown in public services, the desire to express dissatisfaction with facilities and amenities and to respond to redevelopment plans. Many of the groups have taken a strong interest in housing, local physical amenities and planning. Pressure from community groups was successful in amending plans for the redevelopment of the Shankill Road. The 'Save the Shankill' campaign conducted by community and redevelopment groups with the support of paramilitary groups and other organizations finally achieved the acceptance of its demands that there should be no more flats, maisonettes or buildings more than two stories high, and that the area should retain its shops. Such groups have often been in a position of strength in that with paramilitary support they could effectively prevent clearance and new building [24].

At the same time the Housing Executive has come to accept that all redevelopment schemes at design stage should be the subject of discussion with local community groups. In Londonderry after considerable pressure from the Bogside Community Association the Executive agreed to draw up redevelopment plans in co-operation with the Association. The first report of the Housing Executive clearly states that the Executive should encourage responsible and enlightened attitudes by stimulating an informed dialogue with tenants' associations. However the upsurge in community action as a result of civil disturbances has probably forced public bodies to take a more open line and to allow a greater degree of participation than would have occurred otherwise.

The existence of a large number of groups with an interest in housing has led to another recent development; some have formed themselves into housing associations. Northern Ireland has had very few housing associations and their development is desirable for several reasons. They can provide an alternative source of rented accommodation in a situation where the Housing Executive has a monopoly of public rented accommodation; they can assist in rescuing houses in their own areas from decay, and they provide another means of community participation in housing. The government has set up the Northern Ireland Federation of Housing Associations to encourage the development of housing associations and to provide financial assistance. About a dozen former tenants' or community groups, mainly in Belfast, have become Housing Associations, their aim being to purchase, modernize and rehabilitate abandoned or bricked-up houses in their localities. Long-term consequences of this growth of militant housing groups may be increased tenant participation, continuing on existing lines and perhaps also in the new directions of local maintenance schemes and housing co-operatives.

Conclusion

The influence of violence on housing has been most marked in the Belfast area where the main effects on the housing stock have been an increase in the rate and extent of obsolescence in the inner city area and a quickening decline of the privately rented sector. Also significant for the working of the housing system has been the increase in movement from the private into the public sector and increased religious segregation.

As well as contributing to the creation of a comprehensive centralized housing authority violence has resulted in greater government intervention in housing, in more intervention in the private sector through the purchase of evacuated dwellings scheme, in private home purchase through the Home Loans scheme, in the decision to have a large-scale scheme of municipalization, and in bringing communities into participation in redevelopment schemes.

It is an adage of social policy that wartime brings more government intervention and regulation: for example, during the Second World War measures introduced in Northern Ireland included limitations on rent increases, controls over eviction, tribunals to fix fair rents, and schemes to repair war damage. It is also true that in wartime it is easier to justify more government intervention, emergency measures, and crash programmes and that these are more acceptable to society then than they would be at other times. To some extent this has been true of developments in housing policy in Northern Ireland. It has been said that once such government intervention or special measures are introduced it is frequently the case that they become accepted as part of the normal range of policy measures even when the emergency which produced them comes to an end. The extension of the Payment of Debts Act, deducting social security benefits from tenants in rent arrears, may be an example of this. In several directions violence is likely to leave a lasting impression on housing in Northern Ireland.

Notes

1 *Disturbances in Northern Ireland* (Cameron Report), Belfast: HMSO, 1969, Cmnd 532.
2 *See*, for example, H. A. Lyons, 'Riots and Rioters in Belfast', *Economic and Social Review*, **3**, 4, 1972, 605–14, and W. D. Birrell, 'Relative Deprivation as a Factor in Conflict in Northern Ireland', *The Sociological Review*, **20**, 3, 1972, 317–44.
3 *Northern Ireland House Condition Survey, 1974*, Belfast: Northern Ireland Housing Executive, 1975.
4 *First Annual Report 1971–2*, Belfast: Northern Ireland Housing Executive, 1972.
5 *See* W. D. Birrell, P. A. R. Hillyard, A. S. Murie and D. J. D. Roche, *Housing in Northern Ireland*, London: Centre for Environmental Studies, 1971.
6 *Northern Ireland Development Programme, 1970–75*, Belfast: HMSO, 1970.
7 *Housing in Northern Ireland*, op. cit., p. 238.
8 *Northern Ireland Development Programme, 1970–75*, Government Statement, Belfast: HMSO, 1970, Cmnd 547.
9 *Second Annual Report 1972–3*, Belfast: Northern Ireland Housing Executive, 1973, p. 10.
10 Weiner, R., *The Rape of the Shankill, Community Action in Belfast Experiment* (published privately), Belfast, 1975.
11 'Displacement of Persons' in *Violence and Civil Disturbances in Northern Ireland in 1969*, Belfast: HMSO, 1972, 1, pp. 246–9.
12 *Flight*, Belfast: Northern Ireland Community Relations Commission, 1971.
13 Darby, J. and Morris, G., *Intimidation in Housing*, Belfast: The Northern Ireland Community Relations Commission, 1974.
14 Morton, J., 'Varieties of Homelessness' in Butterworth, E. and Holman, R. (eds), *Social Welfare in Modern Britain*, London: Fontana, 1975, pp. 99–105.
15 *See House Condition Survey, 1974*, Belfast: Northern Ireland Housing Executive, 1975, p. 7.
16 *See* article in *Fortnight*, 11 April 1975.
17 *Third Annual Report 1975*, Housing Executive, 1975.
18 Interview with H. Simpson, *Belfast Telegraph*, September 1974.
19 *Second Annual Report 1972–3*, op. cit.
20 *See Intimidation in Housing*, op. cit., pp. 103–6.
21 ibid., p. 108.
22 Birrell, W. D., Hillyard, P. A. R., Murie, A. S. and Roche, D. J. D., *New Building and Housing Need* (forthcoming).
23 Townsend, P., 'Human Need in Ulster', *New Society*, **18**, 478, 25 November 1971, 1037.
24 Weiner, op. cit.

7 Police and Penal Services

Paddy Hillyard*

Introduction

The aim of this chapter is to analyse the ways in which violence in Northern Ireland has led to changes in the police and the penal system [1]. It is necessary, at the outset, to make a number of general points. Any analysis of effects of, or reactions to, violence which presupposes violence itself to be the problem will lead to confusion. Violence results from underlying phenomena. To concentrate analysis on violence, rather than upon the underlying causes, is likely to lead to a narrowing or even distortion of the social reality. The concept of violence contains a constellation of ideas and moral precepts as well as a set of responses which are considered appropriate for dealing with it. By starting with violence all these facets may be taken for granted. If, on the other hand, the causes of violence are taken as the starting point then these features become problematic. For example, if the police react to violence by increasing their manpower and technology, an approach which takes violence as the problem will consider this type of response to be acceptable. However if the causes of violence are analysed then increases in manpower and technology will be seen as very different, and possibly unacceptable.

The second point that needs to be emphasized is that the institutions discussed in this chapter are very different from those described in other chapters. One central function of the police and the penal system is to deal directly with violence either by trying to prevent it or else by detecting and processing the perpetrators of violence. None of the other services described in this book have this as one of their functions. This analysis will, in keeping with other chapters, describe the *effects* of

* Paddy Hillyard lectures in Social Administration at Bristol University, and is co-author of *Law and State: The Case of Northern Ireland* (1975).

violence and it will also describe changes which have been introduced to *deal* with violence.

Another important distinction between the institutions described here and others described elsewhere is the degree to which they have gained the consent of the population. Certainly many of the social services in Northern Ireland have not enjoyed the popular consensus which appears to be a generally accepted feature of social services in the rest of the United Kingdom [2]. However, the degree of consent extended to the police and the penal system has been both quantitatively and qualitatively different. The Roman Catholic community has held a long-standing distrust in all the institutions of justice. There are many reasons for this distrust. One important factor is the way in which successive Unionist governments perceived and responded to Republican violence. Some understanding of these perceptions and responses is essential if the changes introduced as a result of recent violence are to be fully understood.

The beginnings of devolved government in Northern Ireland in 1920 were violent and bloody. The Protestant community was determined to preserve the constitution which enabled them to remain in the Union. Many Roman Catholics on the other hand were equally deter-mined to oppose it. From the outset, the institutions of law and order were therefore developed to preserve the constitution and the parlia-ment of Northern Ireland. The institutions of law enforcement and the administration of justice were whenever possible placed directly under the control of the Minister of Home Affairs.

In 1922, following the recommendation of a Departmental Committee of Inquiry, the Royal Ulster Constabulary was established [3]. It was organized under a single command structure for the whole of Northern Ireland and made directly answerable to the Minister of Home Affairs. The suggestion that the force should be organized on a local basis was firmly rejected and no attempt was made to set up a force which was independent of the executive by establishing watch committees or similar organizations. Another feature was that it was trained from the start to perform a military as well as a civilian role. To provide extra police strength, the RUC was backed up by an auxiliary force known locally as the 'B' Specials.

In the same year as the RUC was established, the Civil Authorities (Special Powers) Act was passed. It conferred wide powers of arrest, questioning, search, detention and internment on the police and gave the Ministry of Home Affairs almost completely unrestricted power to make regulations with the force of law. It was directed and used almost exclusively against Republicans who, of course, were opposed to the existence of the state of Northern Ireland.

A concern with developing institutions which would safeguard and maintain the constitution, was also reflected in penal policy. There were few developments in the penal system over fifty years and, as a consequence, provision in Northern Ireland in 1968 contrasted sharply with provision in the rest of the United Kingdom. The two prisons, Crumlin Road in Belfast and Armagh Women's Prison, were very old and were in need of extensive renovation. There were few changes in the institutions for young offenders until the building of a modern training school at Rathgael in the sixties. The probation service was never considered a priority and as a consequence in 1968 there were only thirty probation officers for the whole of Northern Ireland. Many of the reforms introduced in the Criminal Justice Acts of 1961 and 1967 in Great Britain were ignored by the Northern Ireland government and it was not until the Treatment of Offenders (Northern Ireland) Act in 1968 that some important reforms were introduced.

The official explanation for this lack of development in the penal system was that the crime rate had been much lower in Northern Ireland than in the rest of the United Kingdom and a number of policies introduced into England and Wales to deal with high crime rates had been inappropriate for Northern Ireland. It was further argued that devolution had permitted an assessment of a number of experiments carried out in England and Wales and a number of these proved not to be worth introducing [4]. Although there is some substance in these points, particularly in relation to policy development during the sixties, there is much to suggest that the primary cause of the inaction was the question of security. The IRA campaign during 1921–2 and the subsequent campaigns in 1938–9 and 1956–62 served to confirm the need to maintain top security in all penal establishments. During each campaign internment without trial was used and people were detained in the prisons and in other makeshift accommodation. The problem of security was always a central concern and it tended to be carried over into periods of peace, preventing or retarding any innovations in the penal system.

The policy of successive Unionist governments to derogate from the rule of law, maintain control over the police and keep in existence the 'B' Specials, played a fundamental role in engendering distrust among the minority towards the police and the whole of the administration of justice. Lack of confidence extended to all institutions of the state and played an important part in maintaining the minority's disaffection from the Unionist government.

The extent of the disaffection of the minority became a problem for the Unionist government in the early sixties as new developments in the field of trade and the economy required changes in political relations between the North and South. Roman Catholic support for the régime was essential for the maintenance of good relations with the Republic and also for the very survival of the Stormont system [5]. One section of the Unionist party fully supported a move towards a more liberal system of government but another, more powerful, section of the party totally opposed it. This group was composed of members of the social classes which had the most to lose from reforms.

When Westminster politicians began to take an active interest in Northern Ireland from 1968 onwards, following the breakdown of order, they clearly considered as unacceptable the Unionist government's reluctance to uphold the principles normally associated with democratic régimes. They recognized that support for these principles served as a very powerful legitimating force. They therefore insisted that reforms be introduced that would give Northern Ireland citizens, irrespective of political views or religion, the same standards of treatment and freedom from discrimination in all legislation and executive decisions as existed in the rest of the United Kingdom. A communiqué to this effect was issued jointly by the two Prime Ministers in 1969 [6]. Social and other policies from 1968 onwards were characterized by the Westminster government's insistence that Northern Ireland be brought into line with the rest of the United Kingdom. But predictably the proposed changes brought opposition from those who stood to gain most from the *status quo*. It is against this background that the analysis of the effects of violence on the police and the penal system is set.

This chapter is divided into two sections, one dealing with changes in the police and the other with changes in the penal system. Each section presents a selective review of changes brought about by the violence since space does not permit a more comprehensive analysis.

The Police

Organizational Changes

Since 1968 violence has caused many changes in the RUC, but the most far-reaching changes during the period were those introduced as a result of the violence which stemmed from the Civil Rights marches in 1968 and 1969. The worst violence occurred in Londonderry in August 1969. For three days the police were involved in a battle with the inhabitants of the Bogside area of the city and the confrontation did not end until the British Army was brought in. Following most of the clashes the police were accused of brutality and partiality. Relations between them and the Roman Catholic community reached an all-time low. Changes were very necessary and as part of an overall reform programme a committee of inquiry under the chairmanship of Lord Hunt was established to 'examine the recruitment, organisation, structure and composition of the Royal Ulster Constabulary and the Ulster Special Constabulary (the 'B' Specials) and their respective functions and to recommend as necessary what changes are required to provide for the efficient enforcement' of law and order in Northern Ireland' [7]. The committee presented its report in October 1969 and made forty-seven recommendations most of which were introduced in 1970.

A number of major recommendations changed radically the role, accountability and organization of the police. The first was that the RUC should be relieved of all duties of a military nature and it should adopt the role of a civilian police force. To this end it was recommended that it should no longer be assigned military duties and all vehicles of a 'warlike character' should be replaced and the police should no longer be armed. Secondly, it was proposed that a Police Authority reflecting the proportions of different groups in the community should be established and charged with the responsibility of maintaining an adequate and efficient police force. While the new authority should be responsible to the Minister of Home Affairs the clear intention of this recommendation was to remove the overall responsibility of the police from direct government control and make it answerable to some independent body. It reflected a recognition of the need to make the police appear independent of the executive and marked a fundamental change in the administration of justice in Northern Ireland.

Thirdly, it was recommended that the 8,000-strong Special Constabulary should be replaced by a locally recruited part-time force to help with security under the control of the GOC Northern Ireland. As the 'B' Specials had traditionally been used as a back-up force for the police, their disbandment radically reduced the number of men available for policing. To overcome this shortage the committee proposed that the size of the RUC should be greatly increased and that a part-time police reserve should be established.

There were a number of other recommendations aimed at improving police–community relations and restoring public confidence. These included the stepping up of police community relations activities, the introduction of a new system for handling complaints against the police, the setting up of police liaison committees and the handing over of all but minor prosecutions to an independent prosecutor as in the Scottish system. It should be noted that despite the widespread animosity between certain sections of the Roman Catholic community and the police, no other suggestions were made to deal with the problem of public confidence. The committee did not consider other possible methods of policing such as the development of local community police forces as recommended by Boehringer [8]. It was of the opinion that the problem would be solved by a centralized system coupled with changes in the role, accountability, and organization of the police.

The Unionist government accepted all these major recommendations except the suggestion of a Scottish system of prosecution. This was not rejected outright, but referred to a committee for consideration. Early in 1970, the Police Act (Northern Ireland) was passed to make the necessary provisions for the changes. In June, the issue of arms to the police was phased out and the Police Authority set up. It was composed of representatives from local authorities, other public bodies, the universities, the legal profession, trade unions, agriculture, industry and commerce, voluntary organizations and the Ministry of Home Affairs. It was charged with the responsibility for securing the maintenance of an adequate and efficient police force. The Act, however, did not make the Police Authority totally independent of the Ministry of Home Affairs. The Ministry still maintained the power to make regulations in relation to the force and the approval of the Minister had to be sought with regard to a number of aspects including appointments. This lack of independence was soon to be commented upon adversely by members of the Roman Catholic community [9].

Later in the year, following the recommendations of Mr Robert Boyes who was asked to consider what changes would be necessary in the RUC now that it had become a civilian force, the rank structure of County and District Inspector and Head Constable was abolished and replaced by the rank structure used in England and Wales, and a structure of divisions, sub-divisions and sections similar to those used in Great Britain was introduced. One other significant development during the year was the setting up of a community relations branch. It was charged with the task of 'making a maximum contribution to the cause of improved community relations throughout the Province particularly in those areas where it had deteriorated'.

The continuing violence and the growth of guerrilla activity during late 1970 and 1971 effectively thwarted the development of a civilian police force. In late January 1971 two policemen were shot dead in Londonderry and in February two policemen were killed when on riot duty in the Ardoyne area of Belfast. By the end of March it was reported that the police had been fired at on thirty-five occasions and, in addition, numerous police stations had been attacked. As a result, the civilian role of the police became impossible. Saloon cars were replaced by Land Rovers fitted with protective shields. High fences, barbed-wire and sandbagging were placed around police stations. In November, 1971 the Police Authority announced that the police had been rearmed.

One important outcome of the growth of violence was the elevation of the Special Patrol Group (SPG) to a central position within the force. This group, which was formed in 1969, was given the more difficult policing work. For example, often the situation in a particular district made it impossible for policemen who lived in the area to arrest suspects for fear of reprisal either to themselves or to their families. The SPG would therefore be given the task of making arrests using information collected by the local police. Other tasks have included the detection and arrest of assassination squads, control of riots and the break-up of protection or other rackets. The group is made up of volunteers from the rest of the force.

Further organizational changes were introduced in 1974 when a new regional command structure was established. In addition the CID was strengthened. Throughout the whole period the community relations branch was given greater priority and expanded. One other change which the violence precipitated was the setting up of local police report centres. There were, however, a number of objections to this scheme. It was argued that it provided the paramilitaries with the opportunity of joining the Police Reserve and then being in a position to take over policing in a particular area. The police appear to have felt that this was a serious possibility because after a few such centres had been set up, interest in the scheme seemed to decline.

Changes in manpower

The violence from 1970 onwards placed an enormous strain on police manpower. Police in troubled areas were being asked to do massive amounts of overtime without any prospect of time off in the future. Initially, a great emphasis was placed on improving the manpower situation by the civilianization of administrative duties and a reduction in the training programme from 20 to 12 weeks. In addition the Police Reserve was continually being expanded. The establishment size was raised on no fewer than three occasions between 1970 and 1974 and by the beginning of 1975 the authorized establishment for the Reserve was 5,000 men and 1,900 women. These changes, however, were not considered sufficient. In 1975 the establishment strength of the RUC itself was raised from 4,900, suggested by Boyes, to 6,900. Table 1 notes the actual strength of the RUC and Reserve for each year since 1969.

Table 7.1: Strength of the RUC and Police Reserve, 1969–75

Year	RUC	Reserve
1969	3,044	—
1970	3,809	625
1971	4,086	1,369
1972	4,256	1,902
1973	4,391	2,299
1974	4,563	3,860
1975	4,902	4,819

This emphasis on recruitment has resulted in a situation in which approximately 2,800 out of 4,902 regular policemen have been in the force for under five years. In the case of the Reserve Force all 4,819 members have had less than five years' experience of policing. The personnel of the RUC has therefore changed radically over the last six years and as a result the composition of the force in 1975 is very different from what it was in 1969.

Technical changes

The violence has played a part in various technical developments within the force. Violence and the threat of violence have made witnesses reluctant to appear before the courts. The outcome of many prosecutions has therefore depended solely on forensic evidence. In response to this situation the forensic department has not only greatly improved its equipment but it has also introduced and developed many advanced techniques. Development in communication facilities would probably have occurred in normal conditions, but were certainly accelerated as a direct result of violence. A very modern system which gives every policeman direct contact with his local police station, and on request with headquarters, has been introduced into the force.

Police–army relations

The introduction of the British army 'to aid the civil power' in 1969, and its continuing presence ever since, has necessitated a close liaison between the two forces. This has been achieved at various levels. At the highest level, regular conferences have been held involving the Chief Constable and the Army director of operations. There have also been regular joint security committee conferences at Stormont involving the heads of the army and the police as well as the Secretary of State. At other levels there have been numerous contacts. The army has been represented by a liaison officer at RUC headquarters and there was an RUC officer at Army headquarters until he was removed in 1974 because it was felt that he was no longer needed. At ground level local commanders of the police, army and UDR have held local meetings to discuss security. As well as these contacts, there has been considerable liaison between army units and police when the former have been accommodated in a police station.

Although liaison has existed between the police and the army, the two forces handle the security situation in very different ways. Police have tended to follow a traditional police approach of building up contacts, relying on information volunteered by members of the public, and arresting only those persons whom they suspect of having committed an offence. The army, on the other hand, have adopted a heavy-handed approach mounting large-scale screening and arrest operations. As the deployment of the two forces has tended to coincide with the sectarian divide—the police working mainly in Protestant areas, the army in Catholic areas because of the greater danger—this, coupled with the differences in approach, did little to alter the opinion of the minority that the law in Northern Ireland was biased [10].

Throughout the period, various attempts at joint policing have been made, particularly in the more dangerous areas, but these experiments were never long-lasting. In 1969 joint police army patrols were organized and were then used at various times in the East and West of Belfast. Another example of joint policing occurred in 1973. Members of the Army Special Branch were introduced into the RUC causing widespread consternation among the police. Up to this time the army had developed its own under-cover security branch following the failure of the RUC Special Branch to identify the most dangerous and active terrorists for the purposes of the initial internment operation in August 1971. The police therefore considered army assistance as an unwarranted interference with police work. Another element adding to resentment was the fact that up to this time the police had been willing to give information to the Army Special Branch but help had seldom been reciprocated.

It seems clear that the relationship between the two forces has never been very good. Indeed, it has been particularly bad in those areas in which an army unit during its tour of duty created local disaffection by screening and arresting large numbers of people. This approach always caused widespread resentment among the population and as a direct result many people refused to co-operate further with the army and, more importantly, with the police. The amount of information given freely to the police either via the confidential telephone system or from other sources dried up making the police ineffective for long periods. On one occasion relations between an army unit and the police were so bad that a public row developed between members of the unit and the police after a robbery in Belfast. The police arrived on the scene and arrested the offenders. The army arrived a few minutes later and insisted that they be permitted to question the offenders. The police refused, pointing out that there was no need for such questioning as they were handling the situation. When the army persisted the police pointed out that they too would be arrested if there were any further demands.

Effects of violence on police personnel

The analysis so far has attempted to indicate how violence has been instrumental in changing the role, organization and methods of policing. Another important aspect of violence is the effect it has had on the policemen themselves. Although direct effects such as death, injury and violent attacks on police stations are easily assessed, indirect effects such as changes in attitude and behaviour are not. To begin with, the experience of violence will probably affect each policeman differently and it is therefore difficult to talk in general terms about effects on the police. In addition, the information relating to changes in attitudes and behaviour is limited. It is thus possible to offer only a very tentative analysis.

The direct effects of violence on the police have been considerable.

In the period 1968–76 69 regular policemen and 21 RUC reserves were killed and over 2,800 were injured in circumstances associated with the security situation. There were numerous attacks on the private homes of policemen and on police stations. In 1975, there were 85 attacks on police stations and 1,348 armed attacks on personnel. Many of these caused only minor damage but where large car bombs, rockets and mortars were used, damage was considerable and in some cases stations were completely destroyed. The majority of the attacks on police personnel and police stations were carried out by the provisional IRA. Another sometimes neglected direct effect of the violence relates to police work. Police have the responsibility of attending the scene of every violent crime to carry out an investigation. Many policemen have therefore had almost daily contact with the aftermath of attacks in which people have been killed or injured and buildings destroyed. Between 1969 and the end of 1975 they investigated over 1,600 murders and 4,733 explosions.

Although, as has been noted, an assessment of the indirect effects of violence on police personnel is difficult, there would appear to have been observable changes in police attitudes and behaviour as a result of the violence.

Violence has produced noticeable changes in the morale of the police. Following the widespread criticisms of the RUC's handling of Civil Rights marches and subsequent riots in 1969 the morale of the force was very low. Many policemen with between five and fifteen years' experience left the force. Forty-four left without a pension or gratuity and seventy-eight left or were discharged with one. More recently morale has improved as indicated by the smaller number leaving the force and the record numbers taking promotional examinations.

Terrorist violence has produced, perhaps not surprisingly, an increase in the use of violence by the police themselves. This has been accompanied by a shift in opinion regarding police malpractices. A number of different pieces of data support these views. To begin with the number of allegations of police violence has remained high over the whole period. Some of these allegations have clearly been made for propaganda purposes and had no basis in fact. However a significant number cannot be dismissed on these grounds particularly in the light of the medical evidence produced to support the allegations. Further, the number of registered complaints of assault against the police have been steadily increasing over the period. In 1970 there were fewer than 200. In 1975 this figure had increased to 730. Admittedly, only 5% of all complaints are substantiated, and therefore it could be argued that

registered complaints provide an unreliable indication of the increase
of violence by the police. But although the number of substantiated
complaints is very low, this does not invalidate those which are not
upheld. A number of factors make it virtually impossible to substantiate
a complaint against the police however thoroughly it is investigated.
In making an arrest or in bringing a person to the police station it
may be necessary to use force and it can be claimed that injuries
received from an assault resulted from the need to use force. Moreover,
as so few assaults are witnessed it is usually the policeman's word
against the complainant's. Finally, if an assault is witnessed by other
policemen they may be unwilling to provide information to an
investigating team. As in any occupation there is the characteristic
tendency to stick together. In view of these points it is not unrealistic
to use registered complaints as an indicator of the increased use of
violence.

A third effect of violence on police behaviour is to produce a greater
commitment in the ranks of the police to look after their own interests.
This is reflected in the development of a strong organization, the Police
Federation, to represent all federated ranks. This body first came into
being in 1971 and although it might have come into existence in normal
circumstances, as in England and Wales, there can be no doubt that
its strength and orientation owes much to violence. For example, it
campaigned for and in the end obtained the introduction of a special
allowance for all members of the force. Another considered success
was in relation to a policeman who was charged under the Emergency
Provisions Act (Northern Ireland) for a particular offence. The
Federation argued that this piece of legislation was enacted to deal
with terrorists and not policemen. The affair was only resolved after
the police refused to do escort and court duties.

Apart from concerning itself with the welfare and working conditions
of the force, the Federation has played an important role in expressing
the views of its members. As early as 1972 a motion was passed pro-
posing that the force should be disarmed and that it should return to
a civilian policing role. These views were made public. In 1973, at the
annual conference of the Federation, the Chairman of the Federation,
in the presence of the Secretary of State, made a bitter attack on the
Police Authority and said bluntly that the Police Federation had had
little success in persuading the Authority to forsake its 'paramilitary
frontier role'. This theme has been regularly reiterated. The Federation
has also taken up the question of the independence of the force. In
1975 the Chairman released a strongly worded statement telling the

politicians to stop trying to interfere with policing. The police, it was emphasized, was an independent body under the control of the Chief Constable. While the pursuit of these broader issues raises questions about the answerability and accountability of the force, the growth of the Federation clearly owes much to the violence.

The Penal System

Internment and interrogation

Throughout most of 1970 the violence mainly consisted of clashes between rioters and the army. But inevitably it was soon to escalate. The year saw the first fatal shooting of a rioter in the New Lodge area of Belfast and by the end of it the Provisional IRA, which had been non-existent in 1969, had built itself into a strong and well-organized military force receiving widespread support from the Roman Catholic population who perceived little progress towards promised reforms and redress of their many grievances. In February 1971 the Provisional IRA shot dead a British soldier, the first to be killed by them. By the middle of 1971 rioting, although still common, was overshadowed by shootings and explosions. The violence was now on a different level. Up to this time the Stormont government used the courts to deal with violent offenders. But in August 1971, the Westminster government, partly due to the lack of alternative policies to deal with violence and partly due to their reluctance to interfere too radically with the government of Northern Ireland, agreed to let the Unionist government introduce internment. It was clearly contrary to the text of the communiqué issued by the prime ministers in 1969 and also contrary to the advice of the British army. However, it was in keeping with previous Unionist governments' responses to republican violence. Ironically it was to be the last occasion in which any government of Northern Ireland had the opportunity to respond to the IRA in the traditional manner as the response was to be instrumental in the collapse of Stormont and the imposition of Direct Rule in March 1972.

As a full description of the introduction and subsequent history of internment and interrogation is available elsewhere, only a few points need to be noted [11]. The decision to introduce internment was put into effect in the early hours of the 9th of August. A massive arrest operation, named Operation Demetrius, was mounted with the aim of arresting and detaining several hundred people who were suspected of being members of the IRA. In all 354 persons were arrested. The list of those arrested was hopelessly inaccurate and many of them were known in the communities in which they lived to have had no direct involvement in subversive activities. Within 48 hours 104 had been released. During the days following the initial arrest operation, there were numerous allegations that a number of men were being subjected to brutal and illegal interrogation techniques. These allegations were subsequently investigated by the Compton Committee [12]. It was concluded that tough interrogation techniques had been used but the committee reached the thoroughly unconvincing conclusion that while many of the techniques constituted physical ill-treatment they did not amount to brutality. The important issue of whether the techniques were legal and whether they should have been used were referred to a committee under Lord Parker [13]. Lord Gardiner in a minority report concluded that the techniques were unlawful, could not be justified and were counter-productive. The majority, however, concluded that the techniques might be unlawful, but that the situation had required tough interrogation techniques. They therefore recommended that the government should take whatever steps were necessary to protect those taking part in the operation. What is of particular importance from the point of view of this analysis is that the type and level of violence was being used as a justification for the introduction of a policy which was at best on the borderline of legality, and at worst illegal. Eventually, the government accepted Lord Gardiner's view and stopped the further use of such techniques.

The reaction of the Roman Catholic community to internment and the allegations of brutal interrogation was united and violent. The level of violence increased dramatically. In the following eight months, there were, 1,130 bomb explosions and over 2,000 shooting incidents; 150 civilians and soldiers and 17 policemen were killed and 2,505 civilians, 306 soldiers and 107 policemen were injured.

When the Westminster government imposed Direct Rule in March 1972 it was their intention to bring to an end internment under the Special Powers Act. The continuing high level of violence and the problems associated with bringing terrorists before the courts, however, were such as to make the abolition of internment inappropriate. In November 1972, the Detention of Terrorists Order was introduced. Although it replaced and repealed the Special Powers regulations relating to internment and detention, it maintained an executive system of detention but with various quasi-judicial trimmings. These provisions were later incorporated into the Northern Ireland (Emergency Provisions) Act 1973.

In 1974 the government established a committee under Lord Gardiner to consider, in the context of civil liberties and human rights, the measures which were in force to deal with terrorism. Its advice was that while detention could not 'remain as a long term policy' the 'present level of violence, the risks of increased violence, and the difficulty of predicting events even a few months ahead makes it impossible to put forward a precise recommendation on timing' [14].

Notwithstanding the views of the Gardiner Committee and the continuing high level of violence, the Secretary of State effectively ended detention without trial by December 1975 by a policy of ministerial releases. The powers, however, remained on the statute book.

Prison accommodation

The change in the nature of violence and the concomitant increase in the number of persons sentenced to imprisonment, as well as the introduction of internment, placed great demands on prison accommodation. In 1968 there were only 727 persons in prison. By 1971 this number had increased to 944. At the end of 1974 it had risen to 2,848. It had increased four-fold in six years.

The response of the authorities to the problem was varied. To begin with maximum use was made of existing accommodation. The young offenders' centre in Armagh Women's Prison, which had only recently been opened, was closed and the wing incorporated into the rest of the prison. Secondly, new prison complexes were developed at Long Kesh in County Down and at Magilligan in County Derry. Long Kesh was originally built to house internees but it was later extended to accommodate convicted prisoners. The change was accompanied by a change in the name from Long Kesh to the Maze Prison in an attempt to remove past associations of the place with the internment and detention systems.

The urgency with which the extra accommodation was required influenced strongly the design of the complexes, which soon posed serious problems for the prison authorities. Both prisons were developed as compounds with accommodation in huts rather than in individual cells. Each compound was built to hold up to 90 prisoners with sleeping accommodation in Nissen hut dormitories. At Magilligan each prisoner had a cubicle but at the Maze only a few dormitories had partitions. The disadvantage of this type of accommodation from the authorities' point of view was that there was virtually no disciplinary control by the prison warders within the compounds. Compounds, housing either republican or loyalist prisoners but never both, became self-governing communities with little or no contact with the prison staff; prisoners' lives were not organized by prison rules but by the standing orders produced by the prisoners themselves. Day-to-day decisions were under the control of the compound commander. By the end of 1974, 71% of male prisoners—1,881 out of 2,648—were accommodated in temporary premises of a compound type rather than in cells.

Despite the building of these complexes, the Unionist government decided at the beginning of 1972 that a new prison, built on conventional lines, was required. As the decision to build the new prison was directly related to the situation in the province, it is important to consider the history of the proposal in some depth to illustrate the way in which violence may determine penal policy not only in the immediate present but also for years to come. In addition, it will also provide an insight into the development of a policy which in this instance reveals a bureaucratic muddle on a massive scale [15].

The decision to build the new prison came after the government received a report from the Cunningham Committee, which had been set up to review security at Crumlin Road prison in Belfast following the breakout of 13 prisoners. The Committee's principal conclusion was that the prison was a highly unsuitable site for a high security prison [16]. They concluded that the ultimate solution was the construction of a more secure prison on a different and more suitable site. The Committee also noted the problem of overcrowding.

Initially, the government decided that the new prison would replace Crumlin Road entirely. The plans therefore had to include provision for remand prisoners as well as male and female prisoners. It was considered that a site of about 50–60 acres should be selected close to Belfast so that remand prisoners would be close to the courts. A search was therefore begun for a site. At this time it was decided that the land should be purchased voluntarily and compulsory powers should not be used.

As the level of violence rose and more and more prison accommodation was required, the Ministry of Home Affairs and, after Direct Rule, the Northern Ireland Office, continually changed the design to suit the prevailing situation. In April 1973, it was decided that there should be two separate prisons, one for males on a 100-acre site, and one for females on a 10-acre site. But only a month later these plans were changed back to the original proposal of having both prisons on the same site. But now the acreage requirement was to be 140–150 acres. In July 1974, plans were changed again and it was decided to retain Crumlin Road as a remand prison and not to include remand accommodation (except for females) in the new prison. This decision meant that it was no longer necessary to search for a site within a close distance of Belfast.

In June of the same year, the Gardiner Committee looked critically at the existing provisions in the penal system. Their views on what they found were blunt and forthright:

> The present situation of Northern Ireland's prisons is so serious that the provision of adequate prison accommodation demands that priority be given to it by the Government in terms of money, materials and skilled labour such as has been accorded to no public project since the Second World War [17].

They recommended the building of a temporary cellular prison for 700 and a permanent prison for 400–500.

In September 1974 a series of violent protests was begun at the Maze Prison. First, prisoners threw their food and bedding over the wire perimeter fence. Then in October there was a full-scale riot which culminated in the burning down of the prison. In November a prisoner was shot dead during a mass break-out.

Although the Gardiner Committee's report was not published until January 1975, the views of the Committee had obviously been made known to the government much earlier, because shortly after the prison protests the Secretary of State announced that a new prison similar in design to the one subsequently recommended by the Gardiner Committee was to be built at Maghaberry. It was proposed that it should be built in three phases. Phase 1 would provide 'advanced cellular' accommodation for 500 convicted male prisoners. Later these cells would be phased out as permanent cell accommodation proposed in Phase II was completed. Phase II would consist on completion of cellular accommodation for 432 convicted males, a separate female prison and a young offenders' centre for girls between 16 and 21. The most outstanding feature of the proposal was security. It was to be a maximum security prison with two sets of parallel fences 17 feet high, and topped with German 'S' wire. The inner two fences would be illuminated at night and at all times either patrolled or observed by closed circuit television. The cost was to be in the region of £30 million. The acreage requirement was 536 acres. It was all too clear that the design was determined by the immediate security situation.

The announcement meant that the initial plan to replace Crumlin

Road prison changed out of all recognition. Crumlin Road was to remain and to be used as a remand prison. The acreage requirement had grown from a mere 50 acres to ten times that requirement. And compulsory powers were to be employed in the end. The plans produced widespread opposition, the most important of which came from the Northern Ireland Association for the Care and Rehabilitation of Offenders. It claimed that the whole plan was 'retrograde in the extreme' and would leave the Ulster penal system 'a legacy of Dartmoor mentality for years to come'. NIACRO's central argument was that the plans represented an over-provision of secure accommodation on any reasonable projection of future trends in the prison population. Further, it emphasized that the plan would absorb all available finance for prison building in the foreseeable future and would adversely affect the proper consideration of other less costly alternatives for dealing with offenders.

These arguments were rejected by the government in correspondence with the Association and it appears that the prison as proposed will be developed. A public inquiry into the proposal to acquire compulsorily the 530-acre site has been held and predictably resulted in support of the proposal. As an article in *Fortnight* commented:

> The current pressure on numbers certainly cannot be used to justify the present Maghaberry plan, since it has been decided sensibly that this will be dealt with by temporary cellular blocks at the Maze/ Long Kesh. Most of those now serving sentences will be out by 1980, and long before if things settle down and an amnesty of accelerated parole release scheme is adopted. It looks very much as if the bureaucratic bungling in the prison planning department has left us with a plan for a huge top security prison complex at a cost of £30 million which has grown, rather like Topsy, out of an entirely different and much more sensible plan to replace the Crumlin Road [18].

Special category prisoners

Another penal policy development, which was born out of violence, was the introduction of special category status in June 1972, following a hunger strike at Crumlin Road prison. In practice it has meant that any convicted offender sentenced to more than 9 months' imprisonment who claimed political motivation would be given special category status, provided he was accepted by a compound leader at either the

Maze or Magilligan. Prisoners holding this privilege are not required to work, can wear their own clothes and live in compounds in the way described above. It was not long before the authorities became disillusioned with the policy and wished to abolish it.

The first impetus for its abolition came from the Gardiner Committee. While recognizing the pressures on those responsible at the time, the Committee considered that its introduction was a serious mistake.

We can see no justification for granting privileges to a large number of criminals convicted of very serious crimes, in many cases murder, merely because they claim political motivation [19].

In November 1975, the government accepted that the special status category was inappropriate and announced that it would be phased out. The Secretary of State argued that this had become possible as a result of a new scheme whereby all convicted prisoners except those serving very short or light sentences could become eligible for conditional release after half of their sentence had been served. He rejected the introduction of a British-style parole system because of the difficulties of supervision.

Although no reason was given for phasing out special category prisoner status, it was clearly consistent with the authorities' attempt to depoliticize the violence and criminalize offenders. Another and more important reason was that its abolition meant that it would no longer be automatic for prisoners to be allocated to a compound. Instead they would be allocated to new cell blocks which were being built at the Maze and Magilligan. It was hoped that the change in policy would therefore permit the prison authorities to gain control over the daily lives of the prisoners.

It was predictable that the proposal would meet with fierce opposition from the paramilitaries on both sides. To begin with it meant that it would negate the political basis of their violent acts and would radically decrease the amount of control the paramilitary camp commanders could exert over their members. The conflict was therefore not only a battle over labels, with the authorities wanting to label everyone as criminal and the paramilitaries refusing to accept this description. Rather, it was an issue central to the continuing survival of the paramilitary organizations.

By 1976 both Republican and Loyalist paramilitary organizations had registered their disapproval—violently. Two prison officers were shot dead by the IRA and several others were injured in various attacks. The warders reacted by imposing a three-week ban on visits, food parcels and letters. Following the end of the warders' protest a new *modus operandi* was established, but the opposition from the paramilitaries promised to be sustained and intense. Whatever the outcome of the conflict between the paramilitaries and the authorities the decision to introduce the special category status was a product of the violence and its future is likely to be determined by violence.

Other changes in the penal system

Another sector of the penal system which has been affected by the situation, although not to such a great extent as the prison system, has been the probation service. The principal effect has been a decline in the use of probation. The courts appear to consider that it is an inappropriate measure for offenders found guilty of offences associated with politically motivated violence. Probation officers appear to be in agreement and in 1974 when they were asked to prepare social inquiry reports and supervise offenders who were involved with paramilitary groups they refused. Preparation of social inquiry reports and supervision assumed that the offender could be helped. While some paramilitary offenders agreed to a social inquiry report or supervision for opportune reasons, the assumption that help was required in any form was adamantly denied. The *raison d'être* of probation was therefore non-existent and hence there was little point in pursuing a normal course. In these circumstances, it was not surprising that probation officers refused to work with political offenders.

On a more general level, the probation officers' refusal to do this type of work emphasized the implicit assumptions which are normally taken for granted in the probation setting. In particular it illustrates the point that probation supervision can only succeed if the behaviour has been successfully defined as criminal and the offender accepts this label. If the label is rejected many of the normal roles of the probation officer cannot be performed. The political violence of Northern Ireland therefore plays havoc with traditional penological thinking.

Conclusions

A number of more general points may be made in conclusion to this analysis of the effects of violence on the police and the penal system. The first is that the violence has led to far-reaching changes in both the police and the penal system. The police force has been transformed from a centralized force directly answerable to the government, to an independent force responsible to a Police Authority. In addition, personnel has been changed fundamentally with over 50% of the force in 1976 made up of recruits who have joined since 1968. The penal system has also been altered extensively. Two vast prison complexes have been built and a new prison is planned. It has been changed from what was principally a cellular system to a compound system. But although these changes have been extensive, they nevertheless reflect a traditional response. Apart from one or two exceptions there have been no really radical departures from British police and penal practice. For example, despite the high levels of violence and the widespread alienation of the Roman Catholic community from the police, the changes introduced simply brought the RUC into line with the rest of the United Kingdom. There was no attempt to consider other types of police organization, such as local police forces. The regional type of organization was never seriously questioned. Similarly, the decision to build a maximum security prison reflected traditional penological thinking in which security was the dominant consideration of the policy.

The second point to make is that the violence has produced a far greater unity among the personnel in the police and in the penal system. Both have developed powerful organizations prepared to challenge the authorities not only in relation to working conditions, but also in relation to the development of policy. The implications of these changes for the authorities are far-reaching. In the past, the authorities were able to decide on policy and have it implemented through the hierarchical command structure of either the police or the penal system. Policy can no longer be developed in this way; it must either be considered in the light of possible objections from those required to implement it, or, in some cases, actually negotiated with them. These realities are likely to determine the way in which the authorities react on a wide range of issues. They will be much more inclined to back the personnel than pursue a policy which they may consider to be the most suitable. For example, many people have argued for the setting up of an independent system of inquiries for complaints against the police and the army in order to gain the confidence of Roman Catholics. As in the United Kingdom as a whole so in Northern Ireland police have opposed a totally independent system. The complaints procedure negotiated with the English and Welsh police forces is to be introduced into Northern Ireland, despite the very different social circumstances.

The third point is that violence has not only influenced the development of policy which has already been introduced; it will also influence the development of future policy. The building of the new prison is a case in point. It will not only absorb the majority of finance available in the future for other penal developments, but its very presence as a maximum security prison will dominate penological thinking for years to come. Similarly, the structure, size and methods of policing which have been developed over the last six years will determine to a large extent the future type of policing in Northern Ireland.

The final point that emerges from this analysis is the contrast in approach by Unionist and Westminster governments to the problem of violence in Northern Ireland. Unionists have been consistently unequivocal; the constitution and parliament of Northern Ireland must be preserved at all costs. Derogations from the rule of law and other principles normally associated with democratic régimes were made in order to deal with violence. Westminster governments, on the other hand, acknowledged that there was a dialectical relationship between Unionist governments' actions and violence.

Failure to uphold certain democratic principles was seen as a powerful contributing factor to violence. In 1969 it was insisted that, from then on, the rule of law and other principles would be observed in Northern Ireland. But, as has been illustrated in this analysis this policy was not pursued determinedly. Reforms, such as the disarming of the police, were overturned and various measures were permitted which were clearly contrary to the declared intent. For example, the Unionist government was allowed to introduce internment and un-authorized interrogation techniques. Even after Direct Rule, the Westminster government vacillated. Internment or detention without trial was used for another four years before it was eventually phased out.

The reason for these vacillations was simply that successive Westminster governments were intimidated by the continuing high level of violence. Their stance, since becoming involved in the affairs of Northern Ireland has therefore been highly contradictory. On the one hand, they have publicly asserted that failure to observe democratic principles, in particular the rule of law, has been an important factor in the violence, yet at the same time they continually deviated, in the face of violence, from these very principles.

Notes

1   For an account of the changes introduced in the courts, *see* Boyle, K., Hadden, T. and Hillyard, P., *Law and State: The Case of Northern Ireland*, London: Martin Robertson, 1975.

2 Murie, A. S. and Birrell, W. D., 'Ideology, Conflict and Social Policy', *Journal of Social Policy*, **4**, 3, July 1975, 243–58.

3 *Committee on Police Reorganisation in Northern Ireland*, Belfast: HMSO, 1922, Cmd. 1.

4 Commission on the Constitution, *Written Evidence 3*, Home Office, Government Departments of Northern Ireland, London: HMSO, 1969, p. 19.

5 Wright, Frank, 'Protestant Ideology and Politics in Ulster', *European Journal of Sociology*, **14**, 1973, 213–80.

6 *Northern Ireland: text of a Communiqué and Declaration issued after a meeting held at 10 Downing Street, on August 19th 1969*, London: HMSO, 1969, Cmnd. 4154.

7 *Report of the Advisory Committee on the Police in Northern Ireland*, Belfast: HMSO, 1969, Cmnd 535.

8 Boehringer, G. H., 'Beyond Hunt: A Police Policy for Northern Ireland of the future', *Social Studies*, **2**, 4, 1973, 339–414.

9 Commentary upon the White Paper (Cmnd 558), entitled *A record of constructive change*, Belfast: 1971.

10 Boyle, K., *et al.*, op. cit., pp. 41–5.

11 *See* in particular, Boyle, K., *et al.,* op. cit., Chapter 5.

12 *Report of the Enquiry into Allegations against the Security Forces of Physical Brutality in Northern Ireland arising out of events on 9th August 1971*, London: HMSO, 1971, Cmnd 4823.

13 *Report of the Committee of Privy Councillors appointed to consider authorised procedures for the Interrogation of Persons Suspected of Terrorism*, London: HMSO, 1972, Cmnd 4901.

14 *Report of the Committee to consider, in the context of civil liberties and human rights, measures to deal with terrorism in Northern Ireland*, London: HMSO, 1975, Cmnd 5847, p. 43.

15 'Building the Ulster Colditz, The Maghaberry Muddle', *Fortnight*, 10 October 1975.

16 *See* Department of Finance, *Report of the Honourable Mr Justice Murray*, Belfast: HMSO, 1975.

17 Cmnd 5847, op. cit., p. 36.

18 *Fortnight*, op. cit., p. 5.

19 Cmnd 5847, op. cit., p. 34.

Part B: Violence and Communities

8 Emergencies: Two Case Studies

John Darby and Louis Boyle*

Introduction

On three occasions since the beginning of the current period of violence in Northern Ireland—in August 1969, August 1971 and May 1974—the province's crisis intensified to such an extent as to constitute an emergency. During these periods, which lasted from two to three weeks each, social distress deepened, and the problems of social service agencies and community organizations were considerably increased.

The purpose of the two case studies in this section of the book is to observe the effects of these emergencies, and the attempts of statutory and voluntary bodies to deal with them. In particular they demonstrate the increasing confidence and ability of community groups in the province between August 1971 and May 1974, and the growing tendency for welfare departments to co-operate and act through community organizations during these two emergency periods.

*John Darby lectures in Social Administration at the New University of Ulster and is the author of *Conflict in Northern Ireland* (1976).
Louis Boyle is a community worker with the Eastern Health and Social Services Board.

Internment without trial: August 1971

John Darby

During the early hours of 9 August 1971 more than 300 people from Republican areas throughout Northern Ireland were interned under the Special Powers Act. Within hours many parts of the province had erupted in violent reaction. Barricades were erected and extensive rioting broke out in parts of Belfast, Londonderry and Lurgan. Within two days twenty-one people had died.

Although there had been persistent and growing civil disorder in Northern Ireland since 1969, and especially during the spring and early summer of 1971, the three weeks following the introduction of internment were so different in the extent and intensity of violence as to constitute a clear emergency. Quite apart from the violence, the effects of internment were widespread. Non-unionist politicians declared a campaign of civil disobedience which involved the withdrawal of 130 councillors from public life, and a rent and rates strike which by mid-September was costing local authorities £65,000 a week. Parts of Belfast and Londonderry were isolated as essential services were withdrawn; no buses operated in west Belfast during the entire month of August; there were no milk, post or bread deliveries in some areas for a number of days; during August a total of £23,000 was stolen in 35 separate armed robberies. But apart from the deaths, by far the most serious consequence of the disorder was the population movement caused by the widespread intimidation.

Forcible eviction of religious minorities from streets and estates—a sort of demographic purification—had accompanied every major outbreak of violence in Belfast since the early nineteenth century, and August 1971 was no exception. The burning of 240 houses in the Ardoyne district was the most dramatic single incident, but intimidation on a smaller scale was common and produced a serious refugee problem. By August 12 an estimated 7,000 Belfast people, mainly Roman Catholic women and children, had been transported by special trains to the Irish Republic and were being housed in hastily erected camps; few, however, stayed very long. There was also some Protestant movement to Britain, with eighty refugees arriving in Liverpool on August 13. Most of the intimidated families, however, fled to the houses of friends and relatives in 'safe' areas, or to the emergency relief centres which were established in schools and halls throughout the areas affected by violence. About 2,500 families, or 10,000 people, in the Belfast area alone were driven by intimidation from their homes during the last three weeks of August [1].

The combination of these factors—rioting, deaths, arson, robberies, civil disobedience and extensive intimidation—in a relatively small number of urban areas created a welfare crisis which lasted for about three weeks. The relief problems which it caused for voluntary and statutory organizations were qualitatively and quantitatively different from those caused by the general violence which preceded and followed it. Their ability to cope was put severely to the test.

Community Responses

The most serious relief problems of the August 1971 emergency arose from its suddenness. Overnight thousands of people had fled from their homes and some of them urgently needed a place of refuge; transport was needed for themselves and for their belongings; in parts of the city there was a shortage of food and medical supplies. The need to relieve these problems was not only grave, but urgent.

Many of the reporters who visited Northern Ireland during August 1971 completely underestimated the seriousness of the situation. They were simply unable to believe that the normality which they saw in the city centre and in most of the suburbs could coexist with an emergency in such a small urban area. Indeed the worst effects of the violence were confined to comparatively few districts in the city, particularly West Belfast, Ardoyne and the New Lodge area. All of these were working-class Catholic districts. Although about 40% of the families who fled from their homes during the month were Protestants, the large-scale concentration of distress was a feature of the predominantly Catholic parts of the city. Part of the reason for this lay in the fact that all of the original detainees were suspected republicans, but mainly it was caused by the peculiarities of Belfast's demographic structure. Catholics formed only 25% of the city's population, and 81% of them lived in small compact enclaves with their co-religionists [2]. Protestants were able to feel secure in a much larger proportion of the city. As a result, Catholic refugees tended to pour into small, already overcrowded districts, and Protestant refugees were relatively easily absorbed into the rest.

In all these characteristics the events of August 1971 resembled an earlier and more distressful emergency during the civil disorders of August 1969. In that month more than 3,500 families had fled from their homes, and the need to provide and co-ordinate relief activities in the hard-pressed Catholic areas became an overnight priority. On that occasion the initiative had been taken by voluntary organizations and the Central Co-ordinating Committee for Relief (CCCR) was formed. Originally a middle-class group with the support of the Roman Catholic church—two of the early chairmen were priests—it assumed central direction and organized both the provision of relief and the collection of information about distressed families. After 1969 the structure of the CCCR remained in existence, at least in embryo, ready to adopt a similar role in the event of another emergency, and slowly expanded its membership to include representatives from working-class districts. Indeed its real strength shifted from the central committee to local committees. Four co-ordinators were appointed for the Catholic parts of the city. During the same period, as a result of its conspicuous respectability, the CCCR had been invited to send representatives to a number of statutory and voluntary committees. By 1971 the CCCR was well known to both social workers and welfare authorities.

When the emergency broke out on 9 August 1971 the establishment of emergency centres was anything but smooth. Although the CCCR had an emergency plan, relief centres were established in most of the troubled areas without reference to it. Schools and church halls were opened and refugee families moved in. Local community and parish leaders supervised and administered them. In the event, the need for long-term accommodation in relief centres was much less than it had been in 1969 since the majority of people who had evacuated their homes found refuge with relations or friends or by squatting in unoccupied houses; some indeed returned to their own homes after a day or two. The main function of the relief centres in 1971 was as places of refuge or transit camps, and many of the people who sought refuge in them stayed for only one or two nights, before leaving for more permanent homes. On August 17, eight days after the introduction of internment, there were still seventeen relief centres in Belfast, but many of them were unoccupied. That night they held a total of 370 people in full residence and 410 taking overnight shelter. Relief centres were also established in Protestant church halls and in Orange halls but, for the reasons already mentioned, they were largely redundant from the day of their opening.

The establishment of relief centres in Catholic areas owed little to the advance planning of the CCCR. Opening a hall presents few problems; it is much more difficult to secure beds, bedding, transport, food and medical supplies when there is no money available. It was at this point that the CCCR performed a vital and timely function. As the introduction of internment had alienated the Catholic communities, the Northern Ireland government, sensitive to accusations of sectarianism and possibly prompted by Westminster, was particularly aware of the need to be seen to be tackling the relief problem. Consequently there was a political will to provide resources. The difficulties lay in actually administering the relief activities. In the first place, professional welfare agencies and social workers were effectively excluded from Catholic areas by the violence; in addition they were reluctant to hand over resources to *ad hoc* voluntary bodies about which they knew little and which might have unacceptable political undertones and connections. In this context the role of the CCCR became critical. It was manifestly moderate; local traders, who had the only immediate access to food and medical supplies, trusted it and knew that their bills would be paid. It had the approval of the Roman Catholic hierarchy. Even the fact that the committee was not elected became, in the circumstances, an advantage.

So the CCCR was recognized as a *bona fide* organization, indeed the only *bona fide* organization in Catholic areas, and became the channel for government relief. It was provided with credit to buy food, medical supplies and transport facilities, and was given direct lines of communication with top officials at the Ministry of Health and Social Services. It, in turn, used its standing in the communities to provide safe conduct to a number of service agencies, even providing access to premises for the distribution of cash supplementary benefits. In effect, during the two to three weeks of the emergency, the CCCR appropriated some of the functions of statutory welfare agencies as well as co-ordinating voluntary relief activities.

There were, of course, community initiatives outside the auspices of the CCCR. The Association for Legal Justice provided legal advice—a somewhat redundant activity as internment without trial, the very occasion of the emergency, arose from the use of extraordinary legal powers. The Central Citizens' Defence Committee, the St Vincent de Paul Society and other organizations continued their normal relief activities independently or in co-operation with the CCCR, and many *ad hoc* groups sprang into existence overnight; but their influence was peripheral. The Community groups, which were to become such an important feature of Belfast's activities over the next few years, performed only minor roles; they were few in number, their confidence had not yet developed sufficiently and, even at this early stage, they were regarded with suspicion by administrators and politicians. A number of international voluntary organizations, like the Red Cross, were operating in Belfast during August 1971, but were unable to make much impact. Even organizations like the Belfast Housing Aid Society and, to a much lesser extent, the Belfast Council of Social Welfare, which were later to become involved in more long-term rehabilitation work, were powerless during the actual emergency [3]. The very suspicion and fear which had helped produce violence and distress also served to exclude from the communities all but very few organizations which were not locally based and fully trusted. A feature of Belfast's emergencies has been a turning by communities in on themselves and rejection of assistance from external bodies. August 1971 was no exception.

Statutory Bodies

The local government welfare departments in the Greater Belfast area had, like the community organizations, already experienced the social consequences of a political emergency in 1969. Their experiences should have pointed to a number of obvious lessons: one was the inconvenience of storing basic emergency supplies like blankets, cookers and food in a central depot rather than at local centres; another lesson was that they must learn to establish links with local voluntary organizations which could provide those services which welfare departments were unable to provide during a collapse of the civil establishment. August 1971 proved, however, that statutory authorities had learned few lessons from the experience of 1969. For a full week after the introduction of internment, for example, welfare offices in the city were still rigidly adhering to a 9.00 to 5.30 timetable, and closing at weekends. Volunteers in the Community Relations Commission emergency centre were shocked to find that they, and presumably people from the disaster areas, were unable to contact anyone at the headquarters of the Ministry of Health and Social Services except a caretaker at 6.00 p.m. on August 13, when the emergency was at its height.

The performance of the statutory relief agencies was also hampered by the fact that there was a direct conflict of policy between some local welfare departments in troubled areas and the Ministry of Health and Social Services. Within these welfare departments, which employed social workers and implemented social welfare policy, there was institutional reluctance to allocate resources without normal bureaucratic safeguards, or to suspend temporarily the principles of strict accounting, regardless of the severity of the emergency. This reluctance was heightened by the fear that carelessly allocated funds might find their way into the hands of politically suspect or paramilitary groups, and by the realization that the general violence would make it almost impossible for their social workers to operate with any degree of freedom. Their advocated strategy, therefore, was only to provide support when responsible local leaders had been carefully identified. The problems of the Ministry of Health and Social Services, however, were much more complex. On the one hand the government was well aware both of the seriousness of the crisis and of the political need to be seen to be relieving the distress in Catholic areas; indeed, the contingency plans for transport and supplies which had been drawn up in 1969 might have comprised a blueprint for such action. On the other hand, for the necessary action to be taken it would have been necessary to declare publicly that the introduction of internment had led to a state of emergency, and this would have been politically unacceptable to the government. While the government wanted to act, it was not prepared to take some decisions—such as calling the army out of troubled areas—which would have helped to make its actions effective. Its relief policy was in conflict with its security policy.

Notwithstanding this major constraint, the government was determined to apply resources to the afflicted areas, and looked to the local government welfare agencies to implement its policies. Given the caution of some agencies, the result was antagonism and friction between the Ministry of Health and Social Services and local welfare offices. This conflict was exacerbated by such issues as the Ministry's insistence that a social worker should be allocated to each of the rest centres, and by the fact that the CCCR had much more ready access to the Ministry than the local offices. It was all deeply frustrating for social workers in the field, who were a potentially important resource both for monitoring the crisis and relieving the distress, but whose influence was minimal while policy issues were being determined by political criteria rather than by social needs. Nevertheless the difficulties were not insurmountable, and some social workers were allowed sufficient flexibility by their departments to liaise effectively with community relief bodies. Much depended on attitudes at local office level. It was notable that, while social workers employed by Belfast Welfare Department constantly found their hands tied, those employed by the more enterprising County Antrim Department were allowed to respond with efficiency and considerable success.

In retrospect it is clear that the normal functions of welfare bodies became redundant during the 1971 emergency, and that locally based voluntary organizations took over their role. But, although the normally specified activities of social workers became impossible, there is no evidence of serious effort to search for other means of executing their broader function of public service. In particular there was no attempt to simplify the bureaucratic complexities which faced intimidated families. These families, homeless and frequently distressed, often had considerable difficulty in finding out which agency was appropriate to deal with their situation. When they did find the right connection, the compartmentalization of social relief meant that they had to contact up to a dozen different agencies throughout the city centre for their transport, housing, protection, compensation and other requirements. There was no suggestion from the agencies that their activities should be co-ordinated, or even that centres should be established where the different needs of distressed families could be attended to. After seven years of violence, such elementary co-operation is still lacking, even during emergencies.

An Emergency Operation

One agency which did attempt to adjust to the crisis was the Northern Ireland Community Relations Commission; the co-ordinating centre which it established is interesting both for the manner of its implementation and development and as a possible model for emergency operations [4]. The Commission, established in 1969, had adopted a programme of community development and by 1971 ten Community Development Officers (CDOs) were working with community groups in Belfast, Londonderry and Dungannon. Already the spread of violence had created problems for them in the conduct of their work, but the August emergency made normal activities impossible. So on August 11 the Commission's staff met to determine how it might react to the situation. Even at that early stage it was clear that the relief agencies were failing to adjust their procedures to provide effective relief. So, in the Commission's own words, 'the decision was taken to turn the whole resources of the organisation over to emergency relief, and to set up a communications centre for that purpose' [5]. This centre was intended to facilitate lines of communication between those in distress and the statutory and voluntary agencies which were trying to relieve the distress. Thirty-four volunteers helped to man the centre, and the Commission's regular staff of Community Development Officers was released for such specific tasks as liaison with welfare agencies, co-ordination with relief centres, processing requests for assistance and providing transport for intimidated families. The centre was established that evening and continued to operate around the clock for more than three weeks.

Table 8.1: Cases processed by Community Relations Commission Emergency operation 11–31 August 1971

Offers of help			Requests for help		
Accommodation	127	(53·8%)	Accommodation	42	(2.4%)
Transport	49	(20.7%)	Transport	329	(18.7%)
Other offers	60	(25.4%)	Financial assistance	176	(10%)
			Materials or services	267	(15.2%)
			Housing information	205	(11.7%)
			General information	538	(30.6%)
			Intimidation	122	(6.9%)
			Complaints	26	(1.5%)
			Miscellaneous	15	(0.9%)
			Information	37	(2.1%)
Total	236		Total	1757	

During the period of the Commission's emergency operation two developments were particularly notable. From the very first day of the crisis, when the Commission broadcast appeals for offers of shelter and accommodation, only to find that intimidated families preferred to take refuge in relief centres close to their own areas, it was virtually impossible to keep pace with the remarkable dynamism of the emergency. It became necessary to evolve a systematic method of processing requests for help and referring them to appropriate agencies. By the end of the first week, distress calls, which at the peak of the operation exceeded 200 a day, were being analysed and processed every twenty-four hours. This revealed changes in the pattern of need which might otherwise have been underrated and suggested alterations in the administration of the emergency operation itself. Another development was the tendency for the Commission's role to change from an intermediary one to a directly executive one, as inadequacies in relief provision were revealed. For example, almost from the start of the crisis the need for transport of people and their possessions hopelessly outstripped the resources of the welfare authorities and it became necessary on August 12 for the Commission to establish its own transport section, which used voluntary drivers to mount a 24-hour service, which moved an estimated 3,000 refugees and the contents of 115 houses. Later on, as the early violence eased, some families which had fled from their homes wished to return. No statutory body, however, was prepared to accept responsibility for repairing riot damage to homes. So the Commission, which received no extra finance for such activities until late in the emergency [6], had to set up a unit to provide wind- and water-proofing for houses which had been damaged during the disorders.

The Commission's operation contrasted with the reaction of the social services agencies. Although clumsy and makeshift, it had two qualities not shared by the agencies: it was sufficiently adaptable to abandon its usual functions to meet the needs of a new situation, leaving financial worries until the crisis had eased; and it was—largely due to the pressure of circumstances—conscious of the rapidity with which emergencies changed and of the resulting need to be prepared constantly to alter administrative structures. This need to react to a dynamic situation was frequently illustrated: the original telephone-based operation became inadequate as distressed people began to arrive at the Commission's headquarters; so it became necessary to supplement it with a personal interview section. Similarly the addition of volunteers produced a need for a training manual containing basic information and describing the procedures of the communications centre; this, along with another information sheet containing information for rest centres, was duly produced by the information section. Again, although transport remained a constant demand, the nature of the demand changed greatly a number of times during the operation, requiring in turn lorries, cars and minibuses as the situation called for the moving of furniture, people and materials to repair damaged houses.

Conclusions

When the infrastructure of social services collapsed during the emergency of August 1971 the only people who were able to provide effective relief were those who lived in the affected areas. Since in most cases government agencies were unable to operate in these areas, their normal functions could not be carried out.

A disturbing feature of the emergency was the failure of the agencies to find another, more relevant, role. The communications centre established by the Community Relations Commission essentially filled a gap left by the inactivity of the welfare departments and other welfare agencies. It is as clear in retrospect as it was at the time that a major priority was the co-ordination of relief activities and the establishment of a central information centre which would co-ordinate their activities and serve as a contact point for distressed people. The welfare agencies failed to provide such a service in 1971 and indeed did not even extend their conventional working-hours or relax normal procedures for allocating resources, until forced to do so. The lesson of the Commission's emergency operation is that it is possible for agencies to discover a relevant role, if the will and ability to change is present.

In the end, however, contingency planning for emergencies is only possible within very narrow limits. No two emergencies produce identical needs, so detailed planning based on past experience has limited relevance. Consequently, the changes which have been introduced by welfare departments as a result of the 1971 emergency were administrative and general rather than specific. For example, it has been recognized that emergency supplies should be dispersed rather than centralized, and this distribution has taken place. The local nature of emergencies was also recognized in the decisions that community groups should be more widely supported in the event of future emergencies, and that contingency plans should be drawn up on a local rather than a central basis. In some parts of the province, these plans were devised in consultation with local groups. Assuming, however, that distress would probably be concentrated in the Belfast area, plans were drawn up to co-ordinate the distribution of resources and to maintain the normal activities of a modern city. Details of these plans are not publicly available.

Notes

1   NICRC Research Unit, *Flight*, Northern Ireland Community Relations Commission, 1971.
2   Poole, M. A. and Boal, F. W., 'Religious Residential Segregation in Belfast in mid-1969', in B. D. Clark and M. B. Gleave, *Social Patterns in Cities*, Institute of British Geographers, Monograph, Urban Studies Group, London: 1973. Boal and Poole estimated that 81% of Belfast's Catholic minority lived in the Falls and Ardoyne areas.
3   The Belfast Housing Aid Society dispensed more than £100,000 to intimidated families during the eleven months following August 1971.

4 The emergency operation was described by the author in the occasional paper published internally by the Northern Ireland Community Relations Commission in 1971. Issue was restricted to Commission staff.

5 NIRC, *Second Annual Report*, 1972.

6 The Commission embarked upon the emergency operation without having been awarded extra funds. More than two weeks later, it was given a retrospective sum of £5,000. Since most of the extra assistance came from volunteers, the major costs of the operation were for administration and materials. The total cost was estimated at £8,010.

The Ulster Workers' Council Strike: May 1974

Louis Boyle

The Ulster Workers' Council (UWC) is an association of loyalist workers which replaced the defunct Loyalist Association of Workers, (LAW) in the period following the unsuccessful one-day strike of 7 February 1973, organized by LAW. Relatively little was known of its strength or organization until the 1974 strike [1] commenced.

The strike began on Wednesday, May 15, following the vote by the Northern Ireland Assembly ratifying the Sunningdale Agreement. In the first few days, with general confusion about the issue and strong opposition from the official trade union movement and many political leaders, the strike had little support. But the Secretary of State, Merlyn Rees, and his junior minister Stanley Orme, by their refusal to negotiate with the strike leaders, played into the strikers' hands. This, together with the intervention of the UDA in barricading off a large part of Belfast and other districts throughout the province, brought about more widespread support for the strike.

Effects of Strike

As the strike progressed, the UWC demonstrated its ability to control directly the supply and distribution of electricity, gas, public transport, petrol, foodstuffs and animal foodstuffs, and indirectly, many retail outlets, places of entertainment, private motoring and other sectors of economic life. Shortages developed in many foodstuffs, coal and container gas; petrol was being rationed and was in short supply; the electricity service was being run at a reduced level, determined on a daily basis by the UWC, so that each area in the province was getting power on an on–off basis. Water supplies and sewage were threatened; hundreds of thousands were out of work or on strike; thousands queued for the new emergency benefit which replaced unemployment and supplementary benefit; money was in short supply, public transport was severely curtailed, many shops were either closed or open for only a few hours each day, and pubs, cinemas and many places of entertainment were closed.

The impact of the strike varied from place to place. Belfast was most severely hit, but so were also the big towns with loyalist majorities, Lisburn, Portadown, Lurgan, Antrim, Ballymena, Larne and Bangor. The farming community was badly affected, with cuts in electricity, shortages of animal foodstuffs and disruption in the normal outlets for farm produce. Other areas escaped fairly lightly, except for electricity cuts and petrol shortages.

In the back of everyone's mind was the fear that violence would erupt as had happened during two previous political strikes in Northern Ireland, in March 1972 and February 1973. This time however, the two-week period of the strike was largely free from violence, to the surprise of many. On the one hand the Provisional IRA concentrated on defensive precautions and welfare work, while on the other side it was clearly in the interests of the loyalist strike leaders and para-military groups to prevent violence occurring.

The effects of the strike progressively increased during the second week, and both the Northern Ireland Executive and the Secretary of State were powerless in face of it. The army and the police made no attempt up to this point to intervene. Then, following Harold Wilson's famous 'spongers' broadcast on Saturday evening May 25, the army took over a number of petrol retail outlets on the morning of Monday, May 27. With hindsight it was little more than a token gesture, but it was a direct challenge to the UWC. In retaliation they shut down Belfast's gas supplies, and began to close down completely the electricity supply system. On Tuesday, May 28, twenty-four hours later, the Northern Ireland Executive collapsed, and the following morning, the strike was called off. Disaster was just averted [2].

The Community Responds

The UWC strike was remarkable for the unprecedented involvement of a wide range of voluntary groups in welfare activity. The groups involved included the paramilitary groups of UDA and UVF, Orange Volunteers, Provisional IRA, UWC Committees, relief organizations such as the Central Co-ordinating Committee for Relief in West Belfast, church-sponsored groups, and to a lesser extent, existing voluntary organizations such as the Belfast Council of Social Welfare.

The work and influence of each varied from area to area, depending on the relative strength of the group.

In loyalist areas, local UWC committees who, besides their relief work, were responsible for enforcing UWC regulations and issuing passes to essential workers, Orange welfare groups and UDA-linked *ad hoc* groups, formed the backbone of welfare activity. Not only were they the first off the mark, but they had the local strength, greatly swelled by the ranks of the out-of-work. Moreover they had strong inter-community links within Belfast and with outlying areas, a vital component for any relief operation. Many community groups did not realize until late in the day that the strike might be prolonged and have serious effects. When they did attempt to take action they found that they had no role to play, or that the strike was over by the time they were geared to act. This happened in East Belfast, when a relief operation involving a large number of community groups and church organizations got off the ground on Monday and Tuesday, May 27 and 28, only to find the strike over on Wednesday. The paramilitary groups meanwhile had been active in the area for the previous two weeks. In other cases, community groups threw their weight behind the paramilitary organizations, or worked alongside them. In one area, mainly loyalist South Belfast, the South Belfast Community Association, an amalgamation of eighteen community groups in the area, started a relief operation early in the strike with an emergency operation centre and sixteen local relief centres.

In Catholic areas established relief groups such as the Central Citizens' Defence Committee and the Central Co-ordinating Committee for Relief, each with strong links with the church, went into operation as they had done in previous crises when it was realized that the strike could be prolonged. In areas in which groups and paramilitary bodies had been active, such as Andersonstown and Turf Lodge, and the Markets and Short Strand in central Belfast, the established groups found themselves replaced by or in competition with *ad hoc* relief committees comprising community groups and paramilitary organizations. In both loyalist and Catholic areas during and after the crisis, there was conflict over who had the right to work on behalf of the community. One example of this was a fairly bitter exchange which developed between the Central Citizens' Defence Committee and the Central Co-ordinating Committee for Relief in Turf Lodge [3].

On the other side of the city in East Belfast a newly established relief committee, in a subsequent report of the strike, pointed to the need not to place '*bona fide* groups such as ourselves in a compromising position of being forced to work with paramilitary or political groups who may have obtained supplies by dubious means' [4]. In the Catholic Markets area as well, three separate relief centres were in operation, organized respectively by a local community group, and the two wings of the IRA.

In the more middle-class suburbs of East and South Belfast, church groups were the only relief organizations in operation; their involvement generally dated from Monday, May 27 and they found, like some community groups, that the strike was almost over by the time they were geared to act. Established voluntary organizations such as the Belfast Council of Social Welfare, which had been active in previous crises, were anxious to get involved but were faced with two problems which also confronted their statutory counterparts; to what extent could they co-operate with paramilitary groups, and what could they usefully do and where?

In all areas, the problems confronting relief groups were similar, as was the action being planned or taken to deal with the situation. Most groups set up emergency relief and advice centres, usually operating on a 24-hour basis and used for stocking up foodstuffs, coal, wood, paraffin, bottled gas and any other material for which a need was arising. These centres, which were established in community centres, Orange halls, church halls and in some cases school premises, formed the backbone of the relief effort in the community, and up to one hundred such centres were in operation in the Belfast area alone. Emergency transport with identified vehicles and drivers was organized to collect and distribute essential foodstuffs and materials, and in some cases to provide an alternative ambulance service. There was widespread acceptance of the need to concentrate relief activities on people at risk— elderly folk living alone, house-bound individuals, the handicapped, invalids, sick people and young children. Door-to-door surveys were conducted to determine need. Some of these were very comprehensive, and were used as the basis for follow-up work, the provision of meals, the encouragement of neighbours to get involved with elderly people, and the delivery of coal, wood and paraffin. Among other activities undertaken by relief groups were street cleaning and refuse disposal, the organization of youth into work teams to undertake different duties in their own area, and the setting up of field kitchens to provide tea and soup.

In the aftermath of the strike, reports were produced by many of the groups involved in relief activity. These provide a rich source of information on the work of relief organizations during the strike, and show the scale and extent of activity on the ground. One extract from the report produced by the South Belfast Community Association could perhaps sum up the theme of many of the others:

> the operation demonstrated clearly the strength of community spirit throughout the area, the level of community concern, the willingness and urgency with which community groups were ready to rally around and tackle problems and ensure that hardship would be minimised [5].

Catholic areas in Belfast found themselves in a more difficult position throughout the strike. Firstly the geography of Belfast means that there is a large concentration of Catholics in West Belfast, surrounded on all sides by 'hostile' areas. Elsewhere Catholics live in isolated pockets such as Ardoyne, the Markets and Short Strand—areas which feel particularly vulnerable during crises. The relief groups in West Belfast found that the major sources of supply of many foodstuffs, milk, gas, coal and petrol lay outside the area, and thus under the control, or potentially under the control, of the loyalists. While the main concentration of Catholic relief activity was in West Belfast, contacts were established with the isolated Catholic communities and, following the pattern of previous crises, preparations were made to accommodate families temporarily if intimidation occurred. In the event, there was very little intimidation, and no evacuation was required. Links were established between Catholic districts and rural areas for farm produce and other food supplies. Links were also established with the Republic of Ireland for supplies, but distance made communication difficult. Plans were drawn up to bring in large quantities of food and other essentials if this proved necessary.

In the Catholic areas there was a widespread belief that the loyalists had pre-knowledge of the strike, and had been stock-piling for months. loyalist relief groups generally had gone into operation before the Catholic groups, but there is no evidence that they were in any better state of preparedness. In the loyalist communities there was general underlying support for the strike, and this gathered strength as the stoppage was prolonged. There was a general view that the strike should continue, but that hardship should be minimized. There had been a major growth in community associations and paramilitary groups in loyalist areas during the period 1971 to 1973. The loyalists were therefore in a much superior organizational position than had been the case in either 1969 or 1971. Paramilitary groups, as mentioned earlier, were in a particularly strong position to undertake relief operations.

Some of this involvement was shown to be politically motivated when, on May 27 after the army intervened in the petrol supply, the UWC and various local groups washed their hands of any further welfare work, handing responsibility over to the government with the attitude, 'It's up to you.' However, undoubtedly the main motivation for people involved in relief activity in all areas was a concern to prevent human suffering. There is a natural drive in people to get involved and do something in times of emergency, and when such involvement is also in support of a political cause which is dear to them, this adds to the motivation and satisfaction.

Voluntary organizations played a vital role in relief work during the UWC strike. Without doubt the organization of relief activities was superior to previous crises. Few areas were left uncovered; never before had so much community activity been seen in Belfast; public meetings when held were packed, volunteers were numerous and it seemed in some areas that everyone was involved in some way. In one estate of 500 households in South Belfast, two public meetings were held on Sunday, May 26; the 4.00 p.m. meeting was attended by over 400 women and the 5.00 p.m. meeting attended by 500 men. The following evening in a small Catholic community in central Belfast a public meeting attracted the remarkable attendance of 800 people.

Great skill of organization was demonstrated in many of the relief centres, and new leadership emerged which has subsequently been very beneficial to community work. It is clear, for example, that the UDA's subsequent interest in community work stems from its involvement during the strike. There is no evidence of any great planning beforehand on the part of the organizations involved. While some of the established organizations had the benefit of experience in previous crises, most relief groups came into being as a direct response to a deteriorating situation, and had to start from scratch.

There was a widespread feeling of disappointment when the strike ended so quickly on May 29, before many groups had had the opportunity to demonstrate the strength of their organization. Many groups were left with surplus foodstuffs and other supplies which they had difficulty in disposing of, and this added further to a general feeling of dejection immediately after the strike. Had the emergency been more prolonged, these voluntary organizations would have undoubtedly had a crucial role to play alongside the social services in carrying out a relief operation.

The Social Service Department Reacts

Since 1969, social work agencies in Northern Ireland have had to respond to a series of emergency situations, and provide suitable relief measures. Considerable experience had been acquired in dealing with the evacuation, care and re-location of people rendered homeless because of bombing, intimidation or open conflict. The crises of 1969 and 1971 were localized, and marked by a particular event or series of events, following which problems could be assessed and appropriate action taken. Any contingency plans that were available were geared to this type of emergency. An entirely new situation arose during the UWC strike. Existing contingency plans were totally inadequate for the conditions which prevailed particularly during the last few days of the strike [6].

The response of the social service districts was generally slow, cautious and indecisive throughout. In some areas, as has been shown, local UWC-sponsored relief groups exercised effective control over such services as transport, petrol supply, coal, gas and certain foodstuffs. Faced with this, social work staff had no alternative but to accept the *de facto* control of the UWC and co-operate where necessary. There were many pressures on the districts to act but the official view was that, for as long as money and provisions were available and until an emergency had been declared, action should be on a limited basis. Official policy was to try to keep cool and, if possible, keep the situation under control so that panic should not arise. Furthermore it was realized that, once an emergency had been recognized and responsibility accepted, an unlimited commitment would be demanded until the situation was normalized. Response would generate further demand, and what one district did would have to be followed elsewhere.

In line with this policy, a directive was issued to all social service districts early in the crisis, to the effect that Section 164 of the Children and Young Persons Act should not be used to make special cash payments. This provision would have enabled social services to provide emergency help as a last resort, to families at risk. If a more flexible interpretation had been placed on this provision during the strike, the pressure on social services agencies to make cash payments would have been great. This ruling caused considerable disquiet among social workers in West Belfast who found themselves under particular pressure during the crisis. In most districts, preparations were made to have all available resources mobilized in the event of an emergency being declared, and, in the meantime, contact was established with relief committees through social service community workers.

Not until Monday, May 27 did the Department of Health and Social Services accept the existence of an emergency and authorize the full implementation of relief measures. Even at this stage, however, there was delay as the situation was changing hourly, and the enormity of the problems confronting social services were realized. It was quickly recognized that all available resources were totally inadequate to provide an effective response. Limited help was given to relief organizations; social workers were allocated to relief centres; where no relief organizations existed, as was the case in a few areas, urgent steps were taken to form one; in one district an ex-civil defence field kitchen was obtained, mobile soup kitchens, bottled gas heaters, gas cylinders, mobile gas stoves, blankets, bedding, paraffin oil, supplies of processed food were made ready for use. Each district at the same time was endeavouring to look after homes, hostels and other residential establishments, and to maintain the home-help service, luncheon clubs, day centres and field work services in operation. No sooner had the social services established themselves on an emergency footing, however, than the strike was called off. While considerable social problems remained for several days, matters very quickly returned to normal. There was no opportunity or necessity for social services to implement a full relief programme, so no assessment can be made of how effective such a programme would have been.

While there is no evidence of widespread suffering because of lack of official response, in the aftermath of the crisis considerable criticism was directed against government departments. Personal social services, being the department most directly concerned with community welfare, were a prime target. Most of the reports produced by relief groups contain criticism of the role of social services. They were accused of being either slow or unwilling to respond, of having inadequate emergency planning, of being out of touch with the community and at the same time preparing to rely heavily on voluntary organizations, of showing indecision and inflexibility, and of forcing people to go to paramilitary organizations because only they were providing welfare services. Some loyalist groups saw delay as a deliberate ploy on the part of the government to create hardship and thus dissatisfaction with the strike.

A major problem facing social services throughout the crisis was the question of what constitutes an emergency. It has been shown that in 1971, when there was a breakdown in law and order over a wide area together with widespread and serious violence and a mass evacuation of population, there was considerable delay on the government's part in recognizing an emergency. In 1974, it would have been widely accepted that an emergency existed when there was a breakdown or a threat of breakdown in the essential services of electricity, gas, water, sewage, food supplies and medical facilities. In accordance with this definition, an emergency began only on Monday, May 27 when the army intervened. For many people in the community, however, an emergency had existed from early on in the strike.

Social services were faced therefore with a situation which was serious and getting progressively worse, but was not considered bad enough until the very end to justify the declaration of an emergency. Had the strike occurred during winter-time its effects would have been more serious, widespread and quickly felt. In addition to the timing problem, the situation was fraught with major political implications. Social service provision was a central issue in the strike. The UWC were determined to show that they, rather than the government, could ensure the provision of essential services. The social services departments were operating in the middle of a conflict between the government and a section of the community and the provision of services was one of the areas around which the struggle was being fought. Any decision to declare an emergency and implement relief measures could have upset the balance between the two parties in conflict. The local district offices were restrained during the strike by the active role taken by the Department of Health and Social Services, as had been the case in 1969 and 1971. But was the Department itself acting under political restraint? It may not be possible to establish whether there was direct political intervention in the affairs of the Department during the strike, but it is clear that it must have acted with a full realization of the political implications of any decision it made. In all of the crises since 1969 in Northern Ireland, social welfare provision has been caught up in political constraints. The effectiveness of the social services therefore cannot be judged alone on their responses to need. In times of emergency, they have never had a free hand.

Realizing how inadequately they were prepared in 1974, the Department of Health and Social Services requested all social services districts to prepare contingency plans for dealing with future emergencies, taking into account as far as possible the new circumstances of 1974. It is never possible however to predict the exact nature of an emergency, and no one emergency is the same as the one before. Plans therefore need to be as flexible as possible. At the same time all social services districts must sort out their relationships with voluntary organizations in times of emergency. Perhaps they had learned from the 1971 crisis the importance of co-operation with voluntary groups in the community. After 1974 a further problem arose of how to deal with 'political' or illegal groups, as well as with *bona fide* welfare groups. Pragmatism is perhaps the only answer here. But the questions are, when will the next crisis occur, and what form will it take?

Notes

1   Throughout the crisis, the term 'strike' was used generally by those opposed to it, and the term 'constitutional stoppage' was used by the UWC and loyalist politicians. In this article the word strike is used as a term of convenience.

2   For a full account of the course of the strike *see* Robert Fisk, *The Point of No Return*, London, Times Books: André Deutsch, 1975.

3   *Irish News*, 27 May 1974.

4   Memorandum to the Department of Health and Social Services from an emergency relief committee in East Belfast, 15 August 1974.

5   South Belfast Community Association, *Report on Emergency Operation During the Recent Crisis*, June 1974.

6   In the previous case-study, reference is made to contingency plans prepared by the Ministry of Health and Social Services following the internment crisis.

9 Community Reaction and Voluntary Involvement

Hywel Griffiths*

Part I A Survey of Events

1 The Background

Before the outbreak of violence in 1969 the ordinary man or woman in Northern Ireland depended upon others and the myths they purveyed for the condition of their lives and their hopes for the future. The Protestant working man had been encouraged to believe that his right to exist and his livelihood were guaranteed solely by the existence of the Stormont Parliament, the Unionist Party and the Orange Order. His middle- and upper-class counterparts, by subscribing to the same institutions, were guaranteed opportunities for making a comfortable living without exposure to the degree of competition which existed in Britain. Catholic working-class people were encouraged to put their faith in the prospect of an eventual united Ireland guaranteed by the promises and the constitutional arrangements of the government of the Irish Republic. Meanwhile they were encouraged to believe that all social organization, in addition to spiritual guidance, should be left to the professional clergy and religious of the Roman Catholic Church. The Catholic middle class was ambivalent: on the one hand it subscribed to the same beliefs and institutions as the working class and yet the opportunities for entry into trade and the professions forced some of its members at least, to transfer part of their allegiance to the Unionist Government. This was particularly true of the latter part of the sixties during O'Neill's administration when people of the same

* Hywel Griffiths was first Director of the Northern Ireland Community Relations Commission, and is Professor of Social Administration at the New University of Ulster.

class but of different religions found common ground in a form of liberal conservatism.

Although both Protestant and Catholic working-class people tended to be dependent upon and respectful to largely middle-class controlled institutions there were nevertheless interesting differences between them. For their part the Protestants had difficulty in expressing discontent and grievance because to do so would shake the unity upon which the state was founded. Moreover there was the attitude that authority as represented by the state was benign [1] and predisposed in their favour, as compared with the Catholics; consequently to criticize or to oppose would be to demonstrate evidence of both disloyalty and ingratitude. Catholics, however, believed that the Government would not necessarily protect their interests and compounded their alienation from it by refusing as far as possible to acknowledge its existence. Thus for them criticism of and opposition to the state's administration were natural extensions of their political philosophy and religious allegiances and led them further to establish alternative organizations for their welfare and benefit.

The Protestant working-class assumption that authority was benign was matched by a complementary paternalism on the part of those who exercised authority. For example the Northern Ireland Housing Trust, which was established after the war to make up the serious deficiency in house-building of the pre-war years, could not be regarded simply as a house-building and management agency. Local Authority house-building programmes were controlled by councillors who oftentimes used housing to command allegiance from their followers and to reinforce the sectarian divisions which existed in their communities. Against this the Housing Trust sought to build estates of houses which would not be subject to local authority control and in which allocation was made according to criteria which owed nothing to religious affiliation. But overall there was a general housing shortage with many people living in old houses which by contemporary standards were unfit for human habitation. Consequently, up to 1969, tenants' associations, in Protestant areas particularly, developed to express the needs of their members, but within the context of the kind of cosy relationship which is only possible when all parties believe basically that they are all on the same side. The kinds of leaders that this situation threw up were not those who felt and were able to express the discontent which undoubtedly existed but those who could accept the goodwill and the intentions of those who managed housing: those who were prepared to settle for the status of their office, the ritual of consultation and the minor improvements and reforms which were undertaken when time and money allowed.

By contrast Catholic working-class people were always prepared to be more militant in their negotiations with statutory agencies. There were two traditions which sustained their belief in the possibility of alternative models for meeting social need. The first of these was the tradition of charity widely advocated and controlled by the Church. In its more orthodox form it provided for an alternative system of education, which although heavily supported by the state, called for regular financial contributions from all members of the Church. It also provided for direct involvement in social work and some contribution to income maintenance through such organizations as the Society of St Vincent de Paul, and the Credit Unions. In less orthodox fashion in more recent years, various self-help projects, or so-called self-help projects in some cases, had been established by professional members of the Church inspired by the example of certain well-known, not to say charismatic, figures in the Church. Amongst these can be counted the work of Father McDyer at Glencolmcille in County Donegal, who pioneered a type of rural development programme in an area suffering acutely from depopulation, and the entrepreneurship of Father Eustace of Dungannon who promoted a co-operative housing estate and created the Tyrone Crystal Glass Company as a rival in Ulster of the Waterford Glass Company in County Waterford.

The other tradition which was kept alive, at least as an ideal, in certain sections of the Catholic working-class community was closely linked to the political aspirations of those who saw themselves as Republicans. This was the Sinn Fein tradition of self-reliance which ranged in its manifestation from parochial negativism to the active expression of Marxist philosophies and which included that tradition of Irish socialism identified with the names of Griffith and Connolly. But, by and large, this tradition, although it gave the minds of many a particular direction, had not been successful in producing much by way of tangible benefits other than a spread of republican clubs which in the main were drinking clubs for men. What this tradition lacked, because of its rejection of statutory authority and its lack of support from other quarters, was the means whereby it might give practical expression to some of its schemes. The sad irony of the situation is that when the conflict broke out and the call for arms was raised a steady stream of financial aid began to flow, as it had never done before for social development projects, in order to supply the engines of war.

What both Protestants and Catholics alike relied upon for meeting many of their social, cultural and recreational needs were the churches and various semi-religious organizations associated with them. Most meeting halls were provided in this way: the Orange Hall on the one side and the Parochial Hall on the other. Most youth organizations were also affiliated with the religious denominations: the Boys' Brigade, for example, or the Legion of Mary. Beyond this fabric of organization and control the people themselves looked after each other in their small close-knit communities in kindly ways, sharing their poverty, their achievements, their joys and their sorrows.

Before 1969, therefore, although attitudes to the statutory authorities differed between the Catholic and Protestant segments of the population there was no real tradition of community action nor even of community consciousness except in relation to the political-religious divide. The normal expectation was that new policies and arrangements, if they were needed and could be introduced, would come down through the various hierarchies by means of which the population was both governed and controlled. There was only one exception—the emergence of the Civil Rights Movement in the late sixties. This movement rapidly gained support across the sectarian and class divides, but in its origin it owed more to the models of civil rights movements and protest action elsewhere, notably the USA, which had been projected through the mass media, than to the emergence of community groups seeking coalition. It demanded a number of important legislative and administrative reforms and these, largely through the intervention of the Westminster government, were obtained. But before the reforms could take effect the tide of violence had begun to flow and the stage was set for long years of conflict which even at the time of writing has not ended.

2 The response to crisis

There was an apochyphal story told in Belfast of the first reaction to the crisis of communal violence, the burning of homes and the early killings. It was said that so much money was being handed out by various relief agencies that certain sharp characters hired taxis to do the rounds and took with them plastic buckets to carry away the cash hand-outs which they acquired with plausible tales of need. Whether or not the story is true it is at least characteristic of the early reaction. On the one hand those who had suffered, or who were in need, instinctively turned to the kind of agency, church, voluntary organization or welfare department which they had learned to trust and depend on in emergencies. For their part, the agencies also accepted their responsibility and mobilized to do their share in looking after those who turned to them for help. This was manifested in many ways. Advice centres were set up in many urban areas and to these were linked channels of aid from various quarters. Reception centres for the homeless were created in schools and on church premises. Alternative transport systems, emergency services, evacuation schemes and even a rebuilding programme were all introduced in an immediate compensating reaction for the early horrors which had been experienced.

But by and large all these schemes were introduced and guided by external agencies or came about on the initiative of middle-class or professional people. The Agnes Street advice centre on the Shankill Road was the product largely of the inspiration and the application of the Methodist minister for the area. The Bombay Street house rebuilding scheme owed its success to the intervention of a socially conscious Catholic architect. The Central Citizens Defence Committee which was established to provide a comprehensive range of relief services to Catholics in the ghetto areas of Belfast had as its chief promoter an extremely successful Catholic businessman. The Belfast Council of Social Welfare, mainly through its constituent organization, the Voluntary Services Bureau, initiated numerous schemes from playgroups to house removals.

So accepted was the idea that these kinds of agencies and people would not only meet the immediate demand for relief but would enable the province to return to normality that the government made supporting them its main contribution towards dealing with the situation. It established a Ministry of Community Relations with, as its major responsibility, the administration of a social needs fund to support financially the schemes of established voluntary and statutory agencies. And in the terms of reference of the Community Relations Commission, which it also established, it mentioned expressly the task of promoting and co-ordinating the activities of these agencies, particularly those in the voluntary sector.

By way of contrast in the working-class area the primary community response to the crisis was concerned, not with the relief of need, but with the problem of security. In Catholic areas there followed a massive upsurge of recruitment to the IRA. This was not in itself surprising because the movement had always existed in these areas and sympathy for it was always, latently at least, present. There was, however, one curious by-product in the increase of casual violence and vandalism amongst Protestant Tartan gangs who had hitherto carried on a partly ritualistic campaign of confrontation with their Catholic counterparts. Now that these were absent, learning how to conduct a 'real war', the Tartan gangs were left to turn in upon themselves and upon their own communities. Even more novel was the emergence of Protestant vigilante groups composed of adult men and led frequently by men who held some position of responsibility in the work-place or in the unions. These groups formed to protect residential areas from the threat of attack from adjacent Catholic areas. They met regularly every day and operated a rota system of patrols which ensured that through-out each night someone was on guard to protect the neighbourhood. This development was highly significant even if the participants were not to realize it fully until much later. In the first place they had accepted personal responsibility for the guarantee of security, a respon-sibility which hitherto had been exercised on their behalf by the state. But, perhaps more immediately significant, they began to meet together regularly for and on behalf of their neighbours and, by virtue of under-taking this task, began to learn the skills of organizing and of relating their activities to other organizations. Through meeting as they did and spending long hours together they found the opportunity and the motivation to exchange impressions and ideas concerning their living conditions and the nature of their society which had been shaken so severely by the traumatic events that had taken place.

Here, from this common root, developed the community action organizations, which were in subsequent years to make a significant impact on social welfare and development, as well as the paramilitary organizations which were later to wield power on a province-wide basis. As the fears of local invasion receded and the widespread alarm which the early violence engendered had abated, these groups, finding nothing to do in defence of their communities, turned to other activities. Some moved towards the formation of social clubs which would provide an opportunity for the continuation of the new local spirit of camaraderie and which would allow the members to find their rec-reation within their own communities. Others, more directly, began to look around them at the few amenities which existed in their areas and sought the satisfaction of their own needs by attempting to meet the needs of others in their neighbourhoods. From this there sprang a proliferation of community associations, youth clubs, advice centres and the like, all on a local self-help basis.

In some areas existing tenants' associations or community associ-ations were taken over by the new local leadership but in other areas new organizations were established, by-passing the old. This was in fact a critical period in the development of community action marked by numerous conflicts between the old pre-emergency local leadership and the new men. The established organization and leadership tried to maintain their position by using their connections and their skill in dealing with statutory agencies to obtain formal recognition of their representative status and financial backing for their establishment. One such was the Belfast Amalgamated Tenants' Association which was a confederation of the municipal housing estates tenants' associations in Belfast. In vain the leadership of this organization sought to resist the extension of the concept of community associations to include people living in privately rented accommodation; in vain they sought to gain recognition of their authority and status by attempting to win a government grant which would allow them to establish a permanent central office; and in vain they fought bitterly and with a good deal of resentment, after the many years of service which they had given to their communities, the take-over of all their functions and the destruction of their base of support in the community by the new men. It was a sad experience for them because they could not understand why they were being rejected on the one hand and by-passed on the other. Being involved they could not then understand or appreciate that times had changed and that the style of their operation belonged to the old order which, as a result of the emergency, had changed for good.

When the new men came to the desks of executives and to the negotiating table they brought with them a spirit of independence and confidence which derived from the feeling that they came from the front-line of the battle where they themselves had assumed responsibility and authority. The old compliance had gone and the new relationship was based on a greater degree of mutual respect. Government agencies, which were leaning over backwards to counter the alienation of those who lived in the Catholic working-class ghettos, could not deal with Protestant representatives in a different manner and found in any case that the assumption of common interest no longer bound Protestant community action groups to acceptance of their views. There is no doubt that one of the factors which made an enormous difference to the quality of the relationship was the looming presence in the background of the paramilitary organizations. Frequently statutory organizations dealing with community action groups could not be sure that the representatives who appeared before them spoke on behalf of civil community action groups only. Springing from the same community, the action groups and the paramilitary organizations were always closely linked, and community leaders wore two hats as the situation demanded. Another influence which began to have an effect at this time was the growing encouragement given to community action groups by various individuals employed in a community development capacity, notably by the Northern Ireland Community Relations Commission which pioneered a community development strategy. Catholic community action groups had always attracted the sympathy and support of intellectuals and professionals who could be counted upon from time to time for their advice and help. The same had not been true however of the Protestant working-class groups who, in many ways, were more alienated from their middle class and much more distrustful of intellectuals. But now, needing help in building up their organizations from scratch, these groups received valuable encouragement from a growing number of community development workers. Subsequently they were to learn that in opposing officially sponsored policies which were detrimental to the interests of their communities they would need to recruit their own experts in order to reduce even further the inequalities in their relationship with statutory and other external agencies. This kind of assistance was later successfully employed in the campaign to save Sandy Row and in the campaign which stopped the implementation of the plans for a Belfast Urban Motorway.

One of the most impressive features of the developing network of community action activity was the extraordinary vigour and dedication of the activists. To the craft-skills which they employed in creating premises to meet their needs they added newly acquired skills of organization and leadership which they tested frequently in public meetings with their followers and in delegations to meet their professional protagonists. Moreover they gave an enormous amount of their time to the work which they undertook on behalf of their communities. Some would be out every evening in the week working late and travelling wherever necessary. Others, when the occasion demanded it, were prepared to, and did, give up their work for periods of time thereby subsidizing the work of their associations with their own loss of earnings. It was not surprising therefore that as they developed confidence in their abilities they acquired also a companion contempt for those who worked office-hours and who compelled them to give up a morning's work for a meeting it would have suited them to hold in the evening. Subtly the attitudes they held towards professionals, towards social service organizations and towards all manifestations of authority in society began to change. To some extent this was a product of the general erosion of controls which had taken place, but in very large measure it was also a product of their own experience and involvement.

Two common problems attracted the interest of community action groups in the early years of their development. The violence and the fear which it engendered made people more reluctant to move outside their communities for services and, particularly, for recreation. This exposed the grievous lack of facilities for meetings and for recreation for the young which in the past had been left by the statutory authorities to the church organizations to provide. Thus, much of the early activity was directed towards the building of community centres to serve estates and other definable localities. Associated with this was the organization of clubs and activities for the young and also for the old: both were groups who could not easily move out of their communities to satisfy their needs and who, as a result of the hostilities, were now considerably isolated. But energy and determination alone were not enough to secure the quality and standard of social services and amenities which were desired. There had also to be an injection of resources which, to a large extent, were controlled by agencies outside the community. Thus at a time when, through the mass media, the outside world saw only images of a community locked in conflict and violence, there were repeated all over the province countless negotiations between community groups and statutory agencies over such matters as planning decisions and grant-aid. In Londonderry, for example, a group was building up a football league for youngsters and sought financial aid to provide premises, kit and equipment. In Dungannon the Community Council, despairing of the District Council's inability to promote development and create work, was seeking to promote this itself and even campaigned to have the Council suspended. In Belfast one group was seeking to demolish a row of houses to create play-space whilst another was negotiating with the Housing Executive to convert two derelict houses on their estate into a community centre. In Ballymurphy, after raising most of the money themselves to construct a purpose-built community centre, the association negotiated a grant from the Government to finish the job. In east Belfast where Tartan gangs had been much in evidence a network of clubs and joint activities was created to provide opportunities for recreation and sport for the young: this organization found itself negotiating with three or four separate Ministries as its needs spanned the various areas of administrative responsibility.

By way of contrast it is perhaps worthy of note that this was a period when well-meaning organizations were actually taking hundreds, if not thousands, of children away from their communities for holidays elsewhere. Some of these organizations were entirely voluntary; others received direct or indirect state aid from a number of different sources. Some of the organizations were based in Northern Ireland where they received much charitable backing from funds made available through the churches or from such associations as Lions and Rotary Clubs. Other organizations were based outside Northern Ireland in the Irish Republic, in many parts of England, Scotland and Wales and in various European countries, notably Holland. Through these organizations, groups of children, in the main made up of both Catholics and Protestants, were sent away for holidays in communities elsewhere: one group was even sent, with local backing, to Mallorca. Although the absolute value of holidays such as these to children who might otherwise have not had a holiday cannot be denied, the implied criticism of the children's social environment cannot be regarded as supportive of the efforts of those who within their communities were trying to create a better quality of life for all.

3 The development of community action as a social force

In attempting to describe however briefly and inadequately the growth of community groups and their various activities during this tumultuous period of Northern Ireland history, two events must be singled out for special mention. The first of these was the introduction of internment in August 1971 and the second was the occasion of the Ulster Workers' Council strike in May 1974. Both of these events had a profound effect upon the development of community action as they had also upon the shape of all subsequent events in the province. What is most significant as far as this account is concerned is the difference in reaction on the part of community groups which, occurring over a period of time, provides us with some indication of their development.

In 1971 the spate of violence which was triggered off by the internment decision led to an immediate polarization throughout the whole of Northern Ireland society. In working-class areas this was translated into direct spatial terms by the flight of frightened families from areas where they had lived for years as individuals or as members of a minority religious group to other areas where they could be with their co-religionists. In Belfast for example it could be said that as a consequence of this event the Catholic ghettos in West Belfast expanded whilst Protestants moved out to fill the empty houses left behind in the city's outer estates. In any event it proved to be a massive dislocation of population which, occurring at a time of increased violence and of substantial administrative reform including the reorganization of local government and the delivery system for all the major services, placed an enormous strain upon all the available resources. In many ways it could be argued that, particularly in Belfast and Londonderry, the system broke down and was unable to cope with the situation which was created. Of course on the surface everything went on very much as before: people turned up for work in their offices and the milk was delivered; but behind this façade there existed a network of no-go areas where the civil writ no longer ran. The total unreality of the situation in which officially there was no emergency can be illustrated by a number of examples: when pressed by a relief worker, the best advice that an official of the Housing Executive could give to a family turned out of their home was to go ahead and squat: the demand for welfare and relief services was met principally by the relief organization established by the Community Relations Commission supported by many groups of volunteers: building sites closed down because Catholic workmen were chased off them: whole streets were cleared of their occupants by means of organized intimidation.

The need for security strengthened the claim of the IRA to be the protectors of the Catholic working-class areas. In Protestant areas the vigilante groups assumed a similar role in their communities and the province-wide organization of the Protestant paramilitary forces to meet the challenge of the IRA began to grow. However the effect on the Protestant community was, if anything, more profound than the effect upon the Catholic community. In the Catholic communities the flare-up of communal violence justified all the old fears, and for the most militant served to prove the correctness of the analysis which they had always propounded. On the Protestant side the reaction was one of shock and betrayal as many realized that the system which they had supported all their lives had failed to protect them in this particular hour of crisis. Psychologically as well as physically the Protestants felt exposed and defenceless: the trust that they had always given to the institutions which had commanded their loyalty was in a very short space of time destroyed. In its place they turned with characteristic energy to themselves and began to organize their own forms of self-help and self-reliance. It was in the context of this sequence of events that the emergence of action groups in the community began to take on a greater significance, for with it there developed an increasing consciousness concerning their reality, a questioning outlook and a capacity for articulating criticism of perceived deprivation.

However for the most part the main activities of community groups at this time were, as has already been described, concerned with the expression of need and the securing of external resources to support local effort to meet those needs. In only one matter apart from security itself did need become so acute in various areas that there was in effect a direct take-over of the function of a statutory agency: this was in housing. The movement of population had become so great that the authorities were unable to check it or to prevent the usurpation of management responsibilities by local groups who declared their right to say who should and who should not join them as neighbours. To some extent these newly declared rights were taken over by the paramilitary organizations which on occasions used their powers of allocation in a manner not dissimilar from the much criticized Local Authority councillors whose control of housing had been taken away from them. Even when the paramilitaries did not themselves assume control there is no doubt that their presence blunted the reaction of the authorities against the wholesale take-over of housing management in some cases, and the enforced sharing of responsibilities between the Housing Executive and local groups in other cases. This loss of control continued for a long period of time in some areas although the Executive never ceased to try to meet its responsibilities. Generally the Housing Executive did win back control over most of its housing but the exercise of management responsibility by local groups on that occasion has left a residual and positive effect upon the relationship between the Executive and its tenants who today have a greater day in housing affairs than did their predecessors in the pre-1969 era.

In 1974 the reaction to the Ulster Workers' Council strike, which paralysed the country more effectively than any violence and in the end brought down the power-sharing executive led by Mr Brian Faulkner, was quite different. The fundamental change in attitude of the Protestant working class in 1971 augmented by the years of experience the community action groups of all persuasions had enjoyed in a wide variety of tasks meant that in every sense they were better equipped to meet the new challenge. From this experience they had developed an independent outlook and a confidence in themselves and the skills which they had acquired. In a sense too it was true to say that during this period the stock of politicians as a group who could be relied upon to provide services and resources had fallen, while the esteem in which many community groups were held had risen as a result of their achievements. Unfortunately this was not true in all cases and there were instances of reaction where the sometimes close association of these groups with the paramilitaries had led to some areas being controlled by gangster elements who themselves took advantage of the paramilitary role for personal gain and satisfaction. But generally speaking it is true that the paramilitary action groups were at this time through, for example, their support for the Green Cross and Orange Cross welfare services to the families of Catholic and Protestant internees, becoming more involved in other social roles than the purely defensive, which gave an added dimension to community action. There was yet another factor which had emerged in the intervening years. This was the growth of a relationship, sometimes begun through professional or quasi-professional intermediaries, between community action groups on either side of the sectarian divide in the community. This had brought about on occasion joint action programmes in respect of common problems and, although permanent relationships were difficult to sustain, did lead to fairly regular contact between community leaders and workers with pronounced, sometimes even hard-line, republican or loyalist allegiances. Although this relationship was of necessity fragile it did ensure at least that there was a system of communication between the different communities and an appreciation of where their interests were shared and where they were opposed. The result was that, whereas professionally controlled organizations were responsible for the ordering and management of the relief programme in 1971, it was the community action groups themselves which took over from the professionals in 1974.

The extent of this shift of control which left the established agencies carrying on, but without the command of events that would normally be expected, can be illustrated by reference to the achievement of the South Belfast Community Association (itself a confederation of smaller, highly localized community action groups) which set up its own emergency relief programme. Not only did this organization take over the functions which had been exercised three years before by professional organizations but it improved upon them. For example, it produced clear criteria by means of which an emergency would be recognized and declared. Along with these it had prepared in advance a complete plan for the preservation of the health, welfare and life of the residents of its area. This plan was worked out in considerable detail and included, amongst other things, the arrangements for securing supplies of food and water and for the care of people at risk in the community. Most impressively, though, it went on to detail how even the streets were to be kept clean and how young people would be given activities and responsibilities which would not only keep them out of mischief but also enlist their support as partners with the adult members of the community.

When the strike started this plan began to be implemented and there is no doubt, from the behaviour and determination of those involved and from the procedures they had already worked out for dealing with information and the management of the organization, that, had the strike continued longer, the plan would have been fully implemented. In the event the full implementation was not required but the strike did not end before the most significant meeting in that area at that time had taken place. This was a meeting between the District Social Services Officer and the members of the Community Association Executive Committee. He had come representing a statutory authority and his role in his own mind was to liaise with the voluntary groups in his area; but at the meeting it was they who took charge and told him that in an emergency they would take over his resources.

Although the strike did end before the threatened local take-over of services could be realized there can be no doubt that, in the period that followed, the attitudes of community action leaders and of the professionals and bureaucrats in the social service system changed fundamentally. The former now claimed a right to be consulted on all matters: some became over-confident and even took off in flights of fancied grandeur, disdaining even to talk again to anyone but the 'top-man'. For their part the professionals realized that they had an uphill battle to re-establish their credentials in the community they sought to serve. The old assumptions upon which they could have based their behaviour, as the police had experienced years before, were no longer tenable and they found that they had to re-negotiate their relationship on new terms acceptable to the community.

It would appear that this period extending through 1974 into 1975 marked the zenith of community action groups' activity in the province. It was the period when the late Sam Smyth (member of the UDA and community worker) could propose a Community Convention representative of all Community Organizations to do the job which manifestly the Convention, composed of elected politicians, was going to fail to do. It was the period when the government passed legislation enabling and encouraging District Councils to give support to the activities and development of community groups in their area; when the Minister, Mr Moyle, announced that he would establish a Community Institute dedicated to teaching and research which would give practical support to community group activities; when the Minister appointed a Standing Committee of representatives of community organizations to advise him on policies with regard to community action. It was the period when traditionally strongly identifiable areas such as the Bogside in Londonderry or the Shankill in Belfast brought to fruition schemes for a rich variety of community development projects with workers who had emerged from the community and who had learned their skills from the community's experience; when numerous meetings took place, within Northern Ireland and without, between representatives of republican and loyalist community action groups to explore common problems and to study such topics as the formation of co-operatives. It was the period during which the Northern Ireland Council of Social Service with more adequate financial backing began actively to promote and support community councils and other similar organizations; when the Belfast Corporation began to build up its complement of community worker staff and to embark on a policy of community centre development. And it was the period during which the paramilitary Ulster Defence Association adopted the policy of promoting the Ulster Community Action Group as a confederation of Protestant community action groups and also, in its turn, as a promoter of community action in Protestant areas.

But it was also a period towards the end of which, particularly, there were signs emerging of a slackening of effort on the part of the community activists. Most programmes continued and most of the leadership remained active but it was as if the engine, after straining hard for a number of years in top gear, had changed down for a longer haul. The unresolved political impasse after so many years had begun to erode hope with the result that the community activists, like everyone else in the province, became uncertain as to the direction in which they were moving. At the same time through the pre-occupation with the province's government and future political development began to loom the even larger problems of inflation and the economic difficulties of maintaining the existing levels of employment, investment and standard of living. The sober atmosphere in which the implications of these new problems were now being considered contrasted vividly with the confidence and excitement of six years before.

Part II The Involvement of the Paramilitaries [2]

1 Paramilitary activity defined as community action

So far in this account the question of the role of the paramilitary organizations has been set to one side. Note has been taken of the common genesis of these organizations with other community action groups in the fearful response to the violence of 1969: and it has also been observed that, on occasion, community leaders pursuing social development goals have been known to exercise leadership functions in other organizations more directly concerned with the issue of violence. But no attempt has been made yet to explore this peculiar aspect of life in Northern Ireland which sets it so far apart from the experience of communities in other parts of the United Kingdom and elsewhere. The difficulty here is that the violence itself and its dreadful consequences tend to block perceptions of the social forces which both sustain and oppose it. The mass media in particular have singled violence out for our attention and have given very little by way of careful consideration to the interaction between the acts of violence and the social fabric within which it occurs. Consequently in the same way that people in other countries like to pretend that what is happening in Northern Ireland is due in part to the peculiarity of the people who live there, so too there is a tendency even within the country to see paramilitary organizations as some kind of freak graft on to society. no doubt this view of paramilitary organizations could be sustained were the organizations completely unknown and had they no support of any kind in the community. But the same cannot be said when the paramilitary organization enjoys active support in the community; for example, when they can attract donations to relief funds for the families of interned or imprisoned members of their organizations. Nor can it be said when the members of those paramilitary organizations enjoy a measure of silent support expressed by a reluctance to apply normal rules of morality or law to their conduct; by a reluctance to condemn and, most subtly of all, a hesitancy in the mind to form an adverse judgement on their behaviour which in other circumstances would be considered abhorrent.

The paramilitary organizations are, in these circumstances, the product of their communities. They are as representative of their community as any other more acceptable institution. If they represent a dark side to the nature of the community then it is because that side exists within the community and within the individuals who belong to it. All those who belong to such a community have no right, therefore, to deny responsibility for these organizations' existence and for their action; and yet this is precisely what those who belong to what is described as 'the silent majority' are always inclined to do.

The implication of this argument, of course, must be that little will be achieved by trying to interpret and understand the behaviour of paramilitary organizations viewed as peculiar phenomenon all on its own which transcends normal social relationships and divisions. Abstracting it from the context within which they occur and relating it to other presumed species of what is sometimes described as a world revolutionary movement, we ignore at our peril the particularity of their origin, and of their development, which in fact determines their existence.

It can be asserted further that, in fact, paramilitary organizations based in the community share more characteristics and features with other community action groups in that community than with other paramilitary organizations. Indeed the inference clearly is that paramilitary groups engaged in militant action are but another species of community action group employing coercive tactics within a direct-action strategy towards some goal, clearly or unclearly identified.

In following this line of argument it is quite clear that one is leaving oneself open to two specific charges. Firstly, it may be argued that by placing paramilitary organizations in the same category as friendly-sounding community associations one is glossing over, and making acceptable, a hideous reality. The true nature of the reality is such that after seven years of violence over sixteen hundred people have been killed, many of whom were innocent of any involvement in the conflict, and many thousands have been afflicted by injury or bereavement.

The other accusation which can be made is that by stopping short of the moral judgement of the behaviour of these groups or by straying from the strict legal interpretation of events one is in some way condoning what has taken place. The implication is that by trying to formulate an alternative framework in order to obtain a deeper understanding of the significance of these groups one creates a convenient apology for behaviour which would otherwise attract the strictest censure.

However it is precisely because neither moral condemnation nor legal judgement has made any significant impact upon the spate of violence that this risk must be taken in order to explore both the degree and the significance of their similarities by attempting to compare these groups.

2   A comparison of paramilitary and civil community action groups

There are, it is true, sharp differences between the civil and paramilitary manifestations of community action but at all essential points the two models are, it is suggested, two different forms of the same phenomenon.

The major difference between them of course lies in their choice of tactics. Paramilitary groups employ violence as their principal tactic whereas civil groups do not. Violence can be described as the taking of direct action to extreme lengths in order to coerce others. Its extreme form marks it off from other types of action. Even so it could not be claimed that civil groups do not themselves employ direct-action strategies nor that on occasion they do not employ coercive tactics, because this is what they frequently try to do. When the Shankill Community Association organized a march up the Shankill Road in Belfast to protest at planning proposals for the area, blocked off traffic, held an open-air meeting to criticize the proposals, considered the possibility of withholding rents, and prepared a campaign film to draw in massive support, it was doing precisely that.

Where the civil community action groups differ mostly in terms of strategy and tactics is with regard to their flexibility. Whereas the paramilitary group, as its name suggests, is almost totally identified with one type of strategy, the civil groups by and large are adaptive and will employ any strategy suited to the occasion. These will range from direct action such as the Shankill protest already quoted to, perhaps, the regular contribution of columns of news to local newspapers, or even the publication of a community newspaper as the Bogside Community Association has done in Londonderry, as a means of community education.

Probably the biggest difference between the two models lies in their respective attitudes towards law and morality. By and large the paramilitaries employ illegal methods and are reckless in their regard for the moral consequences of their action. Their belief is that the importance and urgency of the task which they have undertaken excuses them from conventional legality and morality. For some this comes from a previously acquired ideological commitment but for others this position is reached inductively as a product of the heightened fear and uncertainty regarding the welfare and the prospects of the community to which they belong. Therefore, to become a member of a paramilitary action group requires a fundamental reorientation of attitude as a prerequisite; once this step is taken, of course, subsequent involvement will cement and sustain the new frame of reference.

Becoming a member of a civil community action group frequently also requires a significant shift in attitude, if not in conventional morality and legality at least in terms of self-perception and attitudes towards others, particularly authority figures, in the community. But by and large this is not here a prerequisite for taking action: the growth of confidence and the development of the personality which takes place is a product of the involvement. As this account has already shown the uninformed and hesitant responses of community action groups in the early years were replaced by bold and competent ventures subsequently reflecting this personal development on the part of the activists.

Another important difference between the two types of action group lies in the fact that paramilitary groups take action, in the main, covertly whereas civil groups take action openly. The civil group for the most part is concerned with local problems, is pragmatic in its programme and in its behaviour, and acts openly in the community in order to build up support for its activity. By contrast the paramilitary group, although beginning in the community with local problems of defence, eventually becomes attached to goals of regional importance: their broader policies are not always worked out in local terms and therefore are not revealed so readily to the local community as the essentially local responsibilities which they continue to undertake. Either the local service becomes the justification for the broader policies or the local presence becomes the price which the community has to pay for its acclaimed, or tacit, support for the broader objectives. Sometimes this price can be high because the paramilitary groups, no matter what their purposes, attract to their ranks people who seek only an excuse for violence or crime. Because the paramilitary groups have themselves deliberately turned away from those institutions responsible for upholding legality and morality there is no sanction left to control the behaviour of those who would ignore the rules for personal or perverted reasons other than the arbitrary justice of the kangaroo court and the application of penalties such as knee-capping.

Finally, in this comparison of paramilitary and civil community action groups, some reference must be made to the psychological differences between them. Because of their control and use of violence and paramilitary groups regard themselves as powerful. This sense of power is reinforced by the authoritarian attitudes held by the members and by the code of discipline which is presumed to exist within the ranks of the organization. By contrast the civil community action groups are constantly bedevilled by a sense of powerlessness; by the feeling that they are arraigned against forces over which they have no control and against which they have few weapons to command. Moreover the basic philosophy of these groups is egalitarian and thus is opposed to the use of coercive tactics simply to build up support for authoritarian structures.

Were it to be left at this point this particular distinction would in all probability raise serious doubts regarding the validity of the proposition that these two types of community action groups belong together. An autocratic organization employing tactics which lie outside conventional social processes could not, on the face of it, be compared with a democratic association working within the guidelines that society allows. But looked at from within this distinction is not as sharp as it would appear.

Most members of civil community action groups are imbued with or at least nominally subscribe to, democratic principles. And yet observation of the behaviour of many activist leaders would suggest that there is frequently some conflict between sincerely held principles and a natural inclination to lead and, in some instances, to dominate. This ambivalence is not very far removed from a very similar phenomenon to be observed within the paramilitary groups. In this case the instinct to dominate has been given full rein but is constrained from time to time by reference to the very same political, social and, on occasion, moral principles which guide the behaviour of activists in the civil groups. This should not be a matter for any great surprise because, as it has already been observed, the activists in both groups are drawn from the same community and share a common heritage of upbringing, environment and custom. But it is as well that it should be explicitly stated.

Nor is the appearance of powerfulness on the one hand and powerlessness on the other as distinctive as might be imagined. Civil community action groups have discovered that, where they can mobilize widespread support in the community behind some objective, which when put to the test against generally held standards in society has a quality of rightness about it, they can be, to some degree, powerful, even against entrenched positions. The key to the power which they can exert from time to time is the extent to which they can mobilize public opinion behind them. That principle applies equally to the paramilitary groups who depend upon the community for both tangible and intangible gestures of support. One of the principal reasons why the Ulster Workers' Council strike in May 1974 was completely successful was that the action of the paramilitary groups were supported by many levels of the trade union movement and by the preparedness and competence of the civil community action groups described earlier.

The feeling of powerlessness and the acute consciousness of limitation to action is by no means confined to the civil community action groups. The paramilitary groups also are constrained by an awareness of two realities which form for them the classical horns of a dilemma. In the first place they are aware that the indefinite pursuit of their strategies, although having a certain negative value in preventing others from achieving their objectives, will not achieve their own: that at the end of the day a satisfactory resolution of the problem will only be achieved through the employment of alternative political strategies. Secondly they are aware that despite their distrust of, and lack of confidence in, professional politicians they are themselves unable to take the kind of political initiative which they think is required. The limitations as perceived by one paramilitary group at a meeting in 1975 were

'1. The paramilitary organisation lacks credibility in the community (Except as a defence organisation when the community is under threat of attack).
2. The organisation lacks resources to undertake such an initiative.
3. The organisation lacks experience and skill in this kind of action.
4. The organisation lacks support from the newspapers and from the T.V.'

Anyone who has had extensive experience of work with community action groups of the civil kind could not fail to recognize the familiarity of this kind of self-assessment.

3 Limitations shared by both types of community action

Quite clearly the common problem which both the paramilitary action groups and the community action groups face, and have always experienced difficulty with, is how to relate to political parties and the political system generally. By and large, with some notable exceptions, the politicians have always tried to ignore or bypass this extremely active sub-political system and to depend upon ticket-loyalties to bring out the voters in their support at the ballot. But it does seem that, in the long run, it can only be the established political parties and their representatives who have lost already and again stand to lose most from the political paralysis which followed the re-introduction of Direct Rule in 1974.

The fissures of division run deep in many directions throughout the society and factionalism has become a way of life. One division is readily recognizable: it is that between Catholics and Protestants or, more accurately, between those who seek to maintain the border between Northern Ireland and the Republic of Ireland and those who seek to abolish it. But there is an equally wide division between those who claim to hold authority in the state and those who do not: this division cuts across the other and segments the population into assenting and dissenting (or potentially dissenting) parts. These two cross-cutting partitions of the country reinforce each other. For example, political representatives were elected not in order to govern or to provide a sound administration but in order to maintain the politico-religious divide. In turn this divide provided the foundation for the now virtually extinguished political system (as it did for many other institutions in the society) and obviated for those who controlled the system the necessity of creating anything other than an authoritarian relationship with those who formed the base of their support. However, as the political representatives on both sides failed to achieve or to guarantee the purpose for which they were elected, so too their authority has been correspondingly reduced. In an impasse of this sort time is not on the side of the political parties: they face the prospect of becoming increasingly refined expressions of popular feeling, with which goes decreasing ability and opportunity for political movement.

The position with regard to community action groups is quite different. Despite the uncertainty regarding direction and the reduction of energy and enthusiasm with which they have pursued their goals in recent times which were noted in the first section of this chapter, they can continue to operate, and indeed operate successfully, even in what might otherwise be regarded as a bad situation. They are still limited in the types of action they can undertake but they can expect to obtain greater opportunities for action. Their great strength is their flexibility, their ability to focus upon immediate issues such as redevelopment plans or welfare needs which form part of the day-to-day concerns of the people. Their limitations are that for the most part they are confined in their action to either producing alternative services of the self-help type or to giving expression to negative reactions with such force as will block the proposals or programmes of others. The question which is frequently asked, and one which activists themselves ask from time to time, is can they move further into the political vacuum which has been created in Northern Ireland, a political vacuum which they (certainly the paramilitary groups) helped to create? Can they, in other words, become a revolutionary force which will overthrow the existing order?

To ask this kind of question is to misunderstand the real significance of these kinds of groups. Although the combined effect of their activities can affect the province as a whole, it remains the case at the provincial level, as at the local level, that their power is restricted to the ability to interdict at certain points in time. To do more would require the widespread organization of an alternative system and this is the antithesis of community action. The local base of much community action is not accidental and is of great significance. It determines the characteristics of the issue upon which action is taken; those of immediacy, relevance and intelligibility. It also strengthens the action taken by providing immediate, often face-to-face, contact between activists who are seeking to work within a human dimension which is concrete, as distinct from a societal dimension which is abstract. In taking action in this way the activists seek to assert their own existence as much as to achieve specific goals and are in fact trying to create for themselves opportunities for living; for taking responsibilities and for making choices in areas where once upon a time they were deliberately encouraged to become dependent by agencies, professions and institutions which, since then, they have learned they cannot trust. (In this sense it can be argued that the IRA, which does have an extremely controlled and well-supported organization, is quite mistaken in identifying a large part of what its organization in Northern Ireland actively does as being revolutionary).

Within all this the position of the paramilitary action groups is of great interest. By their existence they demonstrate that action groups can in extreme conditions employ extreme tactics. They also demonstrate, in combination with other community action groups, that where a critical situation exists and the reaction is strong enough they have the power to paralyse the whole political system, even though they themselves are incapable of fulfilling a wider political role.

Part III Some Reflections

1 Leadership in the community

In reviewing seven years of community action experience in Northern Ireland it is possible to conclude that the pattern of development has followed a cycle which, although it obviously owes much to the cycle of conflict in the province, may also have developed according to a pattern of its own. The correspondence between the two developments is most easily seen in relation to two major events which shaped the history of the province: these were the introduction of internment in 1971 and the Ulster Workers' Council strike in 1974. What is perhaps less obvious is that community action in its various manifestations has developed along a separate curve which has been subject to other determining influences than simply the response to violence. Indeed it may very well be that the same kinds of influence have had a concurrent and coincidental effect on both the movements of violence and the movements of social reform and development. In so far as the point has already been made that the paramilitary organizations and the community action groups are but different expressions of the same communities acting independently in their own interest, this, no doubt, could be expected to be the case.

One of the most important elements in the development of community action in the province has been the emergence and growth of its leadership. No-one who has witnessed the development of this phenomenon over these years can have failed but to be impressed by the ability and energy exhibited by those who have emerged to represent their communities. The conclusion which has been widely shared is that in this society there existed strong reserves of talent and skill which simply did not have the opportunity to emerge and to flower under the previous paternalistic system of dominance. The emergence of this talent in 1969–70 created the first watershed in local leadership. Not only, as has already been described, did it displace the representational leadership which then existed but to varying extents it displaced other forms of leadership in the local community as well. District Councillors who were themselves undergoing the traumatic experience of local government reorganization at the time came immediately under threat. Some responded by participating themselves but many held themselves aloof, clinging to a dwindling band of supporters and a diminishing sphere of influence and comforting themselves with the knowledge that their party machines would secure their re-election. Alongside the District Councillors, the status of professionals appointed to work in the community such as the clergy, the doctors, the social workers and the clerks of works, was also significantly reduced, affecting to a very marked extent their own confidence and self-perception. Again talented individuals who were prepared to accept the rules of the new game maintained their own position by dint of their own personal effort, ability and dedication. But there was no automatic right to leadership or power of influence any more, and some became extremely anxious as they watched the old conventions disappear.

Three or four years later it was very interesting to observe some members of the new community leadership expressing fairly similar anxieties with regard to their position in the community, and referring to the years of hard work they had undertaken on behalf of their communities. This was the reaction on the part of some Protestant community leaders to the energy and enthusiasm with which the newly formed UDA-sponsored Ulster Community Action Group was creating new community organizations and winning the affiliation of some of the old to their new confederation.

But in spite of threats of take-over such as these, and notwithstanding the continued existence and strength of influence of the paramilitary organizations, the most significant fact of all is that during the seven-year period there has been relatively little change overall in the pattern of leadership amongst community groups. New leaders have emerged, it is true, to thicken the ranks of those who were first to respond to the challenge; the relative position of some leaders has changed over the years and of course there have been a few dropouts: others again have shifted from being community leaders to becoming community workers as their talents have been recognized and they have been given permanent employment in these roles through the funding of external agencies: but, in the broadest sense these faces and names that came into prominence during the first couple of years of this cycle can be found today in the same kind of activity.

The level of intensity of the involvement in the early years, as has been noted, has tended to diminish, and this raises the question as to whether this is related in a very real measure to the capacity of individuals to sustain their efforts on behalf of their communities over a long period of time. Two things must be borne in mind here: Firstly, the leaders themselves are, in a sense, amateurs working without official recognition, frequently with the minimum of official support and then won at the expense of considerable effort; they work in their own time or in the time that they are prepared to give up at personal loss, from their gainful employment. They therefore bear a very real cost in terms of loss of opportunity for recreation, family life and frequently earnings which in the long run must blunt the edge of their motivation and energy. Secondly, the nature of community action is such that despite the fact that some groups, like the Bogside Community Association, do produce elaborate formulae relating to their structure, the forms of their association and the issue of their representativeness, they remain in a very real sense largely personalized organizations. This is to say that, to a large extent, the organizations consist of the individuals of whom they are composed and, unlike well-developed bureaucracies, acquire no separate existence which can deal with the problems of regeneration and replacement. In this regard their strength, which is their flexibility, becomes, in the fact of their non-institutionalization, their weakness: as long as their leadership continues they prosper but when

it wanes they can only be replaced by new leaders in new forms of
organized community action.

Thus their success as action groups ultimately must be measured not
in terms of their continuation, which may even be undesirable, but in
terms of the changes they were able to produce in policies, and the
modifications in the behaviour of established agencies and
organizations that they were able to accomplish during the period of
their existence. It is to be measured also in the degree of change which
takes place in the self-perception and level of consciousness of the
members of their own communities and thus their capacity to create
other forms of community action to meet other needs in the future.

2 Community action and local politics

Because, clearly, community action is a form of political action the
issue of the relationship between the community action system and the
established political system deserves some comment. Not only in
Northern Ireland but in many parts of the United Kingdom and elsewhere the emergence of any form of community action has frequently
been characterized by a large measure of mutual hostility between
elected representatives and community action leaders. Where they have
been unable to use community action groups to their own advantage
the elected representatives have tended to use the evidence of the ballot
box and their own statutorily defined position in support of the view
that they, not the community action leaders, are the true representatives
of the community and that therefore, for example, they have a
monopoly claim to all communications with external agencies. For their
part community action leaders have tended to accuse councillors of
neglecting their constituents, of being uninformed, of failing to consult
their constituents and of being in the most real of senses unrepresen-
tative of the communities they purport to serve. The validity of these
accusations and counter-accusations obviously varies according to the
circumstances but it must be argued that the emergence of community
action groups on such a large scale in Northern Ireland (a survey in
1975 [3] revealed a number in the region of 500 in a province with
a population of 1,500,000) does indicate both that the local government
system was in many instances unsatisfactory and that it was totally
inadequate in being unable to respond to the emergency created.

The dilemma for all community action groups has already been
referred to. It is that, although they can themselves undertake certain
responsibilities for the provision of services and amenities to their own

communities on a self-help basis, at the end of the day they must turn
to the major institutions of society, not only for services, but even for
the support which they need to do what they can for themselves. But
there is a dilemma here too for the political system. How can it
effectively continue to operate as a form of representative government
if its representativeness is continually challenged and its actions discredited and brought into disrepute by articulate and well-informed
criticism and opposition? As in Northern Ireland that opposition is
reinforced by the employment of arms in widespread violence, this requirement of a broad consensus base for all forms of government is
starkly presented. Although this is a problem which is by no means
confined to Northern Ireland it may be that what has happened here,
particularly as a result of the collapse of the political system (which
because of the cushion provided by the broad legislative and economic
framework of the United Kingdom has not led to absolute chaos) may
provide some clues for the future.

Removal from the local authorities of the majority of their responsibilities for such matters as housing, personal social services, education,
etc, has left the reconstituted District Councils with very little authority
or power in the traditional sense. Many councillors in the new District
Councils were unable, and frequently are still unable, to come to terms
with the effect this has had upon their power-base in the community.
Even within the population generally many have failed to perceive that
the role of the councillor has changed and that he can no longer fix
things in the way that he could when he had some influence upon the
officials employed by his authority. This is why in many areas
community action groups have formed and have continued in existence
because they have made themselves better informed, have acquired
more elaborate skills in communication and negotiation, and have been
quicker to learn how to use the new system than many of the old-time
councillors.

As long as this gap in their respective knowledge and skills continues, it must be to the disadvantage of the political system at the
local level. In effect community action groups are wielding the very
weapons the councillors need to undertake properly the functions en-
trusted to them. In some areas this has already been realized and recently
it is noticeable that some Councils are beginning to change the style
of their approach to the task and also come out to meet community
action groups in an attempt to build up the strength of their contacts
with their constituents. In Londonderry city, for example, the relationship between the council and various regional authorities has changed

from a pattern of ignorance and dogmatism to a more open-ended, tougher, better-informed and skilful negotiation of the city's interests. The authority which councillors now command is that of knowledge, community interests and needs, and a growing base of support in the community for the effort which is being made.

What can therefore be tentatively suggested is that the relationship between the two systems is beginning to be improved in some cases and may be improved further, not by the take-over of community action groups by the councillors, nor by their suppression (which would in any case be impossible) but by the councillors' adoption of the methods, knowledge and skills which the community action groups have employed to such good effect. There is a corollary to this of course, and it is that public representation and party-political systems which are unable to acquire this new competence will inevitably be replaced by political structures which will.

3   The heart of the matter

What then are the lessons, if any, which are to be learned from this account of the development of community action in Northern Ireland during seven long years characterized by violent conflict? If the situation in Northern Ireland is peculiar rather than unique then there must be many aspects of the conflict here, and of the reaction of the population to it, which mirror, even if in magnified or distorted form, features of life elsewhere. It cannot be a simple coincidence, for example, that the growth of community action in Northern Ireland occurred at a time when there was an expansion of the same kind of activity, indeed an active promotion of it in some parts, in the United Kingdom generally. Nor can it be argued that the eruption of violence in 1969 and the heightened tension during a number of periods in the years that followed, which can be held to explain the various upsurges in community based activity which took place, can indeed account for the whole of the development. What could be argued is that the structural elements in the situation, to which attention has been drawn in this account, have played a much more fundamental role in determining the emergence and growth of self-help and self-reliant activities by community groups. To the extent that these structural elements remain unchanged today or resemble structural features of society in other parts of Britain or Ireland, what has occurred here in the past becomes relevant for determining what may happen in the future here or elsewhere. Although the particular experience of violence in Northern

Ireland implies the possibility that it might occur in similar terms else-where, it would be quite wrong to restrict the interpretation of these events so that the focus on the possibility of violence obscures the much more serious and fundamental issues that lie at the heart of the matter. Of these the most important is obviously the issue of the disputed constitutional status of Northern Ireland. But here again there is a real danger of trying to explain everything in terms of a simple dichotomy of allegiances to the extent that other important contributory factors may be obscured. Consequently in offering a general observation on the significance of Northern Ireland experience with regard to com-munity action, it must be done without reference to violence or to the issue of constitutional status; not in order to deny the central importance of these matters nor indeed to imply that there is an alternative analysis which would replace them, but simply to draw attention to an aspect of the situation which deserves serious consideration also.

It does appear from the evidence that, although some form of crisis is required to motivate and mobilize individuals into forming associa-tions for the betterment of their communities, it is not this alone which creates the necessary conditions for the growth of their activity. To some extent it has to be acknowledged, for example, that there are cer-tain psychological factors at work which produce this kind of action. In adopting leadership roles in the community there can be no doubt that some individuals find opportunities for self-actualization normally available only to a few, from which number they had been excluded, which add greatly to the quality of their existence. For some the opportunity to take action in a situation, where the normal rules and the conventional deferences no longer apply, affords great satisfaction and provides the stimulation required for prodigious effort. However the fact that some community leaders enjoy some kind of ego-trip is not in itself sufficient to explain the totality of the process. The crucial factor is to be found in the existence of hierarchies, whether of political or religious control or of administrative service systems, which exclude the vast majority of people and are incapable of adapting to fundamental changes in the society which they cannot or will not com-prehend. It makes very little difference if these hierarchies prefer to remain, as far as possible, stationary—as is the case with the Irish Catholic Church—or whether they are actually attempting to move, but along a path inimical to the interests of those whom the proposed change is intended to benefit—as was the case of the Belfast Corpora-tion's programme for the development of the city. Nor is the often cited explanation of a break-down in communication of much value when the real gap is one between the values of those controlling the agency or institution and the people served by it who have fallen out of sympathy with its purposes; even, perhaps, with its whole establishment.

In these circumstances, with no other means of bringing about the change they desire or of obtaining some measure of control over the change that is to be imposed, community action groups emerge either to supply the need themselves or to campaign against the agencies with whose policies they so fundamentally disagree. The emergence of various forms of community action, particularly to the extent that has been experienced in Northern Ireland, therefore becomes a challenge to those structures to respond and recreate the relationship between, as it were, the agency and its clientele.

Community development then becomes either the response of established agencies seeking to recreate that relationship, or the initiative which the agency promoting change takes to involve people in their communities in a process of change. In both cases peoples' commitment to a development programme is secured in return for offering them some genuine opportunities to influence what will take place. In this there is of course a range of professional tasks to be undertaken with regard to social analysis, communication and stimulation and support of community groups. But there is also a political task and it is the most fundamental of political responsibilities: that of ensuring that the control and management of the services which sustain community life are responsive to community needs and appear always to be acting with the best interests of the community at heart. In this the essential ingredient is not so much agreement as trust.

Notes

1   For some aspects of political analysis in this Chapter I am indebted to S. Nelson, *Developments in Protestant Working Class Politics*, an unpublished paper delivered to the Institute of Irish Studies, Queen's University, Belfast, February 1976.

2   For a more extensive discussion of this subject *see* 'Paramilitary Groups and other Community Action Groups in Northern Ireland' by the author in *International Review of Community Development*, 1974, from which part of this section is taken.

3   *Community Action and Community Perceptions of the Social Services in Northern Ireland: A Feasibility Study*, Coleraine: New University of Ulster, 1975.

Bibliography

1   Books and Articles

Administrative Structure of the Health and Personal Social Services in Northern Ireland, Belfast: HMSO, 1969.

Andrews, Allen, *Earthquake*, London: Angus & Robertson, 1963.

Baer, E., 'Civil disorder: mass emergency of the 70s', *American Journal of Nursing*, **72**, 1973, 1072.

Bates, F. L. *et al.*, *The Social and Psychological Consequences of a Natural Disaster*, Washington, D.C.: National Academy of Sciences, 1963.

Benn, John, *A Commissioner's Complaint* (a personal review of three years of work as Ombudsman), Coleraine: New University of Ulster, Occasional Papers in Social Administration, 1973.

Bennet, Glin, 'Community disaster in Britain', in Jones, Kathleen (ed.), *The Year Book of Social Policy*, London: Routledge and Kegan Paul, 1974.

——, 'Bristol floods 1968: controlled survey of effects on health of local community disaster', *British Medical Journal*, **3**, 1970, 45–458.

Birrell, W. D., 'Relative deprivation as a factor in conflict in Northern Ireland', in *Sociological Review*, **20**, 3, 1972, 317–44.

——, *et al.*, *Housing in Northern Ireland*, London: Centre for Environmental Studies, 1971.

——, and Murie, A., 'Social policy in Northern Ireland', in Kathleen Jones (ed.), *The Year Book of Social Policy*, London: Routledge and Kegan Paul, 1973.

Black, H. D., *Management of Human Behaviour in Disaster*, Ottawa: Department of National Health and Welfare, 1967.

Boal, F. W., Doherty, P. and Pringle, D. G., *The Spatial Distribution of some Problems in the Belfast Urban Area*, Belfast: N.I. Community Relations Commission, 1974.

Boehringer, G. H., 'Beyond Hunt: a police policy for Northern Ireland of the future', *Social Studies*, **2**, 4, 1973, 399–414.

Boehringer, K., 'The welfare jumble', *Fortnight*, 3 September 1971.

Boyle, K., Hadden, T. and Hillyard, P., *Law and State: the Case of Northern Ireland*, London: Martin Robertson, 1975.

Bryant, Richard, 'Professionals in the firing line', *British Journal of Social Work*, **3**, 2, Summer 1973, 161–73.

Clifford, R. A., *The Rio Grande Flood: a comparative study of border communities in disaster*, Washington, D.C.: National Academy of Sciences, 1956.

Critchley, Julian, *Community Violence: the challenge of the urban guerrilla*, Crisis Paper, No. 14, Atlantic Information Centre for Teachers, 1971.

Danzig, E. R., Thayer, P. W. and Galanter, L. R., *The Effect of a Threatening Rumor on a Disaster-stricken Community*, Washington, D.C.: National Academy of Sciences, 1958.

Darby, John, *The Emergence Operation conducted by the Northern Ireland Community Relations Commission*, Belfast: NICRC, 1971.

——, and Morris, Geoffrey, *Intimidation in Housing*, Belfast: Northern Ireland Community Relations Commission, 1974.

——, *Conflict in Northern Ireland*, Dublin: Gill and Macmillan, 1976.

Davies, R., *Devil's Bridge Coach Crash*, London: National Council of Social Service, 1975.

——, *How Do We Know Who's Involved in a Disaster?*, London: National Council of Social Service, 1975.

Diamond, Anne, *Social effects of internment* (unpublished dissertation presented in partial fulfilment of regulations for Diploma in Social Administration, New University of Ulster, 1975).

Economic and industrial strategy for Northern Ireland: report by review team (Chairman: W. G. H. Quigley), Belfast: HMSO, 1976.

'Ethical problems facing the social worker', in *Irish News*, 15 March 1972.

Evason, E., Darby, J. and Pearson, M., *Social Need and Social Provision in Northern Ireland*, Coleraine: New University of Ulster, 1976.

Fisk, Robert, *The Point of No Return*, London: Times Books, André Deutsch, 1975.

Flight, Belfast: Northern Ireland Community Relations Commission, 1971.

'Focus on Northern Ireland, now and later', *Municipal and Public Services Journal*, 5 May 1972, 631–3.

Fraser, R. M., *Children in Conflict*, London: Secker and Warburg, 1973.

Fry, Anne, 'Struggle for power in Newry', *Community Care*, **27**, 2 October 1974.

——, 'Social work in the firing line', *Community Care*, **28**, 9 October 1974.

Gamble, W. W. and Finley, A. H., *Date with Disaster: a model for multi-hospital preparedness*, Washington, D.C.: Office of Emergency Preparedness, 1971.

Griffiths, H. G., 'Parliamentary groups and other community action groups in Northern Ireland', *International Review of Community Development*, 1974.

——, *The Northern Ireland Community Relations Commission: a case-study in agency conflict*, Coleraine: New University of Ulster, Occasional Paper in Social Administration, 1974.

Group of 23 social workers, 'Government policies: ethical problems facing the social worker', *Irish News*, 15 March 1972.

Gurr, T. R., 'Urban disorder: perspectives from the comparative study of civil strife', *American Behavioural Scientist*, **2**, 1968, 50–5.

Hewitt, R., *From Earthquake, Fire and Flood*, London: George Allen and Unwin, 1957.

Jonathan, B. and Bingham, A. M., *Violence and Democracy*, New York: W.P.C., 1970.

Johnson, J. E., 'Tornado as teacher', *Hospital*, **44**, 5, 1970, 40.

Lacey, G. N., 'Observations on Aberfan', *Journal of Psychosomatic Research*, **16**, 1972, 257–60.

Lawrence, R. J., *The Government of Northern Ireland*, Oxford: The Clarendon Press, 1965.

Lyons, H. A., 'Terrorists' bombing and the psychological sequelae', *Journal of the Irish Medical Association*, **67**, 1, 1974, 15–19.

——, 'Depressive illness and aggression in Belfast', *British Medical Journal*, **1**, 1972, 342–345.

——, 'Psychiatric sequelae of the Belfast riots', *British Journal of Psychiatry*, **118**, 265, 1971.

——, 'Riots and rioters in Belfast', *Economic and Social Review*, **3**, 4, 1972, 605–14.

Maltby, A., *The Government of Northern Ireland, 1922–72: a catalogue and breviate of parliamentary papers*, Shannon: Irish University Press, 1974.

McCormack, V., 'Strange facts about the Ministry and the U.W.C. strike', *The Sunday Press*, 11 August 1974.

McCreary, Alf, *Survivors*, Belfast: Alf McCreary, 1976.

McKeown, M., 'Civil unrest: secondary school survey', *The Northern Teacher*, Belfast: Winter 1973.

Nahrendorf, Richard, O., 'Violence and social change', *Sociology and Social research*, **56**, 1 October 1971, 5–18.

Northern Ireland House Condition Survey, 1974, Belfast: Northern Ireland Housing Executive, 1975.

O'Malley, P. P., 'Attempted suicide', *Journal of the Irish Medical Association*, **65**, 5, 1972, 109.

Percival, R., and Duffy, F., *Community Action and Community Perceptions of the Social Services in Northern Ireland* (Report of a research project funded by the Social Science Research Council), Coleraine: New University of Ulster, 1975.

Perry, H. S. and Perry, S. E., *The Schoolhouse Disasters: family and community as determinants of the child's response to disaster*, Washington, D.C.: National Academy of Sciences, 1959.

Pinkney, A., *The American Way of Violence*, New York: Random House, 1972.

Popovic, M. and Petrovic, D., 'After the earthquake', *Lancet*, **2**, 1964, 1169–71.

Price, Richard H., *Abnormal Behaviour: perspectives in conflict*, New York:

Holt, Rinehart and Winston, 1972.

Ragg, Nicholas, 'Benefits in Northern Ireland', *Social Work Today*, **3**, 13, 1972.

Rainsford, T. J., 'Supplementary benefits in Northern Ireland', *Social Work Today*, **3**, 23, 1973.

Report on the emergency operation during the recent crisis, Belfast: South Belfast Community Association, 1974 (cyclostyled).

Robb, J. D. A. and Matthews, J. G. W., 'The injury and management of riot casualties admitted to the Belfast hospital wards, August to October 1969', *British Journal of Surgery*, **58**, 6 June 1971, 413–19.

Rutherford, W. H., 'The accident and emergency departments in the surgery of civil violence', *Recent Advances in Surgery*, Harlow: Churchill Livingstone, 1973.

——, 'Disaster procedures', *British Medical Journal*, **1**, 1975, 443–5.

Social and Economic Trends in Northern Ireland, Belfast: (1975, 1976, published annually, HMSO).

'Social services in Ulster', *Health and Social Services Journal*, December 1976.

Spenser, A. E. C. W., *Ballymurphy: a tale of two surveys*, Belfast: Queen's University, 1975.

Statistics on Security, Belfast: Northern Ireland Office, quarterly.

Strategy for the Development of Health and Personal Social Services in Northern Ireland, Belfast: HMSO, 1975.

Surgery of violence: articles published in the British Medical Journal, London: British Medical Journal, 1976.

Taggart, J., 'Community health services under stress', *Public Health*, **87**, 6, 1973, 225–31.

Theoret, J. J., 'Exercise London: a disaster exercise involving numerous casualties', *Canadian Medical Association Journal*, **114**, 8, 1976, 697–9.

Tidmarsh, Sheila, *Disaster*, Middlesex: Penguin Education, 1969.

Townsend, R., 'Human need in Ulster', *New Society*, **18**, 478, 25 November 1971, 1037.

Tweed, Bill, 'Community work comment in Northern Ireland', *Social Work Today*, **2**, 15, 1971, 2–4.

Ulster Yearbook: the official handbook of Northern Ireland, Belfast: HMSO, 1955–76.

Vigilante, Joseph, 'Urban crisis and violence', *Applied Social Studies*, **1**, 3, 3 October 1969.

Violence in Ireland: a report to the churches, Belfast: Christian Journals, 1976.

Walker, R., *et al.*, *Social Workers and their workload in Northern Ireland*, London: National Institute for Social Work Training, 1972.

Wallace, A. F. C., *Tornado in Worcester: an exploratory study of individual and community behaviour in extreme situations*, Washington, D. C.: National Academy of Sciences, 1956.

Wallace, M., *Northern Ireland: fifty years of self-government*, Newton Abbot: David and Charles, 1971.

Weir, M. B., *Social work in a disorganised society*, privately published, 22 May 1975.

White, Anthony G., *Organised Violence in Urban Areas, a selected bibliography*, Illinois: Council of Planning Librarians, 1973.

Williamson, F., 'Day hospital in a troubled community', *The Nursing Times*, 1972, 1638–41.

Wolfenstein, Martha, *Disaster*, London: Routledge and Kegan Paul, 1957.

Wright, Frank, 'Protestant ideology and politics in Ulster', *European Journal of Sociology*, **14**, 1973, 213–80.

2 Parliamentary Papers relating to Northern Ireland

Allegations against the security forces of physical brutality, Home Office, Report of the Inquiry, Chairman: Sir Edmund Compton, 1971, Cmnd 4823.

Commentary by Government of Northern Ireland to accompany the Cameron Report incorporating an account of progress and a programme of action, 1969, Cmnd 534.

Deaths in Londonderry, Report of the tribunal appointed to enquire into the events on Sunday 30 January, 1972, Chairman: Lord Widgery, H.L. 101, H.C. 220.

Disturbances in Northern Ireland, Report of Commission, Chairman: Lord Cameron, Cmnd 532.

Economic development: Government statement and report of the economic consultant, Professor T. Wilson, 1965, Cmnd 479.

Educational Development in Northern Ireland, 1964, Cmnd 470.

Future Development of the Parliament and Government of Northern Ireland: A consultative document, 1971, Cmnd 560.

Northern Ireland Development Programme, 1970–1975, Report of the three consultants, Professors Matthew, Wilson, Parkinson, 1970, Government statement, 1970, Cmnd 547.

Police in Northern Ireland, Report of Advisory Committee, Chairman: Baron J. Hunt, 1969, Cmnd 535.

Political settlement: Statements issued on Friday 24 March 1972 by the Prime Minister and the Government, Cmnd 568.

Public prosecutions, Report of the working party, Chairman: J. C. MacDermott, 1971, Cmnd 554.

Record of Constructive Change, Report, 1971, Cmnd 558.

Reshaping of Local Government: Statement of Aims, 1967, Cmnd 517.

Text of communiqué issued following discussions between the Secretary of State for the Home Department and the Northern Ireland Government in Belfast on 9 and 10 October 1969, Cmnd 4178.

Violence and Civil Disturbances, 1969, Report of Tribunal of Inquiry, Chairman: Mr Justice Scarman, 1972, Cmnd 566.

Index